Shores of Darkness

Shores of Darkness

By

EDWARD B. HUNGERFORD

Meridian Books

THE WORLD PUBLISHING COMPANY

CLEVELAND AND NEW YORK

A MERIDIAN BOOK

Published by The World Publishing Company
2231 West 110th Street, Cleveland 2, Ohio
First Meridian printing August 1963
Copyright © 1941 by Columbia University Press.
All rights reserved. No part of this book may be reproduced
in any form without written permission from the publisher, except for
brief passages included in a review appearing in a newspaper or magazine.
Reprinted by arrangement with Columbia University Press.
Library of Congress Catalog Card Number: 41-21950
Printed in the United States of America.   MWP863

Not in the legends of the first of days
Studied from that old spirit-leaved book
Which starry Uranus with finger bright
Sav'd from the shores of darkness . . .

KEATS, *Hyperion*

Acknowledgments

Shores of Darkness was published in 1941 by the Columbia University Press. I am grateful to its officers for permission to reissue the book under its present imprint.

Except for the alteration of two or three sentences about William Blake, and for some minor editorial corrections, the text remains as first printed. Recent titles have not been added to the bibliography, which is a list of the books which I used in writing the book.

Shores of Darkness was dedicated to my parents, and I now wish to rededicate it to their memory.

May 1963   E.B.H.

Contents

Part One

Myths and Mythagogues

WHOEVER has read carefully the mythological poems of the early decades of the nineteenth century has been aware of dead presences among them, of vague and nameless influences so remote and shapeless that the mind can scarcely define them. These spectres are no imaginary ones. They are ghosts indeed—the ghosts of a forgotten generation of men who once spoke of each other respectfully as "the learned," of men who believed that by the evidences of elephants' bones, the skeletons of giants, the roots of Greek verbs, Phoenician place names, Druids, and gods, they had traced man and his society and his religion to a pristine time—not more than a very few thousand years ago—when all was in a state of fresh wonder and men walked with God. These men were the speculative mythologists of the latter half of the eighteenth century and of the early years of the nineteenth. They rose quickly from obscurity and plunged so completely into oblivion that they have left scarcely an acknowledged trace upon intellectual history. Yet their pallid and disembodied shades walk with the living poets, like the unburied dead of ancient times who, for the want of a handful of dust thrown upon their bodies, could not descend to the abode of the dead. This chapter shall be that handful of dust which will give them decent burial.

My attention was first attracted toward these speculative mythologists by noticing that in the more ambitious
mythological poetry of the early nineteenth century there
were unusual departures from conventional myth which
were certainly not authorized by classical mythology but
which did not seem to be wholly inventions. A case in
point is Keats's picture of the Titaness Asia in *Hyperion*.
Instead of having Asia born of the usual mythological
personifications which provided the Titans with parents
in Greek myth, Keats names the father of his Titaness as
Caf. No such figure, of course, appears in classical myth.
In the *Oriental Library* of Herbelot some legends respect-
ing a mountain named Caf are preserved, and William
Beckford knew about them when he wrote *Vathek;* but
Herbelot's legends do not explain Keats's use of the name.
When I encountered the mythological speculations of
Jean Sylvain Bailly, however, the allusion was made clear.
Bailly had conceived a remarkable theory concerning the
descent of culture, in which he imagined a prehistoric
Atlantean people to have existed for many centuries in the
region of Caf in the Caucasus Mountains. From this giant
race, Asiatic culture had taken its origin. Keats, as I shall
later point out in more detail, had seized hold of the picturesque theory and employed it as a means of prophesying the rise of Asiatic culture. The circumstance throws
considerable light upon his plans for the story of *Hyperion*, and indicates that not merely classical mythology
but contemporary speculations upon mythology found a
place in the poetry which he based upon classical fable.

Others of the poets were reading not merely the classical
authors and the mythological handbooks based upon them,
but the highly speculative treatises whose brief vogue I

shall describe. Blake in particular was affected by them so much that they constitute a kind of revelation of the world in which his imagination was operating, and it is worth reflecting that, in his poetry and in that of many other poets, ideas which seem mystical and scraps of erudition which seem profound may have been caught up from no more dignified source than Hancarville's ridiculous *Researches* or Wilford's "An Essay on the Sacred Isles in the West."

Who were these "speculative mythologists?" Most of them were men now so completely forgotten that the repetition of their names will not wake many echoes in the mind of the modern reader. The Abbés Pluche and Banier, Dom Antoine Pernety, Court de Gebelin, Charles François Dupuis, Jacob Bryant, Jean Sylvain Bailly, Hancarville, Francis Wilford, Georg Friedrich Creuzer, George Faber, Colonel Vallancey—these are but a few of the legion who made mythology their province. Most of them are too inconsequential to mention. The names of a truly imposing number are embedded in the list of "authorities" which Charles Anthon attached to his great mythological dictionary, and there I shall leave most of them. To review them all in detail might reveal a number of minute particulars in which they had exerted an influence upon the poets, but these "minute particulars," of which William Blake was so fond of speaking, would in the bulk be trivial compared to certain general tendencies in which their influence was most felt. At a time when the conventional myths had become too shopworn for literary fashion, the imaginative and exciting speculations of "the learned" introduced new modes of treating the myths.

It is a curious fact that the Greek Renaissance of the eighteenth and early nineteenth centuries did not express itself in literature as in the other arts. For a period of about seventy-five years, beginning near the middle of the eighteenth century with the excavations at Herculaneum and the publications of Winckelmann and subsiding with the setting up of the Elgin marbles in England and the revolution in Greece, there flourished an intense interest in the classical "antique." The diverse impulses of this latter Renaissance had a common denominator, the influence upon European taste not of a Greece preserved in books, but of an extant Greece surviving in the land itself and in its physical monuments. The fever of archaeological recovery burned high, and the contagion of a new classicism spread even to Russia and America. Never wholly Greek in character, the new classicism nevertheless shook off the rich adornment of the Renaissance and betook itself to what it regarded as a "purer" antique style. There emerged distinguishable styles in architecture, in sculpture, in painting, and in the arts of decoration. But the prevailing influences did not operate in literature in quite the same fashion as in the other arts. Keats's *Ode on a Grecian Urn* and the brief poems of André Chénier, true reflections of the Graeco-Roman taste of the era, did not strike the dominant note in poetry.

The truth of the matter is that men of letters from Dr. Johnson to William Blake had tired of the ancients as a too constant literary theme. The mythology of Greece and Rome had been so steadily exploited ever since the early Renaissance that its freshness as literary material had disappeared. The mythological theme had degenerated into its worst absurdity in the opera, and as Dr. Johnson pointed out, the mythological allusion had too often exhausted itself in puerilities. Mythological allusions were usually, he found, absurd, inappropriate, and dull. Reflecting the weariness of contemporary taste, Johnson resented the intrusion of "heathen fable" in poems dealing with religious themes, and modern attempts to revive mythological stories he regarded as properly doomed to neglect. Writing of Rowe's *Ulysses*, he observed shrewdly: "We have been too early acquainted with the poetical heroes to expect any pleasure from their revival: to shew them as they have already been shewn is to disgust by repetition; to give them new qualities or new adventures is to offend by violating received notions."

Laodamia, Endymion, Adonis, Albion, Prometheus, Helen, and Hyperion might well have been doomed, despite the ever-increasing Greek gusto, to the neglect which Dr. Johnson predicted for them had it not been that the study of mythology took a remarkable turn which was to fasten the minds of the poets upon it again as a new and different material.

After the early Renaissance the study of mythology had taken a fairly pedestrian course. At first books on mythology were concerned primarily with making an adjustment of fables which was satisfactory to the teachings of the Christian faith and the authority of the Bible, and secondly with providing a ready means for the acquisition of that intimate knowledge of the gods and heroes which superficially distinguished the lettered from the unlettered. But with the rise of an independent spirit of inquiry, mythologists followed the increasing rationalism of scientific thought in imposing systems upon inchoate knowledge, and throughout the latter seventeenth and

early eighteenth centuries there appeared a wide diversity
of treatises upon myth, each with a special theory to plead.
When in 1765 the Chevalier de Jaucourt endeavored to
survey for Diderot's *Encyclopédie* the great body of this
literature, he was forced to declare: "Each man has un-
covered in myth what his own particular genius and the
plan of his studies have led him to look for. The physician
finds by allegory the mysteries of nature; the political
scientist, the refinements of the wisdom of government;
the philosopher, the most beautiful morals; the chemist,
the secrets of his art. Each has regarded fable as a country
to be invaded, where he has believed that he had the right
to make expeditions conforming to his taste and to his
interests."

The spirit of this literature was for the most part
Euhemeristic or rationalistic; that is, it was concerned to
demonstrate that the myths were covers for some historical or natural facts. Thus the Cyclops were lighthouse
builders, and their one eye was the beacon. Endymion
was an early astronomer who observed the courses of the
moon. Neither of these schools of interpretation was particularly stimulating to the poetic imagination, but both
were to evolve in directions which eventually provided
the strongest sort of stimulation.

The Euhemerists were attempting to resolve myth into
the corrupted record of historical fact, explaining the
gods and heroes as having had an actual human origin.
This was no modern form of mythological interpretation,
since its adherents were followers of an ancient mythog-
rapher, Euhemerus, whose work has survived only in
fragments. But the motive of modern Euhemerism was
different from that of the ancient world. Modern Euhe-

merism commenced with the effort to explain the myths of antiquity as corrupted records of persons and events mentioned in the Old Testament. It is no accident that old Samuel Bochart, the most celebrated and most eccentric of seventeenth-century mythologists, commenced his studies in the field by lectures designed to support the authority of the book of Genesis. But a study which commenced with the effort to explain the myths of the ancient world as corruptions of facts recorded in the Bible ended in the eighteenth century by questioning whether the events recorded in the Bible were not merely myths. Bochart's original effort to turn the gods into patriarchs resulted in turning the patriarchs into myths. Hence the suspicion with which mythology came to be regarded, and the unexpected alliances which we find between the mythologists and liberal thinkers who were advancing in various directions. Just as it was no accident that Bochart's speculations began with his lectures on the book of Genesis, so it was no accident that the unreligious Bailly formulated his Euhemeristic system in a set of letters to Voltaire.

What happened was this: Whether men were disposed to defend or to attack the authority of the Bible, the way was opened for a new consideration of all the evidences bearing on the earliest history of man, and in this study the mythologist assumed a position of unaccustomed and unexpected authority. Hence the excitement which greeted the rapid succession of new and, from a modern point of view, preposterous systems embracing theories of the origin and dissemination of culture, such as those of Bryant, Bailly, Davies, and Wilford. It is difficult for the modern mind to realize how central a position the mythologist assumed for a brief period in scientific inquiry, or to believe that men like Bailly could receive the approbation of such bodies as the Academy in France or that Wilford's effusions could be received with profound attention by sober men like Sir William Jones, president of the Asiatic Society. Shortly after the beginning of the nineteenth century, "evidences" had accumulated in such great quantity that the theories of what we may now think of as a lunatic fringe of mythologists were swept into oblivion. The statement of Grimm's Law took linguistic science out of the hands of amateurs, and it was no longer possible to speculate wildly about the Phoenician origin of the Celts or the British origin of the Hindus. Evidences as to the antiquity of human society ended efforts to trace all civilizations to the scattering of the peoples after the destruction of the tower of Babel or to describe society in such simple terms as ante- and postdiluvian. Knowledge of the immense antiquity of the earth itself made the oldest myths seem recent. And the Darwinian theory of an upward evolution disposed forever of the widely held belief that society and man himself had degenerated from a Golden Age in which the first institutions of God had been perfect and those which we now possess are, as Volney described them, mere ruins.

The Euhemerism of the middle of the eighteenth century had led, by the beginning of the nineteenth, to a situation in which the mythologist exercised authority over speculation relating to the origin of culture. At the same time, mythology had been advancing in another direction. The fashion of the middle of the eighteenth century had been both Euhemeristic and rationalistic. From the efforts to explain myth in rational terms arose that diversity of special systems of which the Chevalier de

Jaucourt complained. No matter how cogently each specialist pleaded his cause, it was apparent that not every system could be correct. Common to each was the ever-present conviction that the myths rested upon some natural fact, and gradually, without controversy, the doctrine that the myths were embodiments of natural phenomena gained ground. The most interesting development in this direction began in France with Hancarville's theory that most of the myths were merely variants of each other and that basically they were allegories of the procreative powers. The detection of sexual symbolism in the myths became fashionable; in England the work of Richard Payne Knight, who developed Hancarville's theories, caused a suppressed scandal. A development from the new form of speculation was the unsavory recognition of survivals of sexual symbolism in still revered religious forms, and adherents of nature myth found themselves under suspicion as antireligionists. Less preoccupied with sex was another school of symbolists who discovered in myth the primitive language of men who had attempted to express in symbolic language their awe before the face of unknown powers. The increasing recognition, as the study of comparative mythology developed, that the natural language of the myths of one country was common to all, led even to the assumption that in primitive times men had been in a direct relationship to God and that the myths contained a vague but high theosophic knowledge communicated directly in pristine revelation. In Germany it was the mystical feature of the new symbolism which became most significant. The mystic revelation, clothed in the symbols of ancient myth, was of the same character as the mystery of Christianity. The symbolists supported the new movement toward Catholicism in Germany. Voss attacked savagely on this ground. Symbolism became the foe of Protestantism, at least in Voss's attack upon Heyne, Hermann, and Creuzer. Even the moderate Keightley in England pointed out that if the symbolists were right, Christianity became unnecessary.

The Euhemerism and rationalism which prevailed at the middle of the eighteenth century had provided little to stimulate the imagination of the poets. But the subsequent developments, which I have perhaps too hastily surveyed, were of a far different sort. In these was matter for the poetic mind to take hold of. The study of mythology ceased to be, for the poets, merely the instrument of a polite and conventional erudition. It became, indeed, a new sphere in which each, according to his capacities and disposition, could operate. From the eccentric systems of Wilford and Davies it was but a step to that of Blake, and if Blake chose to metamorphose the nebulous figures of mythological personages into equally nebulous figures of his visions, the contemporary reader would at least have recognized the misty region in which he trod. If a mythical Arthur faded into the outlines of an equally mythical Albion, there was little to be astonished at, and Los and Urizen were no more implausible than Bryant's Noah and Bailly's Atlas. Compared to the wild fancies of George Faber and Colonel Vallancey, Blake's work was that of a rigidly disciplined scientist.

To men like Shelley, who had grown mistrustful of what they regarded as the hypocrisy of conventional religion, myth became a new language in which the essential religious truths could be reëxpressed. To the poets of England as to the symbolists of Germany, myth was the

vehicle of religious utterance. It was no accident that when
Blake and Shelley desired to give utterance to the yearning
for a regeneration of mankind through love neither chose
the figure of Christ for the sufferer and the redeemer; the
one took the figure of Albion who should awake from his
sleep, and the other the figure of Prometheus tortured
upon his rock. Even the young John Keats strove to instill
into his *Endymion* an aspiration of the soul for some higher
good; if he failed to give the poem a convincing spiritual
meaning, it was the fault of his youth, not of his desire.

Those mythologists who had attempted to trace, by
their tenuous "evidences," the origin of the races had felt
that they had made important and exciting discoveries.
They had gazed with a wild surmise upon the Golden
Age, and they trembled with the excitement of the ex-
plorer. To the poets they communicated not so much their
wild surmises as their exhilaration. Blake's visions took
him to the origin of things. He saw the giants of antediluvian creation, and he moved backwards in time
through the epochs which had preceded man. Shelley and
Keats lived in a world of myth, and Goethe drew the
vanished beauty of the age of myth down through the
centuries with Helena. Shelley conceived the primordial
Demogorgon, and his imagination dwelt upon the age
when Prometheus brought down the gift of fire. Keats's
Endymion was of a generation before the heroes, and
Hyperion drove his orb of fire to light a world of elementary forms. Mythologist and poet alike shared the
mystery of the remote and the original. As Creuzer, the
most mystic of the scholars, declared that the mythologist
must have the mind of a poet, so the poet found himself
at home in the realm of the mythologist.

If the intellectual interpretations of myth in the eighteenth century had given the poet little stimulation, such was no longer the case. In the poetry of Keats the new nature myth found an inspired utterance. No poet was more skillful than Keats in merging the personages of his mythological poems with the elements which they represent. The most beautiful passages of *Endymion* are of this sort. Sleep (Hypnos), Ocean, the rivers Alpheus and Arethusa are magical translations of personages into natural forms. In *Hyperion* the manner in which the older myth of the sun dies into the rising splendor of Apollo is infinitely subtle and beautiful. Brilliant also is the ingenious manner in which Keats was shaping Enceladus to represent —as he must eventually, had the poem been completed— the volcanic eruptions of Mount Aetna.

Shelley's complex and mercurial mind asserted itself in another direction. Capable of dealing with intricate moral and intellectual allegories, Shelley seized hold of Hancarville and Knight's thesis of the double symbol in myth of the generative powers of nature. The ingenuity with which he applied this theory to his poetic conception of Adonais and Urania, sustaining the allegory in terms applicable to the quickening influence of the poet Keats, gave his peculiar stamp to a mythographical fashion. The immense failure of Goethe's *Second Part of Faust* came from the superabundant diversity of subtle allegories which he attempted to apply to an incongruous mythological theme.

One of the notable influences of the new mythology upon the poets was the growth of interest in very obscure mythological documents containing unconventional variants of the myths. Dr. Johnson's prediction that to give the poetical heroes new qualities or new adventures would offend by violating received notions was met in a curious fashion.

In the effort to foist new theories upon an overworked mass of mythology, each expounder of a new system had to present fresh evidences. The result was a thorough but uncritical exploration of a vast number of doubtful "authorities." Homer, Hesiod, Vergil, and Ovid gave way before a host of minor personages and unfamiliar variants of well-known legends. Recondite notions buried in the most obscure of writings became more important than the usual and the well known. Early Greek logographers and late Byzantine poets, reputed Babylonian priests and nameless mediaeval scholiasts—these became the authorities whose alleged knowledge was cited in support of new theories. In the footnotes of "the learned," Euhemerus, Philo of Biblis, Sanchuniathon, and even the pseudo-Berotus awoke to a brief second life. One encounters names which only the very doughtiest has met upon the verges of bibliography—names like Dionysius Skytobrachion—he of the leather arm—revived for his account of the Atlanteans. Pherecydes, Harpocration, Sallust the Gaul surnamed the Philosopher, Ptolemy Chennus, Antoninus Liberalis—these are names as remote from the course of things as the dwellings of the Cimmerians or Homer's Ethiopians. Minor writers on mythological topics, such as Conon, Parthenius, Hyginus, Heraclides of Pontus, Cornutus (or Phurnutus), Fulgentius, Apollodorus the Athenian, Palaephatus, even the doubtful, but certainly mediaeval, Albricus, became familiar names. Obscure writers on special subjects became fashionable, such as the astronomical writers Eratosthenes, Aratus, Manilius, and the pseudo-Hyginus. Poets as little read today as the

pompous Tzetzes, the dull Nonnus, and the obscure Lykophron assumed a place among the sons of light. Even
Theodontius, whom Boccaccio mentioned and perhaps
invented, was revived, and with him that Pronapides, the
tutor of Homer, from whom Theodontius received much
valuable information, but whose works, unhappily, have
perished.

The great Winckelmann once declared that the Greeks
had one vanity the less, the vanity of knowing many
books. From that modern vanity the Romantic poets were
not exempted. Since the works of the mythologists bristled
with the names of obscure authors, it is not surprising to
find that the poets followed them in their erudite excur-
sions. The insipidity and banality of mythological material was corrected by novelty. The vigorous research of
the mythologists out from the conventional into the adum-
bral regions of myth drew new facts and new ideas from
the shadows. Freshness of theme became possible by developing unusual variants of old legends, and worn classical
figures were reinvigorated by unfamiliar circumstance.

Thus the theme of Keats's *Hyperion* was intended to
turn, as I shall point out later, on an obscure circumstance
hinted by Procopius and Tzetzes. The action concerning
Demogorgon in Shelley's *Prometheus Unbound* rests upon
traditions preserved by the doubtful Theodontius, who
had them from who knows what sources—from that mythical Pronapides, from Conradus de Mure, from Janibiceps
(whom Conrad cites but about whom nothing else is preserved but his astonishing name) and from the nameless
scholiasts upon Lucan and Statius. In his *Achilleis* Goethe
was plotting merely a single part of his action by putting
together hints from a fragment of the Cyprian poems

preserved by Proclus, a prophecy reported by Lykophron in the *Alexandra*, another from Quintus Smyrnaeus, a story in Pausanias, and an unusual and otherwise unrecorded piece of information in Ptolemy Chennus.

Even the most unostentatious of the poets drew, in matters pertaining to classical myth, upon circumstances far outside the limits of information which the ordinarily well-read man might be expected to possess. Thus a stanza of Wordsworth's *Laodamia* seems to have been suggested by a passage in Tzetzes' *Antehomerica*. Several of the Titans in Keats's *Hyperion* stepped from the pages of Hyginus. Keats's friend Woodhouse speaks of "the very dark hints in the mythological poets of Greece and Rome" which went into the making of *Hyperion*. Shelley turned a whole scene in *Prometheus Unbound* upon a trivial piece of information contained in a scholium upon Aristophanes. The classical erudition necessary to design Goethe's plans for the activities of the Thessalian witches in the *Second Part of Faust* is bewilderingly minute. In one case —in his choice of Manto—the identification as a Thessalian sibyl rests only upon an insignificant notice by Suidas.

There was, perhaps, an element of vanity involved in the display of the most minute classical erudition. When Byron confessed to reading Diodorus Siculus in preparation for writing *Sardanapalus*, he explained that it was merely to refresh his memory, as he had long been familiar with the story. Goethe's humor in the Classical Walpurgis Night and in the reproaches leveled against the character of Helen of Troy depends upon such out-of-the-way information as to make one suspect that the poet was deliberately puzzling and confounding the learned among his readers. But there was more than vanity involved. The poets had invented a new kind of pleasure. The thing was to take the most daring liberties with the received notion of well-known myths and yet not really depart from the authority of ancient texts. There was a challenge to the reader to detect that the writer had kept his fable within authorized limits. The critic who failed to discern might easily make a fool of himself. Shelley, for instance, could have cited reputable authority for every circumstance of his barely discernible identification of the cave of Prometheus with Colonus. Novelty was combined with authority, and the learned reader might have the additional pleasure of perceiving the deft manner in which a new turn to a mythological fable had been executed upon an old fact. Much of the action of the last book of *Endymion* depends upon a story recorded briefly in one of the fragments of a mainly lost work of Hesiod, a story amplified by a scholiast upon Apollonius of Rhodes. The reader's pleasure was intended to be increased by perceiving that although the story had departed far from the well-known story concerning Endymion, it was yet operating within limits allowed by the Hesiodic story. The extraordinary flights of Euphorion in the *Second Part of Faust* are quite puzzling unless one has turned to Ptolemy Chennus to discover that Helen's child was born with wings.

I too, perhaps, have been guilty of alluding familiarly to obscure and minor mythologists without providing the reader with much information about them. To pass in review all of the names to which I have referred, attempting to describe the various systems of mythology and the theories of interpretation which each man developed, would be both tedious and fruitless. Some of the leading figures, however, deserve a brief account.

The most delightful and the most bizarre of these was old Samuel Bochart, minister of God at Caen. Pierre Bayle described Bochart as "one of the most learned men in the world." Born at Rouen in 1599, he had early distinguished himself as a scholar, writing verses in Greek and studying the oriental languages. Bayle tells a quaint story of a controversy in which Bochart engaged with one Father Veron, who was "provided with a special mission from the court to dispute, and as it were invested with the office of a Warranted Controvertist all over the kingdom." This redoubtable challenged Bochart "and did not cease to make a noise, till he had obtained a day and place to enter publickly into the lists with him." The dispute, which was held in the presence of a great many distinguished persons, "lasted from the twenty-second of September to the third of October, and the two disputants went through almost the whole wide field of controversy." Veron at last quitted the field, long before Bochart was done. Years later Bochart died disputing on the floor of the academy at Rouen. His French biographer observes that for a savant to have died in such a fashion was truly to have died on the field of honor.

Bochart should be regarded as the father of speculative mythology. Before the era of reliable philology he attempted to trace all words and all myth back to a Phoenician origin. He was really in pursuit of the language of the world which had been confounded at the tower of Babel, and in Phoenician he thought that he had found its most nearly related form. By a system of incredible and breath-taking etymologies he attempted to recover the primitive form of the confounded and corrupted original language—a process considerably aided by the fact that practically nothing was known of Phoenician. The myths he found to be corruptions of original Hebrew history. Bacchus was Noah by virtue of the latter's addiction to the vine on the occasion when he left the Ark, and Moses and the Muses were one. Despite Bochart's absurdities he trembled on the edge of a great discovery. Many of his linguistic analogies were excellent. He made the mistake of assuming a common origin for all languages. Finding true analogies in the Indo-European groups, he extended his method too far and was himself confounded in Babel.

When in 1774 Jacob Bryant in England commenced the publication of his *A New System; or, An Analysis of Ancient Mythology*, the spirit of Bochart walked again. Jacob Bryant was an astonishing person. Financially well off, a protégé of the Marlboroughs and a friend of the king, he devoted a very long life to scholarship, during the nine decades of which he came to not a single correct conclusion. His erudition was equaled only by his capacity to misuse it. He proved that Chatterton did not forge the Rowley poems, that there had never been a Troy, and he set up a system of mythology which dazzles the imagination. At last, as if Learning could no longer endure the outrage, a book fell on him while he was at work in his study, and he died from the injury.

In addition to the works of Bochart, Bryant had been impressed by that group of early chronologists, Josephus Scaliger, Newton, Marsham, and others, who had attempted to work out the real chronology of history by the comparative method, adjusting the periods of the recorded histories of one nation to those of the others. Marsham in particular had attracted his attention by laying side by side all the important chronologies, and by the method of the Procrustean bed, stretching out the short ones, and lopping off the long ones, until all agreed in an absolute chronology, the limits of which were the Flood and the period of reliably dated Greek history.

Bryant had a gift for perceiving mysterious and dramatic analogies in the most obviously unrelated things. The bulk of his work consists of deductions drawn from such observations. He was particularly disposed to resolve all the myths into variants of the story of the Flood; and Noah and the *Noachidae*, as he calls Shem, Ham, and Japhet, engage in the most remarkable transmarine appearances. The nucleus of the treatise, however, is Bryant's basic idea that the descendants of Ham formed a great Amonian family who were the disseminators of culture. As Bochart had attempted to re-create the antediluvian language, so Bryant attempted to re-create Amonian, setting up, in the modern manner, radicals comparable to the hypothecated forms of present-day philology. He fell into the same error that Bochart had made, of hypothecating a single original for all the languages. The ramifications of his Amonian theory need not be repeated here or elsewhere; suffice it to say that Bryant found evidence of the migration of this distinguished people in such separated places as Syria and Japan. Greek fable was a bad corruption of Amonian tradition. Aside from the attention which the Amonians received throughout the six volumes of the *Mythology*, and the unifying influence of Bryant's constant preoccupation with the Deluge, the systematic character of Bryant's work was largely an illusion of his own. The work is in reality a varied set of essays on comparative mythology, full of wild guesses which are often contradictory. Nothing in it seems to be true, and yet it is not altogether absurd. Bryant was fumbling toward a scientific treatment of comparative mythology. A hundred years later, with the protection of modern philology, he might have been a great mythologist. He had raked through the whole literature of myth, bringing to bear evidences from the most difficult sources. His chief fault was a kind of delight in the mysteriously obscure. He had little sense about the comparative weight of evidence, having convinced himself, by a long train of reasoning, that in matters of Greek myth, late Roman and even mediaeval sources were superior in authority to early Greek ones. He was totally unable to perceive the motive underlying the attitudes of early writers. That Euhemerus or Philo of Biblis had an ulterior purpose in writing as they did seems not to have occurred to him. And yet the oddest part of the whole performance is that Bryant's remarks on the scientific consideration of evidence and the necessity for an open mind are excellent.

Bryant had felt a modest but deep confidence in himself. He was thrilled by the feeling that he had penetrated the mists of history, that he had devised a method by which man could reach, through science, to unrecorded periods of time, disentangling from obscurity the long history of man. He was not ashamed to admit that he sometimes contradicted himself, nor was he afraid that his findings should be proved wrong. He was very willing that they should. It was his method which he cherished. He concluded his immense *Mythology* with the statement that if anything remained to be said on the subject, it might wait for a time.

It did not have long to wait. Almost immediately after the appearance of Bryant's *Mythology*, two documents were issued which gave a remarkable stimulus to the study of myth. The first of these to appear was the first volume of the *History of Ancient Astronomy* by Jean Sylvain Bailly; the second was the *Epochs of Nature* by Buffon. The latter of these two books is still memorable for the clarity and beauty of its style. It contains Buffon's theory of *refroidissement*—now a geological curiosity. Of interest to us is Buffon's statement that the cradle of human culture was a region between the fortieth and fifty-fifth degrees latitude, in southern Siberia and the north of Tartary, where the proper conditions prevailed for the development of a great society. There, he concludes, flourished a wise and happy people who, for a period of several thousand years, living in peace and leisure, cultivated a superior society. This society was at length overwhelmed, to be followed by thirty centuries of ignorance, in which successive societies retained merely the debris of the lost culture and faint reminiscences which survived in the varying myths of different peoples.

This happy and wise people who inhabited the Caucasus Mountains were an invention not of Buffon, but of his friend Jean Sylvain Bailly, whose *Astronomy* appeared in the same year.

Through errors needless to repeat here, Bailly had come to the conclusion that a profound knowledge of astronomy had existed at a period prior to recorded history. He developed a fanciful theory of a pristine culture, existing some fifteen hundred years prior to the Deluge, in which astronomy was a highly developed art. Early evidences of astronomical knowledge among the Egyptians, Persians, Chaldeans, Chinese, and others, he attributed to the faint and imperfect recollections of an earlier time. The most ancient of known knowledge was but the debris of this pristine culture. Bailly subsequently became involved in a friendly dispute over the matter with Voltaire, who inclined to the belief that the culture of the Brahmins was the most ancient of all. In a series of letters, written in a sparkling style, Bailly explored his own hypothesis. It is difficult to give an exposition of the actual theory contained in these *Letters on the Atlantis of Plato*, because Bailly had developed an ingenious technique for forcing the reader to make mistakes while the writer committed himself to not a single statement. We are led to the inference, however, that Bailly's lost people were Atlanteans, that they emerged at a very remote period from the Far North, from one of the isles of the glacial sea. Perhaps Spitsbergen was the home of this superior race. The reigns of Uranus, Hesper, and Atlas took place there. Greenland, we infer, was the kingdom of Saturn. In successive waves of emigration, the Atlanteans spread south towards Asia, establishing themselves for a long period of time in the Caucasus Mountains where their culture was developed to its highest point. Eventually the Atlanteans were overwhelmed by a great disaster, and their civilization disappeared. Only some fragments of it, poorly understood, reminiscences which formed the myths of some of its scattered survivors, remained to attest its former existence. The culture of Asia owed its origin to these people, and all the earliest races were indebted to them for what each had preserved from the great catastrophe. Bailly was specific in one interesting respect. He found an exact (if imaginary) location for his Atlanteans during the period of their Caucasian residence. This was that mountain of the Caucasus named Caf to which I have already referred.

The solid accomplishments of Buffon in natural history, and the respectable work of Bailly in astronomy, gave a weight to the theoretical portions of their books which the theory alone would never have received. Men's imaginations were unleashed by the thought of unrecorded periods of history, of a lost race of Titanic people, and by the thought that the myths which had so long been cherished had indeed a germ of truth in them.

A host of imitators followed, who wove from Bryant and from Bailly new and still more extravagant hypotheses. Sir William Jones, offended by Bailly's neglect of Hebrew tradition, made a valiant effort to support the accuracy of Scripture. Edward Davies in his *Celtic Researches* depicted antediluvian society as that of a Golden Age.

Davies' hypothesis was one of the decline of primitive culture from a great original. Referring to doctrines of an upward evolution in society, he rejected them with scorn. Thus in 1803 he declared: "We have consequently been amused with strange and monstrous tales of that mute, as well as ill-contrived quadruped, Man,—a being, who, for a series of ages, crawled upon the earth, before he began, occasionally, to assume an erect posture, and walk upon his hinder feet; who afterwards made slow progress through the monkey, and the savage, accidentally acquired speech and reason; till at length, forming himself into a kind of terrestrial God, he established a dominion over his brethren of the forest."

Davies accepted substantially the Biblical account of origins. His great period of culture was that of the patriarchs. He made the not unreasonable suggestion that men like Methuselah, who lived, retaining the use of their faculties for a space of six to nine centuries, could well be supposed to have brought their inventions to a higher degree of perfection than is allowed to such short-lived creatures as ourselves. He estimated that when Noah got into the Ark he carried with him the accumulated culture of some one thousand six hundred and fifty years of ante-diluvian history, a culture that had been built up by rational beings formed and disposed by the hand of a good and wise Creator.

Davies was particularly concerned with the Druids, whom he believed to have retained the patriarchal culture. He traces them back to Ashkenaz, one of the three sons of Gomer, among whose descendants were likewise the Titans. The Titans, after their defeat, went to dwell among the Hyperboreans, who were none other than the early inhabitants of Britain. Apollo was "an accredited Hyperborean," as was also Atlas. Evidence pointed, Davies believed, toward the fact that the British Isles were both the Paradise and Hell of Greek mythology, even though, as he said, "the country will not answer the description, either of wretchedness or felicity."

I must follow time's example, and neglect some of Davies' too numerous contemporaries, save to remark that one of the most remarkable, Colonel Vallancey, matched Davies' Celtic Titans with Phaeno-Scythian Irish and that George Faber combined prophecy with mythology to become the forerunner of some of our American prophets. Not less fascinating nor less numerous than the English speculators were the Germans, particularly the Göttingen mythologists. Carlyle has done justice to the inspirer of them all, Heyne, with a delightful biographical sketch in which the learned German bears a marked resemblance to the hero of *Sartor Resartus*. Most of the lesser mythologists may safely be left to obscurity, but two little-known figures, Hancarville and Wilford, clamor for recognition, and with them I shall conclude this essay.

Pierre François Hancarville (or d'Ancarville, but really Hugues) was the editor of Hamilton's great folios of Etruscan vases and the exponent of the Etruscan theory of the origin of Greek art. His great work, however, was his *Researches on the Origin, the Spirit, and the Progress of the Arts of Greece,* of which only two introductory volumes were published at London, in 1785, in French. He became so incensed at the criticism of them that he interrupted his labors to write a third volume in answer to the critics, and the remainder of the work never appeared. The two volumes are extraordinary. Hancarville's notes, printed in large letters at the bottom of the page, are so extensive that most of the time they overwhelm the text. Sometimes one loses sight of the text altogether because a whole page is swallowed up by the notes. One seems to be reading six or seven different books at once, on the most diverse subjects, and since the important steps in the development of Hancarville's theory are now in the text, now in the notes, it is never entirely clear just what were the origin, spirit, and progress of the arts in Greece. Appreciating this difficulty, one of Hancarville's first critics declared that as he attempted to review the book, the ground shook under him at every step.

Hancarville was enough of a person, however, to have won the friendship of Winckelmann. Richard Payne Knight became his disciple and the eventual exponent of his ideas, and through Knight and through Charles Towneley, the collector, he exercised a considerable influence in England as consultant in the formation of some of England's most conspicuous collections of antiquities.

Hancarville's basic idea was that in primitive times, when the worship of the true God prevailed, men strove to represent God in works of art. That being ultimately impossible, they succeeded in giving an imperfect expression to some of God's attributes by means of emblems or symbols. Thus the grandeur and immensity of God were expressed in great stones revered in primitive temples such as Stonehenge. Others of God's attributes were expressed in symbols of light and fire. Men strove to represent not alone his attributes but his titles, and Hancarville etymologizes a connection between the symbol of the bull and the Deity. The art of sculpture arose from the effort to embody the idea of divinity in a symbol. But as the representation of forms became more skillful, the original significance of the symbols was nearly lost in the creation of works of art, and worship was transferred from the object to the emblem itself. Nevertheless, the underlying religious symbolism of these evolved forms was never wholly lost to sight, and it is that original meaning which the scholar of art and myth may hope to trace. The theory was involved in all sorts of subsidiary matters, such as the descent of the Greeks from the Titans and the Titans from the Scyths, together with the idea that Greek art was borrowed by the Greeks from Asia (apparently a later idea than the Etruscan theory). One of Hancarville's most interesting beliefs is that the mythological and the symbolical meanings of a work of art are two different things. Mythological fables were late associations of the emblems, attached to works of art when the significance of the emblem had been all but forgotten—an idea of which William Blake made use in his print of Laocoön.

Despite his reputation in society, Hancarville was a dishonest fellow who at one time landed in prison for his activities. He was not above forgery, having invented and printed a number of obscene drawings which he passed off as drawings made from genuine antique gems. He seems, however, to have been as fascinating as he was ingenious and talented, and he and his works were well known for a generation among antiquarians, collectors, the fashionable dilettanti, and the mythologists.

The most interesting and most pathetic figure among my eccentric mythologists was Francis Wilford.

For a long time while I was puzzling over some of the utterances of Blake and of Sir William Jones, it seemed to me that there must have been some mythologist who had attached to his system the notion that events referred to in the very earliest myths had taken place in England. As an astronomer feels the presence of an undiscovered planet by detecting the lag in the movements of the known, so I felt, but could not discern, the existence of some great luminary among the mythologists. The publications of Lieutenant, later Captain, Francis Wilford in *Asiatic Researches*, a journal established by members of the Asiatic Society of Bengal and published at Calcutta, aroused my suspicion, and Wilford seemed a likely choice for the only begetter of such nonsense. Considerable mystery attached to the various numbers of Wilford's "An Essay on the Sacred Isles in the West" which appeared irregularly in the journal. Their most remarkable feature was that they seemed to have no bearing on the subject announced in the title, and that they made little sense. They had no beginning and no end, only an interminable middle, which I was perpetually at a loss to understand. At last the mystery was revealed in the following sorry facts.

Wilford was an English officer living in India who had early joined the Asiatic Society and who was held in high esteem by its president, Sir William Jones. He conceived the notion that there was some connection between Albion and a certain fabulous White Island mentioned in Hindu myths. In order to facilitate his researches, Wilford hired the services of some learned Hindus, the "pundits" to whom he constantly refers. Wilford's pundits sized up their imaginative, naïve, and gullible English patron. They saw that he was interested in collecting evidence which would show some connection between the mythology of India and the legendary history of Britain. Obligingly they commenced to forge documents which they supposed would interest their patron. They altered existing documents, inserted extra pages, wrote variants of their own legends. One entered with such spirit into the deception that he forged a whole poem twelve thousand lines long.

Wilford would discuss his rapidly and startlingly evolving theories with his pundits, and shortly thereafter the pundits would surprise and delight him by producing evidence in support of them. Early in the process Wilford must have had his great conception: that England was the actual spot where the events of antediluvian time, as they are recorded in the history of the Hebrews and the myths of other nations, had taken place. His hypothesis appears to have been nothing short of that.

The pundits went about the extensive forging necessary to support this hypothesis. They read to him "extracts," pretending that these extracts had been taken from their sacred writings. These passed into Wilford's notes. He showed his notes to his friends, especially to Sir William

Jones. The forgeries were not detected. His friends shared in advance the excitement of the amazing thing which he was going to prove. Wilford commenced a series of reports and essays designed to clear the ground for the great event. By word of mouth the news spread, and persons in England knew what was to be revealed. Had the great proof ever been published the relevance of matters in Wilford's essays would doubtless be apparent. Friends who were in on the secret understood what he was about. When Sir William Jones translated one of the documents which contained a purported Hindu version of the story of the Flood, closely parallel to that in the Bible but with striking differences, he was well aware that the document was an important link in the proof of Wilford's great discovery.

Then in 1805, before the great work had appeared, Wilford discovered the imposture practiced upon him. In an effort to check his findings with the original sources, he observed evidences of erasures. He investigated further and discovered all that had been done. Wilford was an honest man. He was overwhelmed with dismay and shame. At once he wrote to all his friends exposing the impostures. Notices were sent to English periodicals and duly published. The *British Critic* for April, 1805, prints an account of the whole affair which indicates that Wilford and his theory of the White Island were well known at that time in England. Wilford was desolated and actually ill from the discovery. Disappointed at the failure of what must by that time have constituted his lifework, he attempted to put together the shreds of what was left. Sir William Jones, actuated, I suspect, by that deep kindness and gentleness of spirit which pervades all his works, went over the documents and deleted the forgeries, making a public statement as to the authenticity of what remained. Wilford corrected his essays and published some of them, but they were mutilated fragments of the originals, with nothing very intelligible in them. He still somewhat pathetically declared that Great Britain and Ireland are the sacred isles of the Hindus, "of which Sweta Dwipa, or the White Island, is the most famous; in fact, the holy land of the Hindus." And it was there, he says, that "the fundamental and mysterious transactions of the history of their religion, in its rise and progress took place." But the vague and rambling essays have little remaining in them that really bears on the question. The situation was further complicated by the fact that the publications of the *Asiatic Researches* were reprinted verbatim in England several years after their original issue in Calcutta, so that we have the extraordinary phenomenon of Wilford's garbled essays reappearing from year to year in England long after the exposure had taken place. The whole farce was reënacted for a second generation of readers, of whom William Blake was probably one.

It is not too difficult to see what Wilford had originally intended to prove: that Albion, or England, was a portion of an old Atlantic continent, and that, together with Ireland and certain other islands, it was all that remained of that continent after the violent upheaval which is recorded in the various traditions respecting a deluge and the disappearance of the fabled Atlantis. Wilford did in fact identify Albion with Atlantis and such other legendary islands and fabulous happy places as the Blessed Isles, Elysium, and the terrestrial paradise. It must have been his intention to say that the book of Genesis preserves merely one version of the events of the earliest history of mankind and that the actual cradle of the human race was England.

With the collapse of Wilford, the day of the eccentric mythologist was over. In Germany, mythology entered upon a truly scientific period. K. O. Müller's insistence upon the precise testing of the reliability of evidence had its effect, and although Creuzer and Görres remained popular, there was soon a swing away from the effort to use myth as the evidence on which to build up a systematic view of the history of man or culture. The mythologist of the older order became a comic figure, and passed into fiction. There was "Mr. Ramsbottom, the zodiacal mythologist," of Thomas Love Peacock's *Crotchet Castle*, who advised Mr. Mac Crotchet to "withdraw from the region of Uranus or Brahma, the Maker, to that of Saturn or Veeshnu, the Preserver, before he fell under the eye of Jupiter or Seva, the Destroyer." The "First Chapter" of Teufelsdröckh's monumental work of which *Sartor* gives us so admirable an account, "turns on Paradise and Fig-leaves, and leads us into interminable disquisitions of a mythological, metaphorical, cabalistico-sartorial and quite antediluvian cast." Carlyle gives us a brief glimpse into the "Adam-Kadmon, or Primeval Element, here strangely brought into relation with the *Nifl* and *Muspel* (Darkness and Light) of the antique North," and then Teufelsdröckh takes us "from the Tower of Babel, to follow the dispersion of Mankind over the whole habitable and habilable globe. Walking by the light of Oriental, Pelasgic, Scandinavian, Egyptian, Otaheitan, Ancient and Modern researches of every conceivable kind," Teufelsdröckh takes mythology into his clothes philosophy in Carlyle's most amusing fashion. And George Eliot had her fun with Mr. Casaubon in *Middlemarch*, who aimed to show that "all the mythical systems or erratic mythical fragments in the world were corruptions of a tradition originally revealed," and who had the immense task before him of arranging the formidable notes which he had accumulated. Mr. Casaubon admitted that all this had been done before, but never, he hoped, with so excellent an arrangement.

With mythology in the hands of Mr. Casaubon, we may turn from the mythagogues to the poet William Blake, who was most conspicuously under their influence. More than one post-mortem has been conducted over Blake's astonishing vision poetry. Perhaps if we find symptoms of speculative mythology a diagnosis may be made which will relieve the doctors of further examination.

Blake's Albion

THE poems of Blake which are best known today are his short lyrics, mostly from his *Songs of Innocence* and *Songs of Experience*. These poems are justly admired, and there has never been any dispute as to their excellence. The composition and illustration of his shorter poems consumed, however, but a portion of Blake's time and creative energy. It was in the setting down, the illuminating, and the printing of his so-called "vision poetry," or "prophetic books," that the poet and artist expended the greatest creative effort of his life. Yet few persons today have the hardihood to read very much of the poetry which Blake must have regarded as his chief contribution to the world. Interest in the prophetic books has been limited to a small set of Blake enthusiasts, and interest in the poems has been second to an admiration for the illuminated drawings which adorn but do not always illustrate them.

The difficulty of reading these poems of Blake is not, however, insuperable. There has been too much talk about Blake as a great mystic. He was, in reality, a very simple man who labored all his life to express a few basic convictions. He had a sharp, slightly enigmatic sense of humor, with an element of perversity in it which often led him to be extravagantly whimsical at unexpected moments—to the detriment of clarity. He championed his favorite ideas with a fanatical zeal which made it possible for him to fly in the face of all the facts which history and science had accumulated, and this, not in ignorance, but with a deliberate disregard. Whatever he believed in, he believed in so fervently that doubt provided no inner check upon his outer manner of expression.

His convictions are all dominated by one: that man has departed from the guidance of God and should return to it. The problem in reading Blake is mainly to perceive just how his central conviction dominates the topic under consideration, and then to perceive the particular, and often eccentric, idiom which he is using as a medium for expression.

The greatest obstacle to an understanding of Blake is the difficulty of apprehending the curious and seemingly baffling mythical personages which move through the vision poetry. Efforts to systematize these personages into an orderly and coherent scheme have resulted only in a greater confusion. They do not fit into a theogony. Nor can the places which Blake imagines be located in an orderly cosmos, as one may describe and even map out the places in Milton's universe. The effort to resolve them into a clear meaning leads to still greater perplexity. These difficulties rest, I believe, upon the peculiarities of the medium which Blake chose as a means of expression, a medium which presented itself to him partly from his own visionary disposition and partly from certain notions concerning myth which were entertained in his own day.

I have said that Blake's mind was, for all his extraordinary genius, a very simple one, intent for most of his life upon the expression of a single fundamental idea: that the

ills of the world—of man in society and in his own heart—
have resulted from man's failure to listen to the guidance
of God. Everything that Blake did or was somehow had
reference to his desire to communicate his great message
of man's need of divine guidance. Blake was absorbingly
interested in the problem which his conviction presented:
How was the guidance of God to be discovered? His
mind explored with the most intense excitement the methods by which man might stand in direct relationship to
God. Divine revelation was what he sought, by whatever
means it might be received. For the Bible, which he
believed to be the revealed word of God, he had the most
profound respect. He sought for revelation in the misty
utterances of Swedenborg. He turned to the mystic Jacob
Böhme. But because he was a poet and an artist, with the
instinct to create, and because he was born in the eighteenth century, he turned primarily to two things, to the
imagination and to myth. In both of these he found what
he supposed to be a direct approach to God.

In the psychology of Blake's time the imagination had
come to be regarded as a function of the mind through
which direct apprehension of reality took place. To Blake
it was the receptacle of divine revelation, the direct inspiration of God, who was the ultimate reality. But if that
which enters the imagination is divine revelation, the perception of reality must take some form intelligible to the
mind. The form which the revelation takes is what Blake
describes as a vision. The function of the poet is to set
down, as from a divine dictation, the visions which enter
the imagination. But since words are inadequate and faulty
in the depiction of a vision, the artist supplements the poet
by drawing or painting the visions exactly as they appear.

But why is it, one may ask, that Blake constantly explains the visionary figures which appear in his poetry and
illustrations by equating them directly or indirectly with
figures which are faintly recognizable from mythology,
or by describing them in such a way that one perceives
analogies with recognizable mythological figures? Why,
for instance, does he give to one of his figures the name of
Albion, who is well known to us as a figure in Greek
myth and in legendary British history? And why, having
done so, does he explain that Albion is King Arthur? And
why again, if Albion is really Arthur, does he make a
drawing of him in which he looks exactly like Laocoön?

The answer is not so difficult or confusing as might at
first appear. In the first place, one must consider the difficulty which Blake's hypothesis presents. If God communi-
cates directly to man by means of visions which appear in
the imagination, how are we to know what the visions
mean? What communication has taken place? It is clear
that the visions must be symbolic in character and communication take place through man's capacity to understand what the symbols mean. If he cannot understand the
symbols, he cannot understand the message. Now Blake
appears to have had no difficulty in understanding his own
visions, and we should expect that he would understand
them, since his own imagination shaped them. But since
he could not suppose that everyone else would understand
them, he employed his remarkable device of symbolic
equation.

In the speculation ardently pursued in Blake's time concerning the nature of myth, symbolism played a conspicuous part. Most noted among the "symbolic" mythologists
was the learned Creuzer, who had come to regard myth

as a development (or perhaps a degeneration) of an earlier symbolism by means of which men had, in the very earliest times, expressed their consciousness of divine power. Symbols were the pristine language in which men spoke of God. Creuzer does not go so far as to say that the symbols were actual revelations at a time when man in his original society was close to God. In fact, he raises the question only to refuse to answer it. But less scholarly minds, perceiving analogies among the myths of the world and reading into their common elements recondite and lofty meanings, had been led to suppose that God had, in antediluvian times, made important revelations to men. Thus Edward Davies, finding evidence of a high theosophy among the Druids and supposing the Druids to have inherited patriarchal culture, expressed the opinion that long before Christ, and long before the Mosaic revelations, God had instructed the patriarchs in such matters of doctrine as the immortality of the soul, the resurrection, and the future judgment, obscure traditions of which he found preserved both by Jews and Gentiles. The promise of Christ, Davies considered among the antediluvian communications, as well as the knowledge of a supreme God, whose unity the Gentiles perceived under a great variety of symbols and allegories. Blake appears to have taken the step that Creuzer was unwilling to take and to have assumed, like Davies, that God had made original communications to men, that these communications had been embodied in symbols, and that the myths of the world had developed out of these symbols, perverting their original significance but not wholly losing it.

But if Blake conceived the myths of the world as retaining, in however vague and vestigial a manner, symbols which embodied high revelation of God, one may perceive how he could equate them with the visions which appeared in his own imagination. Both were to him symbolical representations of divine revelation. By equating the symbolic visions which appeared in his own imagination with the mythological personages by means of which other men had striven to portray the meaning of similar revelations, Blake supposed that the one would help to explain the other. Moreover, by professing an identity between myths and his own visions, he could make the myths serve to authenticate his visions by showing the continuity of God's message and its fundamental and universal character.

Blake sincerely believed that the visions which appeared in his imagination were divine communications, but he would not have hesitated, I think, to admit that the form which they took in his mind was influenced and perhaps determined by his personal experience. Certainly such was the case, and one cannot doubt that Blake was conscious that his visions, as they expressed themselves in his imagination, took forms which could be understood only by those who had shared his experiences. The more personal the visions were, therefore, the greater the need to identify them with a universally recognized symbol: hence the frequent situation in Blake's poetry in which a highly personal experience is incongruously identified with something that seems wholly disproportionate to it.

At this point, I imagine, the reader is ready to interrupt. "What you say," he will object, "makes plausible theory, but it does not make it any easier to read Blake. If the theory is right, all that we need to do is to explain Blake's symbols in terms of a personal experience, or, if we do not understand the personal experience, explain them in terms of some myth with which Blake equates them. But the theory does not work in practice. It still is not clear what the reader has gained when Blake declares that Albion is Arthur."

Unfortunately there is more to the theory—but not a great deal more. Anyone who attempts to resolve Blake's poetry through critical analysis is faced with the stubborn fact that it is difficult to explain one thing about Blake until something else has been explained. Hence it is difficult to find a central point from which a critical discussion may take its departure. Yet the aesthetic theory on which Blake's vision poetry rests is not a very difficult one to understand as a whole, once one perceives the elements of which it is composed.

To sum up briefly what I have already said: I have taken as my point of departure the dogmatic statement that Blake's dominating conviction was that man had departed from the guidance of God and that he should return to it. Scrutinizing the methods by which man might receive directly the guidance of God, Blake found the imagination to be an organ of the mind through which, in the form of symbolic visions, he could receive a direct apprehension of God's messages. These visions were, however, too personal to serve altogether as a means of communication to other persons. Believing that myths might also be interpreted as retaining symbolic representations of divine revelation, Blake attempted to clarify his own visions for his readers by equating them with parallel symbols which he found in the diverse myths of the world. The reader's difficulty lies in the fact that Blake's equations merely make darkness visible.

The trouble is that Blake, like the symbolists in mytho-

logical theory, was forced to suppose that myths had
become seriously corrupted in their passage through time.
Before they could be interpreted as symbols of a pristine
divine revelation, it was necessary to divest them of all
that was false, idolatrous, and corrupt. In many cases an
original symbol had come to be associated with merely
historical events and personages of late periods in human
history. The myths, therefore, had to be cleansed of all
accretions before the original symbolic meaning could be
recaptured. But in the process of divesture, Blake so mutilated the myths as to leave them barely recognizable. Their
ordinary features, by which we might familiarly identify
them, were obliterated. Moreover, in the effort to make
them stand for a symbol of divine revelation, the meaning for which they stood had to be reduced to a vague
and dim one—a faint theosophic promise of the regeneration of the soul through love, an intimation of immortality,
or a promise of a redeemer and a judgment. The modern
reader, by no means disposed to believe that the ancient
myths embodied messages of God, fails to discern any
significance whatever in the equations which Blake makes.
He does not even recognize the myths in any intelligible
form. He dimly perceives that the vision poetry and its
illustrations are infused with a spiritual meaning, but he
perceives no clear connection between the meaning which
he understands and the symbolic personages associated
with Blake's utterances. Blake's medium of expression
proved to be an unfortunate one. The fault, however, is
somewhat mitigated by the fact that in the long run all the
symbols resolve themselves into one and the same thing—
their message is always basically the same: that man has
departed from the guidance of God and that he should

return to it. In effect one may actually ignore, without attempting very hard to understand, the whole immense apparatus in which the vision poetry is communicated. When Blake has something to say, he says it very clearly, and it is usually worth listening to.

Regard for the superiority of vision is what led Blake, by a somewhat circuitous route, to his eager adoption of the more extravagant theories of the mythologists. Blake had a deep admiration for the beauty of Greek sculpture. Anxious to claim the masterpieces of ancient art as works of vision, that is, of divine inspiration, he found in the theories of Hancarville and the symbolists a convenient method of so doing. Greek statues, Blake reasoned, could not have been the work of the corrupt Greeks; they must therefore be copies of earlier inspired works. The fables which the Greeks attached to the statues, associating them with heroes and with false gods, were but late accretions, added after the meaning of an original symbolism had been lost. The earlier works from which they were copied were originals—that is, symbolical works executed under the direct inspiration of God. Blake regarded the Torso of the Belvedere as the only surviving original work among the ancient statues. He declared that he had seen these "originals" in his visions and that they all contained "mythological and recondite meaning, where more is meant than meets the eye." An extreme and perhaps partly whimsical instance of his belief is his statement that the Laocoön Group was copied by the Rhodian sculptors from the cherubim of Solomon's temple. Since the cherubim of Solomon's temple were supposedly copies of the cherubim executed by the divinely inspired sculptors who, under God's direction, adorned the ark of the first temple,

Blake fancied the beauty of the Laocoön Group thus to be derived from an original work of direct inspiration. Modification of the figures to represent the fable of Laocoön and his two sons was an unwarranted corruption and perversion.

Eager to recognize the divine works under their accretion of fable, Blake was happy to suppose that fable itself might be a corruption of original symbol. Hence he found himself in sympathy with the symbolists among the mythographers. "Let it here be noted," he announced in his comments upon his *A Vision of the Last Judgment*, "that the Greek Fables originated in Spiritual Mystery & Real Vision, which are lost & clouded in Fable & Allegory . . ." In the same document he declared that the fables in Apuleius' *Golden Ass* and Ovid's *Metamorphoses* "contain Vision in a sublime degree, being derived from real Vision in More ancient Writings."

If the myths themselves retained something of the recondite or symbolic meaning of divine vision, Blake could find it satisfactory to equate his own visions with mythological personages, provided, of course, that the merely fabulous and idolatrous aspect of the myth be regarded as spurious.

As an exemplification of what I have been writing, I propose to attempt to resolve into critical analysis the figure Albion, which appears so frequently in Blake's vision poetry. I have selected this one from the many personages who are involved in the prophetic poems because Albion, similar in kind to the other imaginary figures, plays a central part in Blake's poetry. The resolution of Albion into his component elements may serve as a revelation of the general character of the other mythical personages and provide an explanation of what Blake intended by them.

Although it is at once apparent that Blake's Albion is not the same as the legendary figure whose name he bears, it will be convenient to recall to the reader the lore ordinarily associated with the name.

Albion is a figure known in Greek myth for his participation in one of the famous stories concerning Hercules. He was one of two giants, the sons of Poseidon, who endeavored to prevent Hercules from passing the Rhone. When Hercules had used up all his arrows, he called for help upon Zeus, who rained stones down upon the enemies of Hercules, slaying Albion. The story is told by Apollodorus, Mela, and others, with some variation in the form of the name. The word *Albion* was also commonly used by Greek and Roman writers as the name of Britain. Holinshed, attempting to link the place name with the legend, explains that Albion, the giant, was of the race of Cham. He subdued the ancient Samotheans, earliest inhabitants of Britain, and established himself as its ruler, giving his name to the island. Fearing the power of Hercules, he went to France to subdue him, and met his death. The name Albion also appears in the name Albion Mountain, applied by Strabo to Mount Velika, a mountain which almost joined the ancient Mount Ocra to the Alps. The etymology of the name has been much disputed, the question being whether it derived from a root which appears in various languages, meaning *mountain*, or a similar root meaning *white*. England's coastline may have given the name to the whole island, *Albion* applying both to the whiteness of its chalk cliffs and to the mountainous appearance of the coastline itself.

We are prepared to expect that in Blake's poems Albion may be a giant, a mountain, or England itself, but we are not prepared for the discovery that he is a great many other personages and things. For instance, in Blake's *Descriptive Catalogue*, commenting on his now lost fresco "The Ancient Britons," the poet declares: "The giant Albion, was Patriarch of the Atlantic; he is the Atlas of the Greeks, one of those the Greeks called Titans. The stories of Arthur are the acts of Albion, applied to a Prince of the fifth century, who conquered Europe, and held the Empire of the world in the dark age, which the Romans never again recovered." A little above, in the same notes, Blake had said: "Arthur was a name for the constellation Arcturus, or Boötes, the keeper of the North Pole." Albion, it would appear, was a Greek Titan, Atlas, the legendary Arthur, and the constellation Boötes, as well as the patriarch of the Atlantic.

All these identifications are exceedingly bewildering unless we suppose that Blake's mind has proceeded in the fashion which I have already described in general terms at the beginning of this essay. Finding the name Albion a very ancient one, connected with words which appear anciently in diverse languages and with legendary figures in the earliest ages of the earth, Blake seized hold of it as pertaining to one of those vestigial symbols through which, he believed, men in the most remote times had expressed some original revelation of God to men. A visionary figure having presented itself persistently to his imagination, Blake conceived a resemblance between the visionary figure in his own imagination and the fabular forms into which an original symbol was corrupted in the myths of the world. Albion, Atlas, Arthur, and Boötes are merely

the forms into which fable corrupted an original mythological personage who represented symbolically a meaning
identical with that of Blake's own vision.

We must now ask ourselves three questions: By what
process of the mind did Blake come to suppose that Albion,
Atlas, Arthur, and Boötes were the forms into which his
original symbol had been corrupted? What meaning did
he attach to the symbol which had been corrupted into
such diverse forms? How may an understanding of these
matters simplify and clarify our reading of Blake's poetry?

To the first of these questions a very exact answer may
be given, as it is possible to trace the process minutely as
it took shape in Blake's mind. His identification of Albion
with the various figures enumerated is the result of a coa-
lescence in Blake's mind of a number of bizarre theories
that he had encountered in the works of speculative mythologists.

Blake's Albion is, he tells us, the Titan Atlas, patriarch
of the Atlantic continent. The notion is put together from
the theories of Wilford and Bailly and from some one
of the many writers who, like Gian Rinaldo Carli, held
that a continent had once stretched from Europe to America and had been sunk in a great catastrophe. Bailly had
conceived of Atlas as an historical personage, son of
Uranus, and brother of Saturn, who had ruled in remote
times over a great race, perhaps of giants, which had
inhabited the world before a great catastrophe overwhelmed them. Blake's Atlantic continent would, then,
appear to be the inhabited world before the separation of
the continents in the Deluge, or some early catastrophe.
The identification of this legendary Atlas of prehistory
with the legendary Albion of fabulous British times, must

rest on Wilford's theory that England was the actual geographical spot on which events of the very earliest antediluvian times had taken place. Hence Blake's remarkable
comment on his picture of Albion in his *A Vision of the
Last Judgment*. Among the figures in the crowded picture
is that of an aged patriarch awakened by his wife. "He is
Albion," says Blake, "our Ancestor, patriarch of the Atlantic Continent, whose History Preceded that of the Hebrews & in whose Sleep, or Chaos, Creation began; at their
head the aged Woman is Brittannica, the Wife of Albion:
Jerusalem is their daughter." Wilford, whose remarkable
hypothesis I have discussed earlier in this book, had no
doubt intended to imply that England was the only surviving portion of the antediluvian continent, and that the
earliest myths of the world, those dealing with antediluvian times, were therefore to be traced through their
preservation in the earliest British legend. Blake had
seized hold of Wilford's theory with all its implications and carried it to preposterous lengths from which
even the credulous Wilford must have shrunk. He
converts Abraham, Heber, Shem, and Noah into Druids,
and declares that Albion was "Parent of the Druids."
Jumping at conclusions that Wilford had not dared to
state on the authority of his cheating pundits, Blake imagines England the very spot on which the creation of man
took place. "Is it a truth that the Learned have explored?"
he asks in his *Jerusalem*. "Was Britain the Primitive Seat
of the Patriarchal Religion? If it is true, my title-page is
also True, that Jerusalem was & is the Emanation of the
Giant Albion." And then he abandons the interrogatory
and the conditional to declare triumphantly: "It is True
and cannot be controverted." By "Jerusalem" he means

the right order of things which God established on earth at the beginning. That England was the place where God first walked with men in paradise, Blake believed with intense literalness:

> And did those feet in ancient time
> Walk upon England's mountains green?
> And was the holy Lamb of God
> On England's pleasant pastures seen?
>
> And did the Countenance Divine
> Shine forth upon our clouded hills?
> And was Jerusalem builded here
> Among these dark Satanic Mills?

Having conceived of England as the spot on which the first events of the world took place, it was but a slight stretch of the imagination to combine Albion, a legendary figure of earliest Britain, with Atlas, a legendary figure of the Atlantic continent, since Blake supposed both personages to be merely corruptions of an identical tradition.

That Blake was able to connect Atlas with Boötes rests upon a statement of Dupuis that Boötes was the Atlas of the ancients, because of the nearness of the constellation to the Pole, or axis of the world, which, Dupuis declared, it thus appeared to sustain. The constellation Boötes takes the form of an immense giant, of which the star Arcturus forms a part and which may be conceived as resembling Atlas.

Albion, Atlas, and Boötes are thus amalgamated. But how did Blake link these to Arthur? The answer is to be found in William Owen Pughe's *The Cambrian Biography: or Historical Notices of Celebrated Men among the Ancient Britons*. The volume was published under the name Owen in the same year in which appeared Edward

Davies' *Celtic Researches*. It is interesting to see to what extent in both these extraordinary documents the mythological theories of the preceding generation had begun to take hold of the historical imagination. Owen's mind had become a confused mélange of the doctrines of the mythologists Dupuis, Bryant, and others, which he attempted to apply to the myth of Arthur. Arthur he identified with Nimrod, and the adventures of Arthur were linked in a common origin with legends of Hercules and of the Argonauts. Owen's mind seems affected notably by the theory of Dupuis, with its interpretation of myth as the derivation of symbols written in the constellations.

After giving a sketch of what he describes as the historical Arthur, as exhibited by the bards and triads, Owen declares: "The hero of that name in the dramatic tales, called Mabinogion, is totally of different features; and in fact, is altogether another personage. The last is then a mythological character, of time so ancient as to be far beyond the scope of history. His attributes in the Mabinogion point him out as such: memorials of this being, and of several others connected with him, are traditionally preserved in various parts of the world; and even written in the heavens, for certain constellations bear their names. Arthur is the Great Bear, as the epithet literally implies: and perhaps, this constellation being so near the pole, and visually describing a circle in a small space is the origin of the famous round table."

Owen thus distinguishes an historical and a mythological Arthur, the latter reverting to those very early and very remote times with which the mythologist loved to deal.

"By confounding the Arthur of history with that of

mythology," Owen continues, "the chroniclers of the middle ages have committed a monstrous anachronism, and thus have blended the real facts of the former with the allegorical attributes of the other; and this confusion is still increased by all the succeeding writers of romance."

Owen engages in the fashionable sport of converting one myth into another. "There are some very extraordinary things to be found," he declares, "concerning the mythological Arthur, in the Mabinogion, and particularly in the Story of Culhwch and Olwen, wherein we recognize adventures, which must have had a common origin with those of Hercules, and with the Argonautic voyage. Therein we meet with the Indian Menu, exactly by name, and with similar attributes, acting as one of the agents of Arthur, to recover Olwen, the representative of the fecundity of nature, he having engaged to exert all his means for that purpose against the adverse powers: But he and his heroes fail; are laid to sleep for ages; but at length they are to rise and triumph."

The influence of Hancarville and Knight appears to have filtered through to Owen's mind, for we find him involving Arthur with symbolic nature myth. The mythological Arthur's parents, we are informed, were "Uther Bendragon, or Wonder the Supreme Leader, and Eigyr, or Generating Power."

How all this monstrous fiction had taken shape in Owen's mind would require a disquisition in itself. I shall point, therefore, merely to the fact that Owen distinguishes an historical from a mythological Arthur, that he supposes some connection between the mythological *Arthurus* and the star *Arcturus*, and that he connects Arthur with the constellation Ursa Major, of which

Arcturus was commonly, but erroneously, supposed to be
a part. Correcting *one* of Owen's errors, Blake connects
the mythological Arthur not with Ursa Major but with
Boötes, the constellation of which Arcturus actually forms
a part. To Owen then we may trace Blake's idea that
Arthur and the constellation containing Arcturus were
one and the same, together with the idea that the Arthur
of legend represented a corrupted and local tradition of
an earlier mythological figure, memorials of whom were
preserved in different countries.

Blake's Albion is this original figure. He is named
Albion after the particular legendary figure into which
Greek and British myth had corrupted him, but he is one
and the same with other legendary personages which were
likewise corruptions of the same original.

He appears to Blake in his visions (that is, Blake imagines him) in the identical form in which, so Blake supposed, he was received in the visions of the earliest men.
And he signifies to Blake the same thing that he signified
to early men: He is a symbolic representation of a divine
communication concerning man, his fall, and his eventual
regeneration.

The reader's problem is twofold: He must receive the
communication; and he must perceive that Albion, who
stands symbolically for the communication, will appear in
Blake's visions not merely as the British or Greek giant
whose name he bears, but with vague attributes now of
one, now of other mythical figures, all of whom Blake
supposed to be corruptions in legend of a single original.

Let us consider first the forms in which Albion appears.

Blake has told us that Albion was Boötes, and we have
seen that that constellation, with its star Arcturus, had

been associated with the remote Arthur and with Atlas. We should expect, therefore, that in the terms which Blake uses to describe his Albion, we should sometimes find him using terms proper to the constellation. The constellation Boötes takes the form of a giant figure in the northern hemisphere. Blake's line in *Milton*, "But now the Starry Heavens are fled from the mighty limbs of Albion," would then be quite properly applicable to Albion as a constellation.

One may perceive that most of the physical movements of Albion in the poems are in terms of the movement of the constellation Boötes. In the second book of *Milton*, for instance, we find this curious account of Albion:

Then Albion rose up in the Night of Beulah on his Couch
Of dread repose; seen by the visionary eye, his face is toward
The east, toward Jerusalem's Gates; groaning he sat above
His rocks. London & Bath & Legions & Edinburgh
Are the four pillars of his Throne: his left foot near London
Covers the shades of Tyburn; his instep from Windsor
To Primrose Hill stretching to Highgate & Holloway.
London is between his knees, its basements fourfold;
His right foot stretches to the sea on Dover cliffs, his heel
On Canterbury's ruins; his right hand covers lofty Wales,
His left Scotland; his bosom girt with gold involves
York, Edinburgh, Durham & Carlisle, & on the front
Bath, Oxford, Cambridge, Norwich; his right elbow
Leans on the Rocks of Erin's Land, Ireland, ancient nation.
His head bends over London; he sees his embodied Spectre
Trembling before him with exceeding great trembling & fear.
He views Jerusalem & Babylon, his tears flow down.
He mov'd his right foot to Cornwall, his left to the Rocks of
     Bognor.
He strove to rise to walk into the Deep, but strength failing
Forbad, & down with dreadful groans he sunk upon his Couch
In moony Beulah.

There can be little doubt that the essential content of
that passage is a description of the rising and setting of
the constellation of the giant figure of Boötes in the sky
as Blake had observed it either in or near London.

Indeed, much of the imagery concerning Albion, from
his first to his last appearance in Blake's poetry, is appropriate to the idea that he is a constellation, a giant
figure written in the stars. It is in this guise that his spectre
frowns over the nations, that the starry Heavens flee from
his mighty limbs (an image of the dawn), and that the
symbolic Milton falls through Albion's heart in his journey
through the stars. A plate in *Jerusalem* shows Albion containing various heavenly bodies within his limbs. The
rocky couch upon which Blake so frequently describes
Albion as lying, is the horizon over which the constellation
is seen. The *risings* of Albion, his *turnings* upon his couch
are but the movements of the constellation. The rocky
couch, composed of cliffs, was presumably suggested by
the white cliffs of the coast near Dover, from which it has
been supposed that England took the name Albion.
Albion's *tent* is the sky, and the *caves* beneath his couch
are the regions below the horizon, into which the constellation descends when it sets; wherefore their location
under the couch "in the corner of the Atlantic."

There can be no doubt that Blake's identification of
Albion with Boötes was not a mere whim, but that in fact
he consistently conceived his figure in terms of the constellation. What of the other personages with whom Blake
identified him? How does the Albion of the poem resemble the Albion of myth, Atlas the Titan, and Arthur?

Like the legendary figure whose name he bore, Blake's
Albion is a giant. The mysterious slaying of Albion, to

which the poet constantly alludes but which he never explains, doubtless has reference to the slaying of Albion
by Hercules, but the identification of the legendary with
the visionary figure is slight so far as any story is concerned. Blake seems to have gathered up items concerning
the name rather than the personage. For instance, he is
aware that there was a probable connection between the
word *Albion* and the Latin *albus*, for the whiteness of
Albion is part of Blake's design. He is sick, or pale in
death, and snowy cold. Thus "Milton" saw Albion:

Deadly pale outstretch'd and snowy cold, storm cover'd,
A Giant form of perfect beauty outstretch'd on the rock
In solemn death; the sea of Time & Space thunder'd aloud
Against the rock, which was inwrapped with the weeds of
    death.

So too the *Mountain* and the *Rock* with which Albion is
often connected in the visions, seem to have been merely
etymological. Holinshed, in discussing the legend of
Albion suggested *alp* as a root for the word, and he appears
to have been correct in supposing it connected with the
root of Latin *Alpis*, Gaelic *alp*, and Irish *ailp*, meaning
mountain. That Blake's Albion is England itself, regarded
either as a place or a people, may be inferred from a number of passages, but Albion is also extended to include
the "Atlantic continent." Thus Albion appears to be
merely England in the phrase "Albion's ancient Druid
rocky shore," but a larger geographical division, engaged
in an earthquake, in such lines as

    Albion trembled to Italy, Greece & Egypt,
    To Tartary & Hindustan, & China to great America
    Shaking the roots & fast foundations of the Earth
       in doubtfulness.

As the patriarch of the Atlantic continent, his character fades into that of Atlas, who was the legendary king of Atlantis. Like Atlas, who in Greek myth was the father of the twelve Atlantides, Albion is the father of twelve daughters whose names are drawn from Welsh myth but who are promptly associated with female figures from other mythologies. Indeed, with the introduction of the sons and daughters of Albion, when Blake commences to identify Albion and his family with the persons of other myths, we are plunged into the maddest sort of mythological jumble, in which Blake imposed no limit to his imagination.

Blake's identification of Albion with Arthur resulted partly from the fact that both were legendary figures in the history of Britain, but the main reason was that in the figure of Arthur Blake perceived a symbolism which fitted well with his conception of an original symbolic figure. It would appear that Arthur's "death or sleep, and promise to return again," to quote Blake's own words concerning his picture "The Ancient Britons," appealed to the poet as representing the promise of a redeemer contained in an original revelation, of which the story concerning Arthur was but a faded vestige. Like Arthur, Albion is the sleeper who, after his death or sleep of six thousand years, awakens to bring about the spiritual triumph at the close of the poem *Jerusalem*.

Thus far I have shown that the Albion of the visions takes on some likeness or significance which Blake read into the various personages with whom he identified him: namely, the legendary Albion, the constellation Boötes, the Titan Atlas, and the mythological Arthur.

It would be convenient at this point if we could say

that Albion has now been analyzed into his component elements and that, at least, he is no one other than the British giant, the Greek Titan, the constellation, and Arthur, king or otherwise. But alas, once Blake had conceived of an original figure, the recollection of whom had descended into diverse corrupt forms, there was no good reason why he should not continue to equate Albion with other personages whom he conceived to be similarly derived. He had, moreover, some justification for so doing; for the speculative mythologists of his day, fumbling with the beginnings of comparative mythology, were all attempting to explain myths as variations of common originals. "The antiquities of every Nation under Heaven, is no less sacred than that of the Jews," declares Blake, and he adds the revealing statement: "They are the same thing, as Jacob Bryant and all antiquaries have proved." Blake does not specifically say that his Albion is to be identified with other personages, but just as one may perceive the vague connection between Albion and Arthur, for which Blake has given us the clue, so one may perceive that there are other vague analogies, with the Adam Kadmon of rabbinical tradition, for instance, or with some of the symbolic characters of the Gnostic myths. Certainly through his children Albion becomes involved with a most astonishing collection of relationships. "Saturn, Jove & Rhea of the Isles of the Sea remote," are enumerated in *Milton* as among the twelve spectre sons of the Druid Albion. Among the other "spectre sons" in the same passage are Baal, Ashtorath, Chemosh, Molech, Dagon, Thammuz, Rimmon, Osiris, Isis, Orus, and Belial. In other passages the sons of Albion are given names of their own, and then identified with recognizable figures. Hyle, one

of the sons, is identified as Gog; Coban is described as the
father of Nimrod; Kox is the father of Shem, Ham, and
Japhet, the Noah of "the flood of Udan Adan"; Hut'n is
the father of "the seven from Enoch to Adam"; and Schofield is "Adam who was new created in Edom." He is
described as the ninth of Albion's sons, and the father of
all his brethren in the shadowy generation. Some of these
names have reference likewise to personal experience on
Blake's part. Schofield and Kox, for instance, closely resemble names of men involved in Blake's trial on the accusation that he had uttered seditious remarks. Hyle may
be a short form of the name of Blake's patron, Hayley, or
it may be simply the Greek word for "chaotic matter."
Perhaps it is both. Blake is, of course, identifying the
visions which appear in his imagination, and which have
been somewhat shaped by his own experience, with mythological figures whom he conceives to convey an identical
meaning. But the identifications carry no meaning to the
reader for the simple reason that the poet, insisting that
all mythological figures are degenerated symbols, strips
them of the degenerate fable by which we alone know
them. It clarifies nothing for us to be told that Kox is
Noah, when Blake means by Noah, not the ancestor of
mankind, but a primordial symbol which has lost its meaning in the fable of the Ark. Probably in some of the given
instances Blake is being roguish and whimsical, but his
procedure is identical in serious matters as well.

It would be tedious and fruitless to pursue outward the
ever-widening circle of Albion's relations. For in the last
analysis none of the various identifications in which Blake
engages has much significance. Since Blake himself regarded the personages of myth merely as the debris of

original symbols, the meaning of which had been lost and corrupted, no more meaning should be attached to his identifications than this: By constantly reminding us that the visions which appear to his own imagination dimly resemble and have affinities with visions which have appeared to the imaginations of men in the earliest days, Blake calls upon men to accept the truth of his own visions as a part of God's continuous communication to men.

We are led at last to ask just what it was that Blake supposed God to be revealing to him. When Blake's imagination was filled with his visionary personages, what did they communicate to him?

The answer, I think, is different from what might be expected, but a very simple one. Unlike the Angel of the Divine Presence in Blake's Laocoön Group, the visionary personages of the poems do not deliver explicit messages from God. Rather they are apparitions which by their presence are intended to confirm the authenticity of Blake's message as a whole.

I am forced, therefore, if I am to carry my analysis of Albion to the end, to attempt to formulate Blake's message as a whole, and then to suggest what part of that message Albion, in his visionary appearances, confirms.

Omitting the many "minute particulars" of which Blake is so fond of speaking, the message as a whole I conceive to be this: Blake believed that by denying direct communication from God in the form of inspiration and revelation, man departed from his Creator. As a substitute for divine guidance, man elevated his reason to a position of dignity which it does not deserve. In place of true religion, man, through reason, formulated a system of mere morality, faulty because it lacked the all-important elements of love, mercy, and divine guidance. Rigid and formal morality, untempered by love and mercy and undirected by divine guidance, led to all the countless ills which found expression in the incessant wars among nations. Man likewise elevated another function of the mind, the memory, to a position which it does not deserve. Men had remembered the original institutions of God, but, denying imagination, through which alone God's instructions could keep his original institutions unimpaired, they had falsified and corrupted God's revelations in the effort to preserve them merely by memory and to explain them merely by reason. Idolatry was the result, in which the forms but not the meaning of God's revelations were exalted. With idolatry followed degrading practices, sacrifices, superstitions, and false evaluations. Revelations were corrupted into fables of false gods, and with such idolatrous forms the art of Greece was chiefly concerned. Reason attempted to supply a moral meaning, an allegory, to these fables, but it succeeded imperfectly. The modern world, reviving the art of the ancient world, imitating the ancient poets, artists, and sculptors, succeeded only in creating a barren, imitative, conventional culture based upon an imitated morality. The hope of man was to restore to its proper function the imagination, through which man might reachieve an original art and a culture resting upon a proper relationship between God and man. Only with the guidance of God could men, with mercy and love, achieve that brotherhood which Blake envisioned as the new Jerusalem.

In this message, which it was Blake's constant effort to communicate with authority, Albion stands for mankind. He represents the stages and conditions of man in the progress which I have synthesized above. He is mankind who falls away from God into corruption; but according to the promise which Blake finds in his own visions and all the visions concerning the destiny of man, Albion is also man who shall be redeemed and restored to the divine vision.

Speculative Mythology

WHEN vague notions are errant in the world, it is difficult to predict the direction in which their influence will turn. We have seen that William Blake, incontestably one of England's men of genius, found the misty concepts of the speculative mythologists satisfactory to his mind, and erected upon their unsubstantial foundation a poetic scheme which has never been very intelligible.

Bailly, Bryant, Wilford, and their fellows believed that they had made profound discoveries about the first of days. Doubtless they hoped that they would win for themselves secure places in intellectual history. It has been their fate instead to be forgotten even by scholars upon the mythology which they thought to illuminate, and if posterity remains to them it will be largely because the most eccentric of English poets found their theories compatible with the vagaries of his undisciplined imagination.

Upon other poets the influence of the mythographers must, in the nature of things, be a secondary one. Shelley, Keats, and Goethe might receive from an intellectual fashion, however ephemeral and injudicious, an impulse of the energy which produced it, but from its absurdities the discipline of their minds protected them. Where the greater poets of the Romantic generation are touched by the influence of the mythologists, that influence comes mainly from the general impetus given to the imagination by the renewed zest for the mythological, rather than from the minutiae of its false doctrines. If the greater poets occasionally seize hold of bizarre items from the new store of mythological ideas, these serve rather for convenient novelties in the development of poetic ideas than, as in the case of Blake, for the substantial basis upon which their minds operate.

An illustration in point is Keats's poetic use of Bailly's idea that in the most remote times there had existed a knowledge of astronomy which had perished with the early race which had discovered it, leaving only vestiges of the original knowledge to the world of races which we now recognize as historical. In *Hyperion* Keats gives us an epic description of the progress of Hyperion, the god of the sun, as he passes through the corridors of his underground palace from the sunset to the dawn. At midnight, while the angry Titan waits for the hour of his rising, his "planet orb," the sun, gives off lights which we may interpret as the Aurora Borealis. These "sweet shaped lightnings from the nadir deep" Keats explains as

> hieroglyphics old
> Which sages and keen-eyed astrologers
> Then living on the earth, with labouring thought
> Won from the gaze of many centuries:
> Now lost, save what we find on remnants huge
> Of stone, or marble swart; their import gone,
> Their wisdom long since fled.

Bailly's Atlanteans had similarly in centuries of now forgotten culture acquired a superior knowledge of astronomy which had been all but lost in their destruction. The remote times imagined by Bailly fitted in well with Keats's conception of the era of the Titans' overthrow, and the notion gave him an opportunity for an arresting epic comparison appropriate to the vast antiquity of his own theme.

More integral to the whole pattern of Keats's plan for *Hyperion* was another idea which contemporary speculation upon myth suggested to him. The uncompleted action of the epic was to have turned upon the ultimate exile of Saturn and his fallen Titans to the British Isles—a piece of invention in which Keats intended to make use of current notions of a connection between the Titans and British legendary figures. However reluctant the modern reader may be to imagine so unclassical an element in the epic argument, he will nevertheless find that the plot seems to point to such a conclusion. The device, however, was a matter of superficial design, rather than of essence, and one does not find Keats's invention swollen with the wind which Blake mistook for inspiration.

So with Goethe, the whimsical joking about the Cabiri in the *Second Part of Faust* is merely a gentle thrust at the mythologists for their endless and pointless discussions concerning the significance of the most mysterious of the mythological figures of antiquity. Whether Goethe knew Faber's extravagant *Mysteries of the Cabiri* or was contenting himself with a jibe at the learned Creuzer on the question is unimportant. Goethe could turn his wit upon mythologizing with as much zest as, in his less sarcastic moments, he engaged in the practice himself.

In the case of Shelley the situation is somewhat different. Brilliant as Shelley's mind was, there was a treacherous element within it which constantly betrayed his judgment.

The dexterity of his poetic invention permitted him to engage in subtleties harmful to the sterner qualities of his mind. He was often distracted from the forthright business of communication by the temptation to juggle with attractive intricacies. When complicated theories about mythology were in the making, it was almost inevitable that Shelley's avid mind would come in contact with them, and not for his own good.

Whoever has struggled to force the conventional editorial comments upon *Adonais*, attempting to perceive Plato in one stanza, Spinoza in another, and the ever-convenient "pantheism" in another, may welcome my suggestion that the difficulty which one encounters in following the movement of ideas in the latter portion of *Adonais* is not due to a confusion of genuine philosophical thought. Shelley was merely trying to develop, in an intricate fashion, a bit of symbolic mythology borrowed from Richard Payne Knight and Hancarville. Moreover, he was not making anything very clear of it.

In the subsequent portions of this book I have something more important to do than to labor the influence of minor mythologists upon the great poets. But before I close the discussion of the subject I should like to trace a few more routes by which mythological extravagancies straggled into poetry. Then, with their meed of laughter and of praise, we may dismiss my speculative mythologists.

It would be fair to attribute to them a secondary literary influence, not less remarkable in kind than the primary influence which they exercised upon the mind of Blake. I refer to their part in the development of a highly romantic conception of the British Druids: an intellectual phenomenon which resulted in a large body of second-rate poetry and third-rate scholarship and aroused a deep veneration for a spurious British past which had next to no connection with sober British history.

Speculation concerning the early inhabitants of Britain was, in the eighteenth and early nineteenth centuries, the Serbonian bog into which an army of poets and scholars sank. In the quest for antiquarian knowledge no object was more alluring and none more formidable than to achieve a satisfactory theory of the ancient Druids, those oak-worshiping priests whose ancient repute had spread from British forests as far as Plato's Greece.

One is not unprepared to discover that old Samuel Bochart, the prime mover in mythological absurdity, was initiator of the Druid mania. Bochart was not, indeed, the author of the theory that the Druids were children of the Biblical patriarchs. He did not, in fact, raise any problem concerning them beyond including the names of the Druids and their bards among the Gallic terms which had affinities with the Chaldean, the Hebrew, and the Phoenician. But when we recall Bochart's penchant for resolving all things into Phoenician, and when we find William Stukeley citing Bochart in the same essay in which Stukeley converts the Druids into Phoenicians, we cannot withhold from the savant of Caen the honor of being at least the inspiration of Stukeley's theory. As Plato's Demiourgos, the supreme artificer of the universe, commenced the work of imposing order upon chaos and then retired to his dark cave leaving the rest of the work for lesser deities, so Bochart, reversing the procedure, commenced the work of imposing chaos upon order and left the details to Stukeley, Davies, Vallancey, and their disciples, who soon had Pythagoras himself a pupil of the Druids.

It was William Stukeley's belief, first stated in his *Stonehenge, a Temple Restor'd to the British Druids,* that the Druid priests "came hither, as a Phoenician colony, in the very earliest times, even as soon as Tyre was founded: during the life of Abraham, or very soon after." These early visitors were, it appears, "an oriental colony" of Phoenicians, who came from "that very country where Abraham liv'd, his sons and grandsons." They came, moreover, "soon after Noah's flood." Rounding up all the herd of doubtful "authorities," Stukeley developed his hypothesis with ponderous exactness. The leader of the colonists was none other, he contended, than Hercules. This Hercules was differentiated as the Tyrian Hercules, and in a later disquisition upon Abury, our author informs us that the Tyrian Hercules was "a principal planter of Britain," that he was "in the same generation as Noah's great grandsons," and that he was "a worthy scholar of Abraham." We learn without astonishment, therefore, that the great rocking stone near Penzance was, in Stukeley's opinion, "erected here by Hercules, in person," and that "the Druid temple call'd Biscawaon" was "not improbably one of the Herculean labors."

The influence of Stukeley in literary history will be obscure to us unless we consider the significance of this extraordinary piece of Bochartean speculation. Stukeley had reasoned himself into an hypothesis by which he was able to suppose that the Druid priests preserved in an unadulterated form the patriarchal religion of Abraham, that this uncontaminated faith was introduced into England shortly after the Flood, and that it became the property of the primitive bards of the British, who, according to classical authority, formed one of the divisions of the

Druidic priesthood. The Tyrian Hercules, said Stukeley, was taught by Abraham, and the Druids learned their lore from Hercules, taking with them "the patriarchal religion, which was so extremely like Christianity, that in effect it differ'd from it only in this: they believed in a Messiah who was to come into the world, as we believe in him that is come." Stukeley's Druid was a cradle gift to nascent Romanticism.

In the half century following the publication of *Stonehenge, a Temple Restor'd to the British Druids*, the mediaeval Welsh and Irish bards came to be associated through what Algernon Herbert described as the "Neo-Druidic Heresy," with the bardic class of the patriarchal Druids, and scraps of ancient poetry preserved from the late Middle Ages took on a special character and interest as links in the chain of a noble succession. There arose in England that remarkable veneration for the primitive bard with his flowing white hair, his harp, his impassioned and exalted utterance, which found its most notable expression in Gray's *The Bard*, but which permeated the whole Romantic conception of the excellence and importance of ancient British poetry. In vain did the scholarly Gray abstain from sullying his muse with extravagant absurdity. The popular, as well as the poetic, imagination seized upon the patriarchal theory, the bards became the repositories of ancient wisdom, and the imitators of Ossian stamped upon primitive utterance a character which the primitive has never rightly possessed.

At the turn of the century, when speculative mythology was at its most undisciplined, Edward Davies took up the cause of the Druids and the bards. Abandoning the Phoenician hypothesis, he nevertheless traced the Druids by another route to an even earlier and more patriarchal origin than Stukeley had imagined. He allowed them the advantage of a prediluvian direct revelation from God, and he scoured the remnants of mediaeval Welsh poetry for traditions of Noah and the Flood.

From Davies the patriarchal Druid passed into so sober a body of poetry as the *Ecclesiastical Sonnets* of Wordsworth, who, in the third of the sonnets, describes the birds of ill omen, in the corruption of the Druidic priesthood, as

> Portending ruin to each baleful rite,
> That, in the lapse of ages, hath crept o'er
> Diluvian truths and patriarchal lore.

In a note which betrays his indebtedness to Davies, the poet explains one of his birds of ill omen, the sea mew, in the following words: "This water-fowl was, among the Druids, an emblem of those traditions connected with the deluge that made an important part of their mysteries."

If Wordsworth supposed that the patriarchal truth as it passed through the Druidic priesthood was corrupted, Robert Southey was moved by no doubt whatever as to the venerable preservation of the primal lore intact even in the hands of the Welsh bards of the twelfth century. Southey's picture of the Gorsedd, the ceremony of the bards, in the eleventh canto of his *Madoc in Wales*, is a typical piece of bardic romanticizing. Describing the bards, the mediaeval survivors of the Druidic priesthood, as "Heirs and transmitters of the ancient light," Southey imagined them as gathering on the spot where, in days of old, a Druid temple had been built. There they had received

> From earliest ages, the primeval lore,
> Through Bard to Bard with reverence handed down.

Wordsworth, instinctively cautious and far too level-minded to be gullible about the great tradition to which the Druid priests were heir, nevertheless has a fine description, quite in tune with the ideas of Creuzer, of how a pristine knowledge of God filtered through the superstitious forms of the Druidic worship. In the fourth of the *Ecclesiastical Sonnets,* called "Druidical Excommunication," he pays reverence to the Druids who, despite the cruelty of their priestly ignorance, had yet aspired to God, the fountain of wisdom, justice, and order. In words which William Blake would have understood and Creuzer approved, Wordsworth imagined the Druids as heirs and guardians of an original intimation of God:

> Tremblingly escaped,
> As if with prescience of the coming storm,
> *That* intimation when the stars were shaped;
> And still, 'mid yon thick woods, the primal truth
> Glimmers through many a superstitious form
> That fills the Soul with unavailing ruth.

Perhaps the most unshaded piece of Romanticism about the Druid bards was contained in an essay "Druidism Revived," which Colonel Vallancey published in his potpourri entitled *Collectanea.* The essay was not by Vallencey himself, but from a manuscript in his possession written by one Beauford, in whose mind the popular fancy of the Druids had taken its ultimate form, with the mysterious priests not merely worshiping but actually living in the hollow trunks of mighty oaks. Vallancey himself, as we should expect, was much interested in the question of the Druids. Throughout his essays he pursued a labyrinthine argument which was intended to prove the Phaeno-Scythian descent of the Irish and presumably the Druids.

Stukeley and Davies had traced the British Druids to a patriarchal origin; it remained for Wilford to transport the Hebrew patriarchs themselves to British soil and thus, by implication at least, to establish the Druids *ab initio*, as Blake seems to have conceived them. To Algernon Herbert, a decade or so later, fell the task of cleansing the Augean stable of Phaeno-Scythian and antediluvian nonsense. After him the tightening standards of English scholarship put an end to romantic Druidism. Nevertheless, the Druids briefly enjoyed a patriarchal prestige unknown to them in antiquity, and left in their second priesthood a record nearly as mysterious as in their first.

The patriarchal and diluvian hypothesis had one excuse in reason: When men believed that the whole population of the globe, civilized and uncivilized, must be traced back to what George Faber described as "the arkite ogdoad" (the eight persons who embarked in the Ark: Noah, Shem, Ham, and Japhet, together with their respective wives), and when a time limit of but a few thousand years was by common consent imposed upon the development and migrations of the peoples of earth, the temptation was strong indeed to take the road of myth back to ultimate beginnings and not to be skeptical about its historicity. Like the Poet of Shelley's *Alastor*, men believed that the secrets of the very dawn of time were written in the records of ancient men—in stone, in symbol, in myth. The problem was merely one of study. In the end the "evidences" could somehow be pieced together. They could be fitted into a *system* which would lighten the dark of all the past. Scholar strove with scholar to be the first who might push through the darkness to the great illumination. The Poet whom Shelley imagined was a true child of the culture of his day:

> His wandering step
> Obedient to high thoughts, has visited
> The awful ruins of the days of old:
> Athens, and Tyre, and Balbec, and the waste
> Where stood Jerusalem, the fallen towers
> Of Babylon, the eternal pyramids,
> Memphis and Thebes, and whatsoe'er of strange
> Sculptured on alabaster obelisk,
> Or jasper tomb, or mutilated sphynx,
> Dark Aethiopia in her desert hills
> Conceals. Among the ruined temples there,
> Stupendous columns, and wild images
> Of more than man, where marble daemons watch
> The Zodiac's brazen mystery, and dead men
> Hang their mute thoughts on the mute walls around,
> He lingered, poring on memorials
> Of the world's youth,—through the long
>   burning day
> Gazed on those speechless shapes, nor,
>   when the moon
> Filled the mysterious halls with floating
>   shades
> Suspended he that task, but ever gazed
> And gazed, till meaning on his vacant mind
> Flashed like strong inspiration, and he saw
> The thrilling secrets of the birth of time.

Shelley's mournful and lonely Poet died without revealing just what "thrilling secrets" were disclosed to him by his study. Since the final inspiration seems to have had something to do with zodiacal monuments, perhaps Shelley imagined his Poet reading the myths astronomically, and finding in the ancient Aethiopian temples remnants of a primordial culture such as Keats had imagined in *Hyperion*, and Bailly and Dupuis had described in their "systems."

Other persons who, through study of memorials of the world's youth, had been suddenly inspired by a revelation of thrilling secrets, were less reticent. One of the most voluble of them was Richard Brothers, a student of the prophecies contained in the Bible and a prophet himself. Brothers belonged to the monstrous brood born of speculative mythology. At a time when it was the fashion to trace the cultural history of races to a hitherto unsuspected origin, Brothers described the English as descendants of the ten lost tribes of Israel.

A French and an English biographical dictionary describe Brothers respectively as an "*illuminé*" and as an "enthusiast." A committee of the Privy Council described him as a "criminal lunatic." He described himself as "the nephew of the Almighty."

Born in Newfoundland, Brothers spent his early years in service in the British navy, from which he retired after twelve years with a commission as lieutenant, and a right to half pay. He went to London to live out an unhappy life and a self-imagined martyrdom. In 1794 he commenced the publication, under divine order, of a series of prophecies relating to political affairs in England and the continent, and to the destiny of the Israelites. He declared that his *Revealed Knowledge of the Prophecies & Times* was "Wrote under the direction of the Lord God," and that it contained "with other great and remarkable things, not revealed to any other person on earth, the restoration of the Hebrews to Jerusalem, by the year of 1798: under their revealed prince and prophet." This prince and prophet was to have been Brothers himself, and for a short time, under the promise of his destiny, he enjoyed a considerable reputation, both at home and abroad. Disciples, admirers, and pamphleteers gathered to his cause, and continuations of his prophecies appeared in print. *God's Awful Warning to a Giddy, Careless, Sinful World* was the title prefixed to editions of 1795 in London and in New London, Connecticut. American printings attested Brothers' widespread reputation. In 1797 Asaph Chilton of Buckland was having the pamphlets printed for him at West Springfield, Massachusetts, to be sold "by the dozen or single." When, however, the year 1798 had come and gone, with nothing more revolutionary than the appearance of the *Lyrical Ballads*, the prestige of Brothers waned. It was not until 1822 that he published a complete statement of his great hypothesis. In that year appeared his *Correct Account of the Invasion and Conquest of This Island by the Saxons &c., Necessary to Be Known by the English Nation, the Descendants of the Ten Tribes.*

That Brothers was legally declared a lunatic should not deny him the posthumous privilege of a place among my speculative mythologists. Indeed, Brothers' influence yet lives. The extraordinary credo known as Anglo-Israelism recognized Brothers as its first exponent, and Anglo-Israelism flourished so luxuriantly that over two million adherents to its tenets were to be counted in England and America at the turn of the last century. The literary influence of Brothers is more intangible, but it is probably to be detected in two of the most remarkable works of the visionary imagination, Blake's prophetic poetry and Joseph Smith's *The Book of Mormon.*

We have no record of an acquaintance between William Blake and Brothers, yet it would be strange if the prophet political and the prophet poetical were unknown to each other. Brothers at one time actually published plans for the rebuilding of Jerusalem, with Eden in the center, a project which could hardly have failed to attract the attention of Blake, whose visions were likewise of Eden and the rebuilding of Jerusalem. Blake may have had Brothers in mind when he wrote the words "Would to God that all the Lord's people were Prophets" at the close of the beautiful poem in which he declared:

> I will not cease from Mental Fight
> Nor shall my Sword sleep in my hand
> Till we have built Jerusalem
> In England's green & pleasant land.

It seems not improbable that Brothers' conception of a Jewish origin for the English found some expression in an otherwise inexplicable passage in Blake's poem *Jerusalem*, in which the poet divides the fifty-two counties of England and Wales into twelve "gates," naming each after one of the tribes of Israel. The passage goes thus:

The Gate of Reuben in Carmarthenshire: the Gate of
    Simeon in
Cardiganshire, & the Gate of Levi in Montgomeryshire:
The Gate of Judah, Merionethshire: the Gate of Dan,
    Flintshire:

and so on through the twelve tribes and the twelve counties of Wales, and then all over again for the forty counties of England. If Brothers is, as seems likely, the inspiration for the passage, we may suppose that as usual Blake's subconscious mind has, to carry out the semblance of authenticity, partially correlated his own visions with the misty calculations and prophecies concerning the Hebrews which Brothers and his followers mistook for fact.

The connection between Brothers and *The Book of*

Mormon lies in a kindred problem, speculation concerning the origin of the American Indian.

It is difficult for the twentieth century, long accustomed to regard the antiquity of man as immeasurable and his ultimate origin a problem of biochemistry, to adjust its mind to the conception that human history was once traced in the narrow span of a very few thousand years. Yet when Shelley, in *Prometheus Unbound*, wished to conceive a time remotely in the age of myth, proper for the commencement of the Titan's suffering, a span of three thousand years from the present sufficed him; and Shelley's contemporary, the Baron Cuvier, was able to state that if any fact was firmly established by geology, it was that the present epoch of the world, that in which man was created, was not older than five or six thousand years. Even chronologists who extended the span of man's existence upon earth, thought in terms of only an added few thousand years. If we consider that recorded history, accurately dated, consumed a considerable portion of the small time allowance, how brief a period remained to be spanned! Small wonder that the mythologist believed he could aid the historian by tracing through the imperfect language of myth the cultural and racial descent of the nations.

Never before was there a time when greater curiosity was excited about the origin of mysterious peoples not satisfactorily accounted for by history. The Cimmerians, the Hyperboreans, the Scyths, the Etruscans—how were these and all the other peoples of earth to be traced to the progeny of Noah or, at least, to an ancestry not much more remotely imagined? Specialists in culture-history lived in the hope of establishing an identification. Ireland, said Vallancey, was the Thule of the ancients. The Greeks, said John Jamieson, were derived from the Scyths, and the Scyths were the progeny of Magog, second son of Japhet, who was the Titan Japetus of Greek myth. Magog's brother Gomer, said the same author, was the progenitor of the Cimmerians, and they were the first people who populated Europe. The Hyperboreans, said Stukeley, were the inhabitants of the Shetland Isles. The Etruscans, said Hancarville, were Phoenicians. And so on, until Darwin simplified the problem by suspending the common ancestor of all of us by his tail from a tree of the jungle.

The American Indian, by virtue of his separation from the other peoples of the earth, constituted a problem of particular fascination. Speculation concerning his origin was as old as Columbus, and many bizarre and imaginative theories had been set forth. But in the early nineteenth century, concomitant with the aroused mytho-historical curiosity represented by such men as Bailly in France and Bryant in England, speculation concerning the early inhabitants of America received a fresh impetus, and a flood of books on the subject appeared, written by both Europeans and Americans. The connection between these writers and the speculative mythologists already familiar to us is attested by the appearance of the names of Bailly, Bryant, Sir William Jones, Faber, and others in supporting footnotes. Even so late as 1839 one finds the unfortunate Captain Wilford's essay in the *Asiatic Researches* cited as a "work of undoubted authority" by John Delafield in his *Inquiry into the Origin of the Antiquities of America.* Delafield's declaration that the question of the common descent of all men from a single stock had been "forever settled by the researches of Bryant, Faber, and Sir William

Jones," certifies his obligation, and we may regard his argument that the American Indians were of "Cuthite" origin as a ripple from the great stone which Jacob Bryant had dropped into the pool of scholarship.

Among the more picturesque theories of the sort which have come to my attention was that of the Spanish savant, Antonio de Ulloa, who, on authority suspect, concocted the idea that at the time of Noah more than one shrewd family, who saw how things were going, had the foresight to construct little arks in imitation of Noah's capacious one. Such an ark-load came to rest upon the Andes when the waters subsided, and the American Indians, descendants of these lucky derelicts, had thus a co-diluvian origin with their European cousins.

Another theory was that of the Italian, Gian Rinaldo Carli, which attracted sufficient attention in America to demand a Boston edition of *Delle lettere americane*. Carli had studied Bailly's theory of the Atlantean culture developed upon Mount Caf in the Caucasus Mountains, and had come to the conclusion that the theory was a weak one. Nevertheless he had been fascinated by what appeared to him vestigial knowledge on the part of the American aborigines which could be explained only by a belief that this knowledge had been derived from a common cultural descent shared with the inhabitants of the other hemisphere. The myth of Atlantis suggested to him a wholly different means of explaining the widespread vestigial knowledge from that which it had suggested to Bailly. Bailly had been somewhat cavalier in his treatment of the Indians; hence the frigid but deprecating politeness which Carli showed toward his predecessor. Plato's Atlantis, it appeared to him, was a continent which once extended across what is now the Atlantic ocean. Upon it men and cultural traditions spread to the western hemisphere, and those common possessions of moral custom and religious practice which had attracted Carli's attention were thus explained.

There was little novelty in Carli's conception of an Atlantic continent. As early as 1598 Albinus, historiographer of Saxony, had suggested that America itself was the lost island of the fable, and in the seventeenth century Kircher had supposed the Canary Islands and Azores to be the surviving summits of an Atlantic continent which had sunk beneath the ocean which bears its name. The startling novelty of Carli's hypothesis was rather the explanation of how the continent happened to sink. In approximately the year 4000 B.C., reasoned Carli, a comet—the same which revisited the world in 1759—struck the earth so violently as to knock it off its axis, disturb the calendar, upset the climate, and sink the Atlantic continent beneath the waves. Recollection of this catastrophe is retained, not alone in Plato's fable of Atlantis, but in the myth of Typhon, in which the monster of Greek fable represents the monstrous comet.

Theories became, as time passed, not less, but more bizarre. One of the most engaging works which I have perused is the *American Antiquities, and Discoveries in the West*, by Josiah Priest, who was publishing at Albany in the eighteen thirties. Priest's eclectic archaeology permitted him to discover in America early evidences of the Carthaginians, Phoenicians, Hindus, Chinese, Japanese, Romans, and Greeks. He was of the opinion that Noah was an American, and he speculated on whether the Ark was erected in New York state or farther west. He refers to

the belief held by some, whom he does not name, that
Adam was created in America. Priest, I think, deserves to
be called the American Wilford.

Speculation upon the origin of the American Indian was
not neglected by the Muse. In 1772 Philip Freneau was
attracted to the theme. In *The Rising Glory of America*
Acasto, Leander, and Eugenio, whose blank verse conversations constitute the lengthy poem, discuss the question of origin. Eugenio having queried:

> How shall we know their origin, how tell,
> From whence or where the Indian tribes arose?

Acasto undertakes the answer, with this prefatory caution:

> And long has this defy'd the sages skill
> T' investigate.

Acasto continues at length, drawing into his discourse
ideas which had been under discussion for two hundred
years and more. He appears to have been familiar even
with the work of Ulloa, which had appeared in the year
the poem was written:

> Tradition seems to hide
> The mighty secret from each mortal eye,
> How first these various nations South and North
> Possest these shores, or from what countries came;
> Whether they sprang from some primœval head
> In their own lands, like Adam in the East;
> Yet this the sacred oracles deny,
> And reason too reclaims against the thought.
> For when the gen'ral deluge drown'd the world,
> Where could their tribes have found security?
> Where find their fate but in the ghastly deep?
> Unless, as others dream, some chosen few
> High on the Andes 'scaped the gen'ral death,
> High on the Andes, wrapt in endless snow,

> Where winter in his wildest fury reigns.
> But here Philosophers oppose the scheme,
> The earth, say they, nor hills nor mountains knew
> E'er yet the universal flood prevail'd:
> But when the mighty waters rose aloft,
> Rous'd by the winds, they shook their solid case
> And in convulsions tore the drowned world!
> 'Till by the winds assuag'd they quickly fell
> And all their ragged bed exposed to view.

He suggests the theory of the ten lost tribes of Israel—a possibility old enough to have been examined and rejected by Hugo Grotius in his *On the Origin of the Native Races of America* published as early as 1542:

> Perhaps far wand'ring towards the northern pole,
> The straits of Zembla and the Frozen Zone,
> And where the eastern Greenland almost joins
> America's north point, the hardy tribes
> Of banish'd Jews, Siberians, Tartars wild
> Came over icy mountains, or on floats
> First reach'd these coasts hid from the world beside.

The theory of a lost continent takes the following form:

> And yet another argument more strange
> Reserv'd for men of deeper thought and late
> Presents itself to view: In Peleg's days,
> So says the Hebrew seer's inspired pen,
> This mighty mass of earth, this solid globe
> Was cleft in twain—cleft east and west apart
> While strait between the deep Atlantic roll'd.
> And traces indisputable remain
> Of this unhappy land now sunk and lost;
> The islands rising in the eastern main
> Are but small fragments of this continent,
> Whose two extremities were Newfoundland
> And St. Helena.—One far in the north
> Where British seamen now with strange surprise

Behold the pole star glitt'ring o'er their heads;
The other in the southern tropic rears
Its head above the waves; Bermudas and
Canary isles, Britannia and th' Azores,
With fam'd Hibernia are but broken parts
Of some prodigious waste which once sustain'd
Armies by lands, where now but ships can range.

Leander, the third of the speakers, animadverts upon
Acasto's "sophistry," and in turn suggests a Carthaginian
hypothesis which I shall not here repeat.

A few years later Joel Barlow, the Hartford Vergil,
resumed the discussion in verse. In *The Vision of Columbus*, first published in 1787, the poet imagines an angel
spreading before Columbus a panorama of the Americas.
Columbus questions the angel concerning the Indians, and
is told that they originated in the same fashion as the other
races of mankind, but because of climatic and other influences they had become differentiated in color and disposition. To Columbus' query as to how the gap of ocean had
been bridged, the angel volunteered the following information. After man had learned the art of navigation, and
before Hercules had conceived the impudent plan of confining all maritime operations within the Mediterranean by
closing the Strait of Gibraltar,

Driven from these rocky straits, a hapless train
Roll'd on the waves that sweep the western main;
While eastern storms the billowing skies o'ershade,
Nor sun' nor stars afford their wonted aid.
For many a darksome day, o'erwhelmed and tost,
Their sails, their oars in swallowing surges lost;
At length, the clouds withdrawn, they sad descry
Their course directing from their native sky;
No hope remains; while, o'er the flaming zone,

The winds still bear them with the circling sun;
Till the wild walks of this delightful coast
Receive to lonely seats this suffering host.
The fruitful plains invite their steps to roam,
Renounce their sorrows and forget their home;
Revolving years their ceaseless wanderings led,
And from their sons descending nations spread.

So the Indians of the south and middle regions were accounted for satisfactorily:

While northern tribes a later source demand,
And show their wanderings from the Asian strand.

Thus the researches of the scholars passed into epic poetry.

One of the most extravagant of the current ideas which found its way into the pages of Romantic verse was the tenacious and exceedingly popular idea that American Indians who spoke Welsh had been found living along the Missouri River. Robert Southey's pair of epic romances, *Madoc in Wales* and *Madoc in Aztlan*, were based upon this notion. The tradition was that Madoc, a Welsh prince, disgusted at the quarrels of the Welsh leaders, abandoned his native country and sailed to the West. Having reached a land which pleased him, he left there some of his followers in order to return home for more colonists. As Southey says in his Preface: "Strong evidence has been adduced that he reached America, and that his posterity exist there to this day, on the southern branches of the Missouri, retaining their complexion, their language, and, in some degree, their arts." Thus wrote Southey in 1805, when the poem was first completed. In 1815 he felt it necessary to add a note informing his readers that "That country has now been fully explored, and wherever Madoc may have settled, it is now certain that no Welsh

Indians are to be found upon any branches of the Missouri." Before the Welsh theory was exploded however, the conviction had become so widely held that a project to send missionaries to the Welsh Indians had been started in England.

Welsh Indians on the Missouri River were to Robert Southey merely a literary idea. They were born of a rumor, and died in a footnote. It was not so with other Indians who were engendered by the imagination. The notion that the ten lost tribes of Israel wore the war paint of the Iroquois and that the Children of the Setting Sun would repossess Jerusalem—this was a conception which could not be confined to poetry: it was to become the inspiration of a prophet and the binding power of an empire.

The link between the speculative mythologist in his study and the religious leader in the wilderness was one Elias Boudinot, one-time president of the Continental Congress.

In the year 1816 Boudinot, then a very old man, published a book on a subject which had intermittently occupied his attention for a period of forty years. The title was *A Star in the West, or a Humble Attempt to Discover the Long Lost Ten Tribes of Israel, Preparatory to Their Return to Their Beloved City, Jerusalem.* His general hypothesis is merely an independent and American variant of that which Richard Brothers was formulating in England. The one found in the American Indians the fulfillment of Biblical prophecy; the other found that fulfillment in the English. Boudinot's scholarship is in the tradition of the speculative writers. He had studied the work of Faber, Jacob Bryant, and Sir William Jones, and his methods and critical standards were those of his predecessors in the genre of mytho-culture history. In support of his "evidences" he converted the Indian war whoop into "Y-O-He-Wah," a corruption of "Jehovah," and he declared that the Choctaw Indians intermixed the word "Hal-le-leu-yah" into their lamentations for the dead. Yet so fine a line distinguishes success from failure in scholarship that whereas Richard Brothers, Boudinot's English compeer, was confined to a madhouse, Boudinot served as a trustee of Princeton College.

Speculation concerning the ten lost tribes of Israel took Protean forms, of which Anglo-Israelism and Lehite Americanism were the least amorphous. No race was too decayed, too remote, too improbable to be denied some claim to the heritage of prophecy or a nineteenth-century advocate to argue its cause.

For the most part the matter of the ten lost tribes is compounded of Biblical lore, some canonical, some apocryphal. It is reported that after the defeat of Israel by Tiglath Pileser, or by Shalmaneser, in the time of Hosea, the greater part of the northern kingdom was removed to Assyria, whence eventually the tribes wandered away and became "lost" to history. Since the reiterated promise of prophecy is that Israel will at length return to the Holy Land, the problem of the total disappearance of so large a part of the once disinherited nation has never failed to puzzle and trouble those who have looked for a strict fulfillment. Of the prophecies, that contained in the thirteenth chapter of the second book of Esdras has borne most directly upon the problem and given rise to the greatest amount of speculation. Esdras dreamed a dream, in the interpretation of which we learn that shortly before the second coming of Christ, among the multitudes gathered together for the occasion at Sion there shall be a certain "peaceable multitude":

> Those are the ten tribes, which were carried away prisoner out of their owne land, in the time of Osea the king, whom Salmanasar the king of Assyria ledde away captive, and hee caried them over the waters, and so came they into another land.
> But they tooke this counsaile amongst themselves, that they would leave the multitude of the heathen, and goe foorth into a further countrey, where never mankind dwelt,
> That they might there keepe their statutes, which they never kept in their owne land.
> And they entred into Euphrates by the narrow passages of the River.
> For the most high then shewed signes for them, and held still the flood, till they were passed over.
> For through that countrey there was a great way to goe; namely, of a yeere and a halfe: and the same region is called Arsareth.
> Then dwelt they there untill the latter time; and now when they shall begin to come,
> The highest shall stay the springs of the streame againe, that they may go through: therefore sawest thou the multitude with peace.

The topographical terms in which the migrations of the lost tribes are thus described, and similar prophecies relating to the return of Israel to Jerusalem, are sufficiently vague to lend themselves to various interpretations. But when to the errors of mediaeval and Renaissance speculation on the subject were added the hypotheses made possible by the new culture history based on the study of comparative mythology, interpretations of the prophecies became even more erratic and bold.

Anglo-Israelism identified the British Isles with the "further country," Ireland standing for Arsareth. There the tribe of Dan, carrying with it Jacob's stone, had found its way. The stone was believed to be the very one on which the kings of Scotland and England were subsequently crowned. Prophecies from Hosea, Isaiah, Micah, and various statements from Genesis and Deuteronomy were gathered up to show that England best suited the predictions concerning the destiny of Israel: namely, that Israel would change its name; that it would be numberless; that it would dwell in islands; that it would have colonies; that it would be the chief of the nations; that it would be north and west of Palestine. The English and Irish were the descendants of the ten lost tribes who should repossess Jerusalem, whereas those admittedly "Jews" were of the other two tribes, and it was their fate to fulfill the direr prophecies.

In America, Boudinot worked out his Indian hypothesis from the same data but with different results. Whereas Richard Brothers had seen himself as the prince who should lead Israel to the repossession of Jerusalem, and that at no distant date, Boudinot was motivated by a selfless piety and genuine humanitarianism. He saw the duty of white men, once the nature of the Indians was perceived, to cease the persecution which had been the fate of the Indians since the usurpation of their lands by the white men. Before the advent of European civilization the Indian had been at least closer to the noble heritage of his descent and had retained traditions which had been dissipated and forgotten under the degrading influence of his conquest. Thus Boudinot set the doctrine of the noble savage upon a new ground.

But the "latter days" foreseen in the prophecy were at hand, and the great events of the promise were hastening to fulfillment. The Lord would be faithful to the pledge made to his chosen people. Their discovery in America served to demonstrate with startling exactness how literally the prophecies had been fulfilled already regarding their tribulations and their wanderings. Let the white peoples in America ignore to the peril of their own salvation the advent of the hour of fulfillment.

Such was the message of Elias Boudinot, a grave and honorable man who combined learning with humility to serve a high purpose with conviction. It must have been received attentively by many of the earnest zealots who, in the fervor and confusion of an expanding pioneer civilization, were conceiving visionary and grandiose religious schemes.

During the middle decades of the nineteenth century, when the rapidly growing Mormon empire was considered a political and moral threat to the structure of American society, many efforts were made to discredit the integrity of Joseph Smith and his *The Book of Mormon*. Nor has the heat of controversy yet been sufficiently qualified to have permitted a cool examination of one of the most remarkable products of the visionary imagination. Whatever a critical analysis may eventually reveal *The Book of Mormon* to be, it has already proved itself historically a document of sufficient vitality to have instigated one of the most vigorous religious movements of the nineteenth century and to have sustained for over a hundred years a stable and powerful society.

Joseph Smith was one of the craggy originals whom, now that the nineteenth century has faded into perspective, America cherishes as a type and symbol of her vast pioneering. It is easy to treat his visions and his chicanery in a jocose spirit. Much that he is reported, by his enemies, to have said and done is preposterous. But Joseph Smith deserves better of history than to be made the butt of a biographer's jokes. He was a patriarch of the frontier, a prophet of the violent West, tricky, ignorant, astute, fanatical, brilliant, mysterious, devout.

Inevitably this nomadic servant of an Old Testament Jehovah, whose character was modeled upon that of the Hebrew patriarchs, would have been fascinated by the current notions of a brief relation between modern culture and a pristine time. His imaginative mind seized hold of the belief that the Indians were descendants of the ancient lost tribes of Israel, and from the fervor of an excited mind his *The Book of Mormon* poured forth as if from a divine dictation. *The Book of Mormon* was "translated" from the golden plates between 1827 and 1830. An official summary issued at Nauvoo about 1843 describes its historical content as follows:

In this important and interesting book the history of ancient America is unfolded from its first settlement by a colony that came from the Tower of Babel at the confusion of languages to the beginning of the fifth century of the Christian era. We are informed by these records that America in ancient times has been inhabited by two distinct races of people. The first were the Jaredites and came directly from the Tower of Babel. The second race came directly from the city of Jerusalem about six hundred years before Christ. They were principally Israelites of the descendants of Joseph. The Jaredites were destroyed about the time that the Israelites came from Jerusalem, who succeeded them in the inheritance of the country.

The principal nation of the second race fell in battle toward the close of the fourth century. The remnants are the Indians who now inhabit this country. This book also tells us that our Savior made his appearance upon this continent after his resurrection; that he planted the gospel here in all its fullness and richness, and power and blessing, that they had apostles, prophets, pastors, teachers, and evangelists; the same order, the same priesthood, the same ordinances, gifts, powers, and blessings as was enjoyed on the Eastern continent; that the people were cut off in consequence of their transgressions, that the last of their prophets who existed among them was commanded to write an abridgement of their prophecies, history, etc., and to hide it up in the earth and that it should come forth and be united with *The Bible* for the accomplishment of the purpose of God in the last days.

The concern of the book is but secondarily with narrative history. It is primarily the vehicle for Smith's ideas, social, moral, and religious—a complex set of doctrines which do not concern us here. The significant thing is to discern that the pattern of thought worked out by Brothers in England and Boudinot in America is complemented by indirect revelation in the imagination of the visionary prophet. The whole history of the Israelitish migration, together with intimations of what will happen in the latter days, is packed with allusions to the prophecies concerning the dispersion of the peoples and their repossession of Jerusalem. All the terms significant to Anglo-Israelism and American Israelism are emphasized in the envisioned history and the warnings. Did not Joseph Smith reshape the pattern with himself in mind? One is tempted to infer that it was originally his intention to assume the leadership of the Indians in the latter-day fulfillment of the prophecies and that *The Book of Mormon* was devised to support a conception of himself as the leader of a gentile religious movement which should culminate in the return of the Indians and the repossession of Jerusalem. *The Book of Mormon* was a youthful work, published long before the actual role which Joseph Smith was to play in history had begun to shape itself, even in outline. As one reads the book, looking backward upon the historical movement to which it lent inspiration, one may understand how the faithful may be reluctant to disengage the Mormon Bible from events and to suppose that its purpose was originally far different from the use to which it was put. But Joseph Smith's *The Book of Mormon* reads curiously like a sequel to Boudinot's *A Star in the West*.

Smith was at one time charged with having stolen his ideas from a manuscript novel by one Solomon Spaulding, an inexperienced and incompetent writer who composed a trifling story based on a conception of pre-European civilization in America. The charge may be dismissed as inconsequential. The eventual publication of Spaulding's story should have sufficed to refute the accusation, as Joseph Smith's subtle and powerful work could have owed little or nothing to such a model. But that Smith's basic concepts may be derivative from Brothers and Boudinot is an hypothesis not to be lightly set aside. Criticism may yet unveil to my speculative mythologists a monument carved in mountain granite.

Part Two

Part Two

Prognosis

FROM midway in the second decade of the nineteenth century, and for a span of about twenty years, the poets were attracted by a form of composition in which invention played very ingeniously and intricately with mythology. The interests of the modern world have shifted, and the time has passed when cultivated readers may be expected to possess the minute knowledge of unimportant mythological documents which forms the necessary equipment to follow the poets through their thematic material. Indeed it is by no means certain that even well-informed contemporaries, at a time when a close knowledge of myth was the fashion, were ever able to follow all the elaborate devices. Nor have editors since taken the pains to work out fully the mythological detail which the reader must possess if the poet is to communicate with him.

My plan in preparing these essays has been to examine the sort of erudite information which the fashion of the day sought out; to trace the labyrinthine inventions of the poets through the mythological action of their poems; and to arrange my findings in essays intended to resolve the difficulties which one meets in the mythological contrivance.

The process has resulted in more than a mere series of notes on the various poems. It has provided a technique

for criticism of some of the most famous poems of the
Romantic period—a criticism which may, in many respects, modify our admiration of them.

So solid is the reputation of Keats and Shelley and
Goethe that the modern reader, puzzled perhaps by the
mazy narrative of *Endymion*, the subtle involvements of
Adonais, the lyric profusion of *Prometheus Unbound*, and
the sly incomprehensibility of the classical *Second Part of
Faust*, may yet accept as substantial, poetic designs which,
if examined with energy, he would reject as of little worth.
Close analysis of the mythological bases of the poems
makes it easier to discern the structural workings of the
poets' minds and to reveal—in some cases, unhappily, to
expose—weaknesses and trivialities of conception or execu-
tion which cannot be admired. In other instances no such
disparagement results from examination. Keats's *Hyperion*,
if one considers its probable development from its thematic myth, appears to have been more ably designed than
critics have perceived. The grandeur of Shelley's moral
allegory in *Prometheus Unbound* can be only the more
admired the more closely it is scrutinized. But for the most
part the critical approach of these essays does not show
the poets to their advantage. With no predisposition to
detract, my examination should puncture once and for all
the inflated reputation of the *Second Part of Faust*. If
more than one reader has suspected that his bewilderment
on reading that work was the fault of the author and not
of himself, he will find here the material to convert suspicion into conviction. Even *Hyperion*, which gathers
strength from the reader's perception of its design, is
revealed as devised to turn upon a doubtful mythological
mechanism. The moral excellence of *Prometheus Unbound*

is in curious contrast to the trivial and florid devices by which the action is conducted. Shelley chips his monumental idea into bric-a-brac. In *Adonais* one is forced to admit the too finely stretched invention of the poet and his inability, for all his dazzling dexterity, to manipulate the too intricate theme.

Modern taste scarcely permits us even a realization of the lengths to which some of the Romantic poets went in mythological innuendo. Shelley found pleasure in imparting to bare circumstance a shimmer of allusiveness which we can now regard with mere astonishment. In *Prometheus Unbound*, for instance, his account of the succession of the primal gods reads:

> There was the Heaven and Earth at first
> And Light and Love; then Saturn, from whose throne
> Time fell, an envious shadow.

The lines continue with a description of the state of men under the reign of Saturn.

At first sight it would appear that Shelley is imagining four successive generations: Heaven and Earth (Uranus and Ge); Light and Love (his own contribution to the theogony); Saturn; and then Time. But Time is apparently an allusion to Cronus, whose name in Greek signifies *time*, and Cronus did not succeed Saturn. The two are merely the Latin and Greek equivalents of a personage who plays identical roles in the primal succession before the advent of the Olympian gods. The inference is, therefore, that Shelley is imagining only three generations. The figure prompts our awareness of the two names under which the father of the Olympian gods was known and says in effect that Saturn (or his Greek equivalent) fell. But the identification of Saturn with Cronus (Time) permits Shelley to give overtones of meaning to the mere statement. We may think of Cronus as a shadow either because he is merely a myth or because, as a variant of Saturn, the one is a shadow of the other. The father of the Olympian gods was envious of his children, whose succession he attempted to prevent. Hence Cronus is "an envious shadow." But by virtue of Cronus' significance as Time, more meaning may be added to the phrase, Time being envious of what comes after, and a shadow because it has no substance. Thus Shelley throws a multiple allusiveness around his words, the recognition of which depends upon our capacity to perceive that in the figure Saturn and Time are one and the same and not successive generations. The question one is inclined to raise is whether there is enough meat in such a nut to make it worth the cracking.

Allusiveness in figurative language, however, is the least of the obstacles which the reader must overcome. The same intricacy is carried over into the entire design, so that to follow the thought of complicated dramas like *Prometheus Unbound* or the *Second Part of Faust* requires more than intense powers of concentration. No amount of mere critical acumen alone will enable a reader to understand what is going on in the more difficult parts of either play. Not only must one observe closely the clues to the meaning in the text; one must possess in advance pieces of erudition well outside the ordinary limits of knowledge. Very few persons, I imagine, know offhand that there is a connection between the legendary Prometheus and a cave at Colonus, near the grove of the Academy outside Athens. My guess is also that very few persons who have read *Prometheus Unbound*—and read it carefully—have perceived that the play has anything to do with the cave or that such a cave is mentioned. Yet the whole allegory of the latter part is bound to a recognition of the circumstance, and to read without making the identification is as futile as struggling for air in a vacuum. Similarly, few persons recall, if they ever knew, that the Haemonian women were reputed to have the power to bring up the dead from the underworld. Yet to read the *Second Part of Faust* without that piece of postclassical information is to lose the whole point of the elaborate transactions leading up to the resuscitation of Helen of Troy in the Middle Ages.

The entire remainder of my book stands as further illustration of the intricacy of invention practiced by the poets who dealt with mythological themes. I state my contention here merely as preface and apology for what follows. The subsequent problem of exposition has not been a simple one. It is difficult to be direct and simple about things which are neither. What I have tried to achieve is an expository arrangement which will lead the reader through the labyrinth to the center and out again with a minimum of effort on his part. The form which each essay has taken is different, according to the nature of the problem.

With *Endymion* the problem is largely one of showing how, in lieu of sufficient plot, Keats struggled to fill out his narrative poem without wholly losing sight of the classical myth of the Latmian shepherd. As one would expect—and certainly excuse on the grounds of Keats's youth—the poet floundered in inexperience. If my exposition reveals that he was mainly in the wake of his story and that at best he steered but a zigzag course, it shows nevertheless that he retained some sort of connection with the myth and it precludes the possibility of attaching to *Endymion* the vapid allegories which criticism has attempted to read into the poem.

In the essay on *Hyperion* I have attempted to guess the uncompleted plan of the epic and then to support my guess by a reinterpretation of the significance to be found in what Keats actually completed. If I am correct, most of the critical objections which have been taken are shown to be irrelevant, and matters which seemed to be difficulties become clear indications of the poet's purpose.

Rossetti's analysis of *Adonais* seems to me the ablest commentary on the poem, but I think that I too have been able to do Shelley some service in showing how he sustained the relation of his theme to the myth of Aphrodite and Adonis throughout the entire poem—a point which criticism seems wholly to have missed. Shelley's ashes will, however, owe me no debt of gratitude for pointing out the instances in which he was unable to make his intricate themes hold together for any good purpose.

Prometheus Unbound has never been submitted to the analysis which it deserves, which it cries out for, but which must certainly expose its too intricate, often almost ludicrously farfetched thematic devices. There is too much that is of superior excellence in the poem to permit its worser parts to obscure them. Some of the noblest of Shelley's poetry is in *Prometheus Unbound*, but the plot lies full fathom five.

If I have succeeded in tracing Goethe's mind through the involutions of the *Second Part of Faust*, it is largely because I have been sustained by the hope that no one would have to perform the labor after me. For that reason I have given in this book a larger space to the drama than its proportionate merit warrants. In the *Second Part of Faust* Goethe concentrated the vices of old age, great reputation, and the Romantic movement. The play will not yield to analysis in a few succinct pages.

Endymion, Hyperion, Prometheus Unbound, Adonais, and the classical portions of the *Second Part of Faust* have, despite the diversity of poetic style and capacity shown in them, a common denominator in their method of thematic treatment. To compare these works with the "classical" poems immediately preceding them is to become aware of their common element. Goethe in his youth, Alfieri, André Chénier, Wordsworth—all made distinguished use of classical themes without placing upon their readers that peculiar obligation demanded by the poems analyzed here.

Goethe's *Iphigenia in Tauris*, for instance, has nothing of the character of the *Second Part of Faust*. Goethe tampered with the classical story somewhat, but he did not play tricks with it as he did with the legend concerning Helen of Troy. The very clarity of the design makes *Iphigenia* memorable. The change in Goethe's manner of dealing with classical legend appears not to have come until his *Achilleis*, for which his notes suggest that he had in mind a very intricate piece of designing. But even the completed portion of the *Achilleis* shows nothing so complicated as he permitted in the *Second Part of Faust*.

Goethe's *Iphigenia* was simply and loftily conceived. It was the poet's attempt to answer Winckelmann's plea for the imitation of the Greek. Like Winckelmann, he idealized the Greek, but in his idealization he escaped the monotony and inertness which one detects in Winckelmann's most ardent disciples—Flaxman and Thorwaldsen in sculpture, Mengs and West in painting. Goethe achieved his idealization by elevating the character of Iphigenia. The wily Greek heroine of Euripides who extricated herself from a predicament by deception was replaced with a gentle, noble, and honest Iphigenia who won release for herself and her brother by telling the truth.

In Italy the poet Alfieri made a fairly traditional use of the tragic themes of classical drama. Except in his style he looked backward upon the drama of Racine and Corneille, ordering his thematic material into the usual conflict between love and duty. Alfieri was moved by a desire to restore dignity in letters to the place which the opera had usurped—the tragic stage. This object he accomplished by powerful management of an unornamented verse and a rigid use of conventional legendary theme. Alfieri was touched by none of the artistic influences which moved Shelley and Keats. He would have scorned novelty of conception or elaboration of design. It is to be doubted whether he possessed any of that love of classical legend in and for itself which was intrinsic in Keats. The *Agamemnon* of Alfieri was an act of duty: the *Endymion* of Keats an act of love.

The classical poems of André Chénier—many of them fragments—were mere experimental imitations. Their object was to recapture a lost spirit, not by making Greek poetry French, but by making French poetry Greek. Intricate manipulation of pseudoclassical thematic material was no part of Chénier's object. Like Keats he loved the Greece which he imagined, but unlike Keats he would not have wished to transmute it into his own nature.

In England no great work, independently conceived and ambitiously executed, had been based upon classical legend successfully for over a hundred years when Wordsworth made his experimental essay in *Laodamia*. Wordsworth brought to *Laodamia* no conspicuous interest in classical mythology. While he had no hostility toward it as poetic material, he felt that for English poets English themes provided stimulus enough. Like Goethe in *Iphigenia* his object was to impart to his legend "a loftier tone than, so far as I know, has been given to it by any of the ancients who have treated of it." He achieved an austere and tenuous style, a note already struck by Alfieri in Italy but not to be heard again in England until the maturity of Landor.

The poem has conspicuous faults. Wordsworth does not sufficiently reveal the immoderate passion for which Protesilaus rebukes his wife. Unless the reader is fresh from the classical sources of the tale, he does not know—nor does the poem indicate—that Laodamia has been so immoderate as to take to bed with her, in her husband's absence, a wax statue of him. To all outward appearances Laodamia in Wordsworth's poem is a matronly person with no abnormal lust for her husband's embraces. When Protesilaus so sharply rebukes his wife, the reader is shocked by what seems to be an unwarranted and puritanical attitude on the part of the husband. In classical legend Protesilaus had no reputation for the kind of virtue with which Wordsworth endows him. His virtues were heroic rather than ethical. The moral lesson of the English poem lies too coldly upon the classical fable. In the *Heroides* Ovid treated the theme nobly by contrasting the unworthy wishes of Laodamia with the fact of the heroic self-sacrifice which, the reader well knew, Protesilaus had already made. In Ovid's poem Protesilaus did not need to return to rebuke his intemperate and cowardly wife. The rebuke was implied, not stated, and the moral is the stronger. The English poem is, in a sense, a sequel to the Latin. Like Goethe in *Iphigenia*, Wordsworth altered, not the fable itself, but the moral character of the protagonist. He gathered up details of the story from a diversity of classical sources, ranging, it would seem, over such wide opposites as Homer and Tzetzes.

One poem based on classical fable attracts an attention which far outweighs its merits. Mrs. Tighe's *Psyche*, completed in 1795, may have suggested a method in the treatment of classical legend which affected a later generation of poets. She built the first part of her allegory upon the legend of Cupid and Psyche as it was told by Apuleius. At the point in the story where Psyche, after sinning against her lover, commences her wanderings and her atonement, Mrs. Tighe abandoned the classical story and invented a Spenserian allegory. The wanderings of Mrs. Tighe's Psyche have no connection with those in Apuleius' poem. Apuleius had made a charming allegory of the atonement of Psyche, but Mrs. Tighe, dissatisfied with the moral tone of it, divorced both her morals and her details from her model. Had she invented her own allegory and yet kept it in terms identifiable in relation to Apuleius, she would have had a subtler and more ingenious piece of narrative. One feels that Keats and Shelley would have seen the opportunity which Mrs. Tighe missed. It may be that her fault suggested to them their method of tying a modern improvisation into a traditional theme. At any rate, *Endymion*, which was much affected by the diction of Mrs. Tighe, was actually such an improvisation, though Keats's success in keeping it linked to the fable was not all that he desired.

With this forewarning of literary and mythological complications to come, we may turn to the sort of analysis which, like diagnosis in medicine, must precede critical judgment.

Keats's Endymion

No MATURE reader reproaches Keats for the obvious defects of *Endymion* as a work of art. *Endymion* was a youthful work, the first ambitious poem which Keats attempted. Its faults are those of immaturity and inexperience, and the best criticism of it will always remain Keats's own deprecating, modest, and honest comment with which he prefaced the work.

Keats's reputation rests securely upon nobler and more beautiful poems. But though the best of Keats is not to be found in *Endymion*, no one who loves his greater poetry and the memory of the man will wish to turn too quickly from it. The inconsequential narrative grows wearisome. The lush lines become cloying: some of them are absurd. But the very exuberance of the poem is a delightful thing to witness. One shares with the young poet the intoxication which he felt at the thought of so much beauty to be encompassed, so many legends to be told in glowing verse, so many images of the sense to be transmuted into words. And everywhere there is present that peculiar quality of the mind which was soon to express itself in transcendent genius. *Endymion* remains the faulty expression of a superior mind, rewarding because even the imperfect expression of Keats's mind is interesting, and because occasionally one finds authentic quality in the poem.

Endymion is difficult to read consecutively because of the remarkable meandering of the narrative. To lose one's place is dangerous, for there are few clues in the devious plot to show what is going on at any one time, or what Endymion has to do with it. Most of Keats's difficulty in the poem, and consequently most of the reader's, comes from the poet's mismanagement of the narrative. It has seemed to me that it might be useful to consider the poem in terms of the myth on which it is based, attempting to point out how the narrative proceeds away from the fable without ever quite losing sight of it. Many of the baffling turns which the poem takes become, in that fashion, intelligible, if not defensible. For the chief problem in understanding *Endymion* is not any difficulty in understanding what the poet is saying, but in perceiving why he has been prompted to lead the narrative in the peculiar directions which it takes.

I think that after Keats had begun *Endymion*, he became aware of a fact that a more experienced narrator would have seen beforehand—that there was not enough story to go around. After all, the story of *Endymion* consists of little more than this: that a sleeping shepherd lad upon Mount Latmos was beloved by the moon, who kissed him while he slept. To stretch such a story into four cantos of a poem would be well nigh an impossibility. Keats began in a leisurely fashion, elaborating in rich descriptive passages wherever he felt the desire, but even with the most leisurely narrative method the fact remains that after the first canto was finished the whole story had been used up. And even at that he had been compelled to stretch it out a good deal.

If one thumbs through the index of a great many

scholarly editions of the classics or consults a very complete guide to mythology, one may gather up many pieces of mythological lore about Endymion. But there is not much with which to make a long story, and what there is does not fit well into the kind of amorous heroic that Keats had imagined and begun. Perhaps Keats did actually make an effort to extract from classical lore a sufficient body of fact to build the story up, but if a few stray pieces of relevant classical erudition may be detected in the poem, it is nevertheless apparent that Keats made no serious effort to weld together into a single narrative all of the material which he might have found about Endymion. It is equally apparent that the bulk of the poem has almost nothing to do with the Endymion of classical myth. There is no legendary connection between Endymion and Glaucus, and yet Keats has told a rather extensive story involving the two. There is no "Indian maid" who figures in the story of Endymion in classical myth, and yet such a lady occupies a considerable place in the narrative of the fourth book. Nothing in the myth of Endymion suggests his wandering through the underground cavern of the second book, with his adventures there. The Endymion of Greek myth has no adventures under the sea and no such marriage in the sky as Keats recounts.

Aside then from the padded story of the first book, the narrative in the poem has little solid connection with the legendary Endymion.

I have often noticed that there is some obscure connection between the story told in *Endymion* and the fables relating to Theseus and Ariadne; as though Keats, lacking a substantial story to tell about Endymion, had eked out his narrative by applying to it items from the story of

Ariadne and Theseus which his imagination had already converted into poetic imagery.

It is interesting to notice that many of the actions of the poem which have no real relation to the story of Endymion do have a connection with the other story. For instance, the wanderings of Endymion in the immense underground cavern described in the second book have only a forced connection with Diana's love for the Latmian shepherd. It is true that Keats manages a meeting somewhere in the depths of the cave between Endymion and Diana, though the incident is all but lost in the narrative account of Endymion's wanderings in the cavern itself. But this portion of the poem might be some sort of adaptation of the wanderings of Theseus in the Labyrinth. For Endymion's cavern with its marble floor, its "thousand mazes," its

> winding passages, where sameness breeds
> Vexing conceptions of some sudden change,

its "marble gallery," its "sidelong aisles," and its "courts and passages," seems at times more like the Labyrinth than a cavern. The famous Labyrinth that Daedalus made for Minos at Cnossus was an underground affair, lost in the depths of the earth. If Keats had been reading about the Labyrinth he would have found just such descriptive detail as that which he attached to Endymion's cavern. There is a cavern near Gortyna, in Crete, which in Keats's time had been regarded by many as the remains of the Daedalian Labyrinth. A young French traveler of the eighteenth century, Savary, has left us an account of his exploration of that cavern. He, like Theseus, fastened a ball of twine at the entrance and guided himself through the mazes in classical fashion. The innumerable "alleys," the passages without outlets, the vast empty space supported by pillars, the phantoms and precipices which the imagination conjures up, the "beautiful grotto, rising into a dome," are like those of the cavern of Endymion. And it is interesting, too, to read that Endymion is guided by the light of gold and gems within the otherwise dark cavern, for Hyginus tells us that it was the gleam of gold and gems within the darkness of the Labyrinth that guided Theseus. Endymion himself seems to recall the cavern as a labyrinth, for when he is in the arms of his Indian maid, he cries, recalling his wanderings:

> O destiny!
> Into a labyrinth now my soul would fly,
> But with thy beauty will I deaden it.

There is no connection between the fable of Endymion and that portion of Keats's poem which relates the under-sea journey of Endymion. Endymion was a shepherd lad who lived in the mountains. But Theseus made a journey under the sea, for Hyginus tells us that after he had arrived at Crete he and Minos fell into a quarrel over their respective parentage. Theseus boasted that he was the son of Poseidon. Minos threw a ring into the sea and told him if he was the son of Poseidon to go and get it. Theseus plunged into the sea, whereupon a great multitude of dolphins rose from the sea and led Theseus to the Nereids, from whom he got the ring and a crown which he later gave to Ariadne. It is the Nereids who convey Endymion from the sea, after his extraordinary underwater visit to the palace of Neptune.

There is no classical legend which links Endymion with Glaucus, but a considerable part of Keats's poem—nearly the whole of Book III—narrates a story involving the two. The name Glaucus is interesting in connection with the possibility that Keats is influenced by the story concerning Theseus and Ariadne, for Ariadne had a brother named Glaucus. Keats's story is the well-known fable of Glaucus of Anthedon—not Ariadne's brother—given, however, a wholly invented ending concerning the rescue of the dead lovers. And yet there seems to have been some connection in Keats's mind between the Glaucus of the Ariadne myth and the Glaucus of the poem, for just as the dead lovers were revived by scattering certain leaves upon the dead bodies, so Ariadne's brother had been brought back to life by having leaves placed upon his dead body. It is curious also that when Glaucus gives Endymion his instructions he should say:

> What more there is to do, young man, is thine:
> But first a little patience; first undo
> This tangled thread, and wind it to a clue.
> Ah gentle! 'tis as weak as spider's skein;
> And shouldst thou break it—What, is it done so clean?
> A power overshadows thee. Oh, brave!
> The spite of hell is tumbling to its grave.

These would be remarkably apt words for Ariadne to have spoken to Theseus as he started into the Labyrinth with his clue of thread, but they have very little point as applied to Endymion, merely forming a part of the magic formula which restores the dead lovers.

That Ariadne had some part in Keats's imaginings for the story of *Endymion* is very certain from two incidents of Book IV.

Endymion encounters an amorous Indian maid who sings to him a sorrowful song of her experiences. Now by

all the rights of literary convention that song belongs to
Ariadne, for the story which she tells is that of Ariadne's
awakening upon the Isle of Dia when Theseus had abandoned her, and of her joining the merry crew of Bacchus
and his revelers. The name Ariadne does not appear, but
had not Keats identified the singer as an Indian maid and
put in a few Indian details to render her nationality
plausible, we should at once recognize the poem as a fairly
conventional treatment of the Ariadne theme. And, of
course, there is no Indian maid who belongs to the classical
fable of Endymion.

It will be recalled that when, either through choice or
through lot, Theseus arrived at the court of King Minos
of Crete with the other six youths and the seven maidens
who were to be sacrificed to the Minotaur as a part of the
yearly Athenian tribute to Minos, Ariadne, the daughter
of Minos, fell in love with him and gave him a sword with
which to slay the Minotaur and a ball of thread by which
he might retrace his steps through the Labyrinth. The
Minotaur was Ariadne's brother, but her love for Theseus
had persuaded her to betray her brother in order to aid
her lover. After Theseus had slain the monster and rescued
the other Athenians, Ariadne fled with him to the Isle of
Dia, or, according to another version of the myth, to
Naxos. Here Theseus abandoned Ariadne while she was
sleeping. When Ariadne awakened, she mourned for the
lover who had forsaken her. Then Bacchus and his crew
of revelers came upon her. Bacchus consoled the grieving
Ariadne and subsequently married her in a magnificent
ceremony in the sky, which all the gods attended. The
crown of Ariadne, a famous constellation, is the heavenly
symbol of her triumph.

The awakening of Ariadne is a famous theme, both in verse and painting, particularly the latter. In *Sleep and Poetry* Keats recalled the pleasure which he had received from seeing one such picture, perhaps that of Titian, which portrayed

> the swift bound
> Of Bacchus from his chariot, when his eye
> Made Ariadne's cheek look blushingly.

And the image of Ariadne among the crew of Bacchic revelers recurred to him in *Endymion* when he described the wine in the grotto of Adonis as

> Alive with sparkles—never, I aver,
> Since Ariadne was a vintager,
> So cool a purple.

In poetic accounts of the story, the sorrowful complaint of the abandoned Ariadne when she awakens on the Isle of Dia forms an important part of the narrative. The sorrowful mood of the lament is followed by an exhilarating description of the arrival of Bacchus and his gay followers and an account of how Ariadne joins the company of Bacchus. Thus, in Catullus (in the *Nuptials of Peleus and Thetis*), Ariadne reproaches Theseus for luring her from her home and regrets that she has betrayed her brother and her father for a faithless lover. The sadness of the lament changes to gaiety as the consoler arrives:

> Bounding along was blooming Bacchus seen,
> With all his heart aflame with love for thee,
> Fair Ariadne! And behind him, see,
> Where Satyrs and Sileni whirl along,
> With frenzy fired, a fierce tumultuous throng!
> Evoe! they yell, Evoe! that jocund rout,
> And clap their hands, and toss their heads about.

There some wave thyrsi wreathed with ivy, here
Some toss the limbs of a dismembered steer;
Around their waists some coiling serpents twine,
While others work the mysteries divine
With arks of osiers, mysteries of fear,
Which the profane desire in vain to hear.
Others with open palms the timbrels smite,
Or with thin brazen rods wake tinklings light;
And many a hoarse resounding horn is blown,
And fifes barbarian shriek with hideous drone.

(Theodore Martin's translation)

In the *Dionysica* of Nonnus, Ariadne mourns that she has awakened, because in the vanity of her dreams she had been happy with her lover, and now even these had fled away. She calls upon Morpheus to fill her mind again with the shadowy image of her happiness. She grieves that she has abandoned her mother and father to follow Theseus and that she will never see her home again. Bacchus appears (Book XLVII), and to console her offers her a place in the sky among the constellations.

Like Ariadne, the maiden whom Endymion encounters is grieving that she left her home and longing to return. She sings a lyrical lament which tells how she sat weeping by the river side, with no one to tell her sorrow to:

And as I sat, over the light blue hills
There came a noise of revellers: the rills
Into the wide stream came of purple hue—
    'Twas Bacchus and his crew!
The earnest trumpet spake, and silver thrills
From kissing cymbals made a merry din—
    'Twas Bacchus and his kin!
Like to a moving vintage down they came,
Crown'd with green leaves, and faces all on flame;
All madly dancing through the pleasant valley.

The stanzas that follow relate how she joined the merry throng, and tell the famous story of the expedition of Bacchus into the East.

The whole incident, with its sequence of the lament and the joyful arrival of Bacchus, seems to have been designed upon the theme of Ariadne's desertion, and then deliberately modified for another story.

In the middle of Book IV, Keats introduces a lyric passage which purports to be the voices of the pinioned multitude celebrating the marriage of Diana in the sky. Since Endymion is still embroiled in the affair of the Indian maid, and since the marriage is supposed to be that of Endymion and Diana, Keats represents the ceremony as a kind of mask prophetic of the ceremony to come. It is a vision. The poem is mainly concerned with the constellations, which would, of course, be appropriate to the conception of a marriage in the sky. Aquarius, Castor, the Lion, the Bear, Pollux, the Centaur, Andromeda, Perseus —all are mentioned. The whole poem is abruptly introduced, with little to account for its sudden intrusion into the narrative.

This inserted lyric, fitted so loosely to the theme of Endymion, might well have had a place in a poem about Ariadne, for one of the most famous legends about her relates to the placing of her crown among the constellations. Aratus tells us that after Bacchus had married Ariadne, he placed her crown among the constellations, and Hyginus tells various stories of how the gods attended the marriage of Bacchus and Ariadne, how she received the crown as a gift, and how Bacchus placed it in the sky among the constellations.

There are certainly many circumstances to suggest that

Keats's mind had been dwelling upon the theme of Ariadne and Theseus and that elements of the theme may be discerned in *Endymion*. If I am correct in believing that Keats found it difficult to stretch out his fable to the desired length—and such must have been the case—then he had the problem of filling it out in some other way. It is plausible enough to suppose that he would try to adapt the circumstances of some other stories to the theme at hand.

What happened was, presumably, something like this. Endymion was supplied with a cavern in which to wander in search of Diana, but certain features of the Labyrinth, retained in Keats's mind, were applied to the cavern. Glaucus of Crete was amalgamated with Glaucus of Anthedon, and the rescue of the Athenians developed into the story of the rescue of the dead lovers. The sea journey of Theseus was shifted to a sea journey of Endymion and linked with the story of the marine Glaucus. Ariadne was converted into an Indian maid, probably from a hint in Ovid's *Fasti* that Bacchus fell in love with an Indian princess whom he took captive on his Indian expedition. The placing of Ariadne's crown among the constellations was converted into a mask of the marriage of Diana and Endymion. And the Indian maid was at last converted into an embodiment of the moon in order to justify her presence in the Endymion legend.

The influence of the story of Theseus and Ariadne accounts for the presence in *Endymion* of a number of matters which are inexplicable merely in terms of the classical myth of Endymion. Nevertheless, a good deal of the action remains somewhat puzzling. What, for instance, is the second book about? The apparent formlessness of

this part of the poem has led many writers to attempt to
read into it various allegories, most of them fantastic.

It seems to me that when Keats had finished the first
book, and had discovered that most of his legend had been
used up, he at first attempted to make it last a little longer.
The legend connected Endymion with the caves where
he was visited by the moon, and Keats conceived the idea
of having Endymion wander in a cave until he encountered the moon goddess. But since the encounter with
Diana had already been described three times, it was apparent that the "bare circumstance," as Keats described
it, must be embellished by something of additional interest.
The cave itself would be a likely topic, and perhaps other
legends might somehow appropriately be brought in. At
about this point in the composition of the narrative,
Keats's mind must have seized hold of the idea of having
Endymion wander through the famous Corycian Cave in
Cilicia, commencing with the discovery of the remarkable glen that leads to the entrance of the cavern, continuing through the underground cavern itself, and emerging
at last through the passage that leads from the Corycian
Cave under the sea. Such a plan might have recommended
itself to him because the beauty of the cave would lend
itself advantageously to poetic description, and because
the belief that it was inhabited by the gods would make it
possible to introduce legendary material by the simple
device of having Endymion encounter legendary figures
during his wanderings.

The Corycian Cave was the most famous, the most bewilderingly fantastic, and the most beautiful cave known
to the ancients. Described by Strabo, by Pomponius Mela,
and by Solinus, the wonderful cave above the promontory

of Corycus in Cilicia was held in awe and reverence by the Greeks and Romans both for its natural beauty and for its legendary and sacred associations. Its romantic situation in the rugged mountains near the sea; its solitary and difficult path, descending through a wooded cleft in the mountains to the vast and mysterious cavern; its murmuring springs and submerged river; its inner caves and underground passages; its divinely inspired music; its secret regions sacred to the gods; and its final deep passage issuing under the sea—all these strange and beautiful things might rouse the imagination of a young poet.

It does not matter whether Keats intended the reader to suppose that Endymion's cave was Corycium. Had he so intended he would doubtless have named it. What does matter is this: if we perceive that the sequence of the narrative in Book II is that of a person following the topographical and legendary features of the Corycian cavern, then the sequence of the narrative becomes intelligible as a thing in itself, and we do not have to seek for a recondite allegory in the experiences of Endymion. Furthermore, we perceive how it is that Keats got his Latmian shepherd under the sea at the end of Book II—an unusual location for even a mythical mountaineer.

The events of the first book of *Endymion* took place on or near Mount Latmos. There Diana had visited Endymion three times, once in a woodland "nook," once in "a deep hollow," and once, in conformity with the legend, in a cave. All these places were on Mount Latmos. The cave of the second book, however, is not the cave of the first, and Keats makes it clear that the events of the second book do not take place on Mount Latmos. Endymion has wandered a long distance from his usual haunts:

> For many days
> Has he been wandering in uncertain ways:
> Through wilderness, and woods of mossed oaks.

There are other indications that he has wandered far from
Latmos. His reverie at the mouth of the cave refers to his
own "long toil and travelling," and the voice from the
cavern suggests that the dreamer's way has taken him
through some very high mountains:

> Oft hast thou seen bolts of the thunder hurl'd
> As from thy threshold; day by day hast been
> A little lower than the chilly sheen
> Of icy pinnacles.

Oak forest, wilderness, and snow-covered mountains are
all to be encountered between Latmos and Cilicia, and the
distance to Corycus was not too great for the physical
constitution of a hero who, like Endymion, could walk
even on the bottom of the sea or float on a cloud in the
sky.

Corycus itself was a mountainous headland, with the
entrance to the cave some ten or twenty stadia from
the sea. Endymion's position before entering the depths
of the cavern corresponds with these geographical demands. Endymion speaks of himself as standing upon "a
misty, jutting head of land," and again as upon "a misty
peak." Strabo in describing the promontory uses the word
ἄκρα, of which "headland" is the primary, and "mountain
peak" the secondary meaning. Keats's "head of land" and
"peak" would thus be proper to the location. The cavern's
distance from the sea would also be plausible. According
to Strabo the distance from the sea to the cave is twenty
stadia, that is, a little less than three miles. Keats says that
as Endymion goes down the glen,

far away, the blue
Of ocean fades upon him.

There are two notable parts to the Corycian Cave, the glenlike approach and the underground cavern. Solinus distinguishes between the open approach and the cave proper by calling the first *specus* and the second *antrum*. The *specus* is a great cleft in the mountain near the sea. It is not a cave, since it is open overhead and trees grow on the uneven and mostly rocky floor, beneath a high and rocky brow. It is more properly a deep valley or glen leading down from a high summit into the mountain in a long, moderately steep descent for a distance of between a mile and a mile and a half. Mela speaks with great admiration of the wonderful beauty of this part of Corycium. A circle of overhanging trees shades the hollow interior. A single path leads into it, down a narrow and rough descent which passes through delightful shades and wildly murmuring wooded spots, with streams flowing here and there. Solinus speaks of the perpetual splashing of fountains as one approaches the bottom of this first gulf of the cave, and Strabo mentions a great spring sending forth a river of pure and transparent water which empties forthwith beneath the earth. At the extremity of this hollow is revealed the mouth of a cavern.

Keats traces Endymion's movements with some care. Endymion, in pursuit of a butterfly, follows it through the countryside, through heaths, dun woodland, and buried paths. He arrives at a place where one path leads down through a wooded cleft. He follows this path down through the cleft, losing sight of the sea, and descends what Keats describes as a solitary glen. He continues for some distance until he comes to a fountain near a cavern's

mouth. It seems to me that at the point where Endymion
finds the path leading into the wooded cleft, he is entering
the approach to the Corycian Cave.

Several details in Keats's account are suggestive of the
language of the geographers. Mela describes the approach
as *gradi namque hiatu patens*, and Solinus describes it as
patulus hiatu amplissimo. The word "cleft" is a good translation for *hiatus* in its topographical sense, and, in describing the approach of Endymion to the cave, Keats says that
"one track unseams a wooded cleft." The "one track" is
suggestive of Mela's *Unus in eum descensus est*. The word
"wooded" might well be provoked by Strabo's statement
that the bottom of the glen is "full of trees of the shrub
kind, both the evergreen and those that are cultivated,"
or by Mela's *viret lucis pendentibus undique*, or by the
phrase of Solinus, *virens introrsus lucis pendentibus*. The
image created by Keats's phrase "unseams a . . . cleft" is
apt for a cleft which runs profoundly into a mountain's
side and is an excellent translation of the language of both
Mela and Solinus. Mela says that the cavity lays open the
mountain, *montem . . . aperit*, and Solinus says that it
opens up a hollow into the mountain, *montem . . . cavat*.
"Unseams a cleft" gives an accurate notion of both *aperit*
and *cavat*.

Endymion "sinks down a solitary glen" until he reaches

> a splashing fountain's side
> That, near a cavern's mouth, for ever pour'd
> Unto the temperate air.

This recalls the spring of pure and transparent water which
Strabo describes. Keats mentions the purity of the water,
speaking of the fountain as "crystal spout-head," and of

its "waters clear." Solinus, after telling of the distance
which one must descend, and just before describing the
mouth of the lower cavern, says: *hinc inde* [that is, at
the bottom of the glen] *fontium assidua scaturigine*. This
"perpetual splashing of fountains" near the mouth of a
cavern is the very language of Keats, his "splashing" suggested by *scaturigine*, his "for ever" by *assidua*, his "fountain" by *fontium*, and his "cavern's mouth" by the next
sentence of Solinus: *Ubi perventum ad ima primi sinus,
alter rursum specus panditur: quod antrum latis primum
patet faucibus.*

Thus far, then, Endymion's movements and the language in which Keats describes them correspond closely,
and in the order of detail, with the sunken glen of Corycium as Strabo and Mela and Solinus describe it.

There is a second part both to the Corycian Cave and
to the wanderings of Endymion. Endymion is to enter the
cavern which opens near the fountain.

Strabo mentions this cavern, but says nothing of it
except that the river from the great spring by the cavern
empties under the earth and then, after running invisibly
underground, issues forth into the sea. Solinus and Mela
are more explicit about this lower *antrum*. "The entrance,"
says Solinus, "stands open with wide jaws. Presently it
proceeds darkly through narrow passages. In it is a temple
sacred to Jove, and those who dwell near the cave believe that in its inner recess the den of gigantic Typhon
was placed." The description by Mela is more extensive.
"The cavern," he says, "frightens those who approach by
the sound of the divinely inspired cymbals and by a great
crashing noise. Thence for a long distance light, and the
farther it advances somewhat darker, it leads the venture-

some into the inmost part, and deep within admits to a
sort of underground passage. There a huge torrent, rising
from an enormous fountain, barely shows itself, and, when
it has contracted a great force into a narrow channel, disappears again, completely submerged. There is a space
within so fearful that no one has dared advance into it,
and it is for that reason unknown. It is believed, however,
that it is all majestic and truly sacred, and worthy to be
inhabited by the gods, and that nothing is revealed to the
sight unworthy of worship, and it is as though imbued
with the divine will of the gods. There is another cavern
beyond, which they call the lair of Typhon, with a narrow
mouth, and, so those who know have reported, tightly
compressed, and on that account suffused with perpetual
night, and never easy to be seen. But because it was once
the lair of Typhon, and because it immediately exhausts
whatever descends into it, it ought to be remembered both
for its nature and for its story."

In the underworld journey through which Keats traces
the progress of Endymion, there is a considerable coinci-
dence between Keats's cave and this part of the Corycian
Cave. Although Keats does not refer to Typhon, there is
correspondence in other respects, both in plan and in detail.

Endymion had encountered a naiad in the pebbly margin
of the fountain near the mouth of the cavern. She has told
him that he must

> wander far
> In other regions, past the scanty bar
> To mortal steps,

before he would find his goddess. While he was reflecting
upon her words and calling upon Cynthia, "from the deep
cavern there was borne a voice" which said to him:

"Descend,
Young mountaineer! descend where alleys bend
Into the sparry hollows of the world!
Oft hast thou seen bolts of the thunder hurl'd
As from thy threshold; day by day hast been
A little lower than the chilly sheen
Of icy pinnacles, and dipp'dst thine arms
Into the deadening ether that still charms
Their marble being: now, as deep profound
As those are high, descend! He ne'er is crown'd
With immortality, who fears to follow
Where airy voices lead: so through the hollow,
The silent mysteries of earth, descend!"

Endymion heeded the voice and fled

Into the fearful deep, to hide his head
From the clear moon, the trees, and coming madness.

We may assume that Endymion has entered the cave
proper, and that it is now not merely an open glen or deep
gorge.

Once Endymion has entered the cavern, Keats allows
his imagination to supply a good deal of picturesque detail.
Perhaps he had explored some of the limestone caverns of
his own country, and here converted his memory of their
fantastic formations and colors into "the metal woof, like
Vulcan's rainbow," the

silver grots, or giant range
Of sapphire columns, or fantastic bridge
Athwart a flood of crystal.

I have already suggested that some of the detail may have
been recollected from reading about Theseus and the
Labyrinth, whether the Labyrinth fabled by the ancients,
or the underground cavern near Gortyna in Crete, long
supposed to be the remains of the work of Daedalus. But

beneath the ornamental description there is a thread of narrative and some details which resemble Corycium.

First of all, there is the word which Keats uses to describe the cavern. He calls it a "vast antre." The word is a very unusual one in English, but it might easily have been suggested by ἄντρον and *antrum*, the words which Strabo and Solinus use to describe the inner cavern of Corycium.

Secondly, there is the fact that Endymion finds deep within the cavern a "mimic temple" and "fair shrine." Solinus mentions a temple or shrine (*fanum*) in the inner recesses of the cavern. Solinus says that the shrine is sacred to Jove, while Keats at least implies that the shrine is sacred to Diana, but the change may have been made for the purpose of the story.

Thirdly, there is the cavern beyond, before which Endymion sits down to rest in the course of his exploration. Solinus and Mela both mention this dark cavern which was reputed to be the lair of Typhon, and which might well correspond with that

> maw
> Of a wide outlet, fathomless and dim,
> To wild uncertainty and shadows grim,

from the contemplation of which Endymion was glad to escape. In this passage, the original reading of Keats's first draft makes it clear that Keats had in mind both an inner chamber and an outlet, more like the lair of Typhon that Mela describes. The rejected reading is:

> And long he travers'd to and fro, t' acquaint
> Himself with every mystery, until
> His weary legs he rested on the sill
> Of some remotest chamber, outlet dim
> To wild uncertainty and shadows grim.

Fourthly, there is the remarkable inner space, which, according to Mela, was sacred to the gods and worthy of being inhabited by them. The major portion of Endymion's wanderings within the cave takes place in a beautiful part of it which is inhabited by the gods.

Lastly, there is the fact that eventually Endymion, after following the course of the subterranean waters of the cavern, emerges under the sea. Such a termination of his course would conform to Strabo's statement that the stream flowed underground and issued beneath the sea.

Endymion explores the natural regions of the cave first. Then, after a prayer to Diana, he is led by a heavenly guide to the supernatural portion of the cave, the "inner space" mentioned by Mela as inhabited by the gods. Here the music which he hears, not louder than the throbbing of his own heart, may be that same sound of cymbals touched by divine hands which the ancients imagined they could hear within the sacred recess. It appears to be Keats's intention to take advantage of this sacred region by amplifying his story with legends which have no real connection with Endymion.

The first legend with which we are entertained is that of Venus and Adonis. Keats links Endymion to it by making him a spectator at the annual return of Venus to awaken the sleeping Adonis and by permitting Endymion to have some conversation with the attendant cupids and with Venus herself. Keats adjusts the story to the situation by imagining that the winter sleep of Adonis takes place in the gardenlike chamber within the cave. The gardenlike bower is a Romantic version of the mythical Garden of Adonis. Endymion's next encounter with a legendary figure is with Cybele, whom he beholds wandering, as was her legendary custom, through the rugged arches of the dusk below the earth. It is in the sacred portion of the cavern that Endymion is carried by Jove's eagle to a jasmine bower where Diana visits him. At the conclusion of this episode little remains except to extricate Endymion from the cave. He continues his wanderings, soon emerging in a cavern beneath the sea. Here Keats introduces a fourth myth, the story of Arethusa and Alpheus. Once again Endymion is merely a spectator. The suitability of the theme is, I suppose, nothing more than that we are concerned with an underground stream. Perhaps the inclusion of this story was suggested to Keats by one of Mela's annotators, who compares the underground stream of the Corycian Cave to the River Alpheus.

The structure of Book II would seem, then, to be a very simple one. Endymion wanders through a cavern, the topographical features of which are those of the Corycian cavern. That portion of the cavern believed by the ancients to be sacred to the gods permitted Keats to amplify and adorn his story by adding to it legendary material introduced by the device of allowing Endymion merely to be the observer. The underground stream of Corycium would lead Endymion out of the cavern, but under the sea, and it is under the sea that we find Endymion at the beginning of Book III.

It is now Keats's problem to continue the story, commencing with Endymion under the sea. Keats has suddenly plunged his hero into a situation utterly incompatible with the legend. It was all very well for Endymion to wander in the cavern of the second book, for legend allowed Endymion to wander in caves, and there, of course, the moon goddess visited him. But having chosen to lead Endy-

mion out of the cavern by a stream which issued under
the sea, Keats had involved Endymion in a situation which
no amount of dexterity could link to the classical myth.
Keats did the only thing he could do: he continued the
story by letting Endymion wander under the sea, while
he, as poet, availed himself of the opportunity to paint
some excellent undersea pictures.

Glaucus and his magical herbs had been in his mind in
connection with the legend of Theseus. He conceived the
idea of having Endymion encounter the famous Glaucus
of Anthedon and of twining the two together into a story.
That portion of the story which Glaucus relates to Endymion is simply the legend of Glaucus of Anthedon. Keats
probably found the story in Ovid's *Metamorphoses*, though
it is told in many places elsewhere. Keats alters the story
only in having Circe kill Scylla instead of having Scylla
turned into a monster. The story of the fate imposed upon
Glaucus—and the collection and ultimate rescue of the
dead lovers—is an invention designed to draw Endymion
into the action. Both the narrative and the descriptive elements of the story of Glaucus are spun to as great a length
as the scanty material permits, the legend forming a light
framework over which Keats stretches his own imaginings.
It is interesting to notice, however, that slight bits of detail
show that he had glanced at various accounts of Glaucus.
Like Philostratus in the famous picture of Glaucus in the
Imagines, Keats makes Glaucus white-haired. And the information that Glaucus in his youth provided the countryside with fish comes not from Ovid but from Palaephatus.

The description of Neptune's palace has no vital connection with the story. Keats seems to have introduced it
merely because he has Endymion under the sea anyway.

and he may as well write some further undersea descriptions. He attempts rather lamely to revert to the main theme of the poem by having Endymion receive from Venus, who appears to be visiting Neptune, a promise that he will soon possess his love. Eventually Keats concludes the garbled story by having Endymion faint, after which the Nereids take him to dry land. Keats's invention had flagged badly, and the narrative had now departed so far from anything remotely recognizable as the myth of Endymion that nothing but a brilliant piece of manipulation could save it.

That brilliant manipulation was not forthcoming. Instead of attempting to draw the story back to its proper subject, Keats began the fourth book with a narrative entirely alien to the myth, the story of Endymion's entanglement with the amorous Indian maid. I think it likely that Keats felt that he had failed to provide his story with sufficient meaning. He had kept dimly in mind that Endymion's love for the moon must have some exalted significance. It was to represent the poet's quest for beauty or, in a more general way, the aspiration of the soul for the ideal. Keats saw the possibility of adding interest and weight to the theme by involving Endymion in an earthly love. His hero's confusion between the attraction of the sense and the attraction of the soul would be a theme proper for poetic treatment, and a resolution might be accomplished by showing that a love of earthly things may be transformed into a love of the spiritual by renunciation. Unfortunately there was nothing in the myth of Endymion to support such a poetic development. Indeed, the myth of Endymion does not easily lend itself to moral, or any other, interpretation. In the low ebb of invention in which Keats found himself at the conclusion of his third book, he was able to find no very satisfactory method of procedure. The amorous maiden with whom Endymion falls in love, and who later turns out to be an earthly embodiment of Diana, was the best invention that presented itself to him, and this, as I have already pointed out, was put together from sources outside the Endymion myth. The Indian maid was a composite of Ariadne, the Indian princess with whom Bacchus fell in love in Ovid's *Fasti*, and Keats's own imagination.

But Keats had not alone the problem of adding weight to the meaning of the poem; he had the increasingly serious problem of bringing the story back into some relation with the classical myth of Endymion, from which it was every moment departing farther and farther.

There were various scraps about Endymion which could be gleaned from ancient writers, but there was nothing much to put together into a narrative. There was, for instance, the story that Endymion had by a naiad—or, as some say, by Iphianassa—a son, Aetolus, who slew Apis, son of Phoroneus, and fled to the Curetian country where he slew his hosts, Dorus and Laodicus and Polypoetes, the sons of Phthia and Apollo, and called the country Aetolia after himself. Such is the story that Apollodorus tells. But obviously the tale could have no place in such a story as Keats wished to tell. Apollodorus also relates that Endymion led the Aetolians from Thessaly and founded Elis. And Pausanias has a good deal to say about Endymion at Elis: how he set his sons to run a race at Olympia for the throne; how Epeius won and obtained the kingdom and named his subjects Epeans for the first time; how his brother Aetolus remained at home, giving his name to the

Aetolians; and how Paeon, the third son, went into exile in Paeonia. But such eponymous legends are not very interesting, and Keats took nothing from them except the name for Endymion's sister. Pausanias says that Endymion had fifty daughters by the moon, but Keats had no intention of making Endymion a father on so large a scale. The stories that Endymion had various wives, among whom were Asterodia, Cromia, and Hyperippe, would have convicted Keats's hero of the loosest sort of fidelity to the moon. Lucian's story that a talkative young girl fell in love with Endymion and would not let him sleep, until Selene, in anger, turned her into a fly, would hardly fit into an amorous heroic; nor would the amusing story about Endymion's kingdom in the moon, told by the same writer. Rationalistic interpretations of the Endymion myth, by which ancient mythographers had tried to explain Endymion as an early observer of the moon's courses—a mythical astronomer—would make dull invention though Drayton had made use of such matters in his poem on the theme.

The story of the moon's infatuation for Endymion was the best of the stories. Keats had, however, one story about Endymion in reserve. The principal source for the legend of Endymion is a long note compiled by the scholiast upon Apollonius of Rhodes (IV, 57). Among the stories which the scholiast has collected is one drawn from the *Great Eoiai* of Hesiod, a poem which survives only in a few fragments. The scholiast says that in Hesiod's poem Endymion was transported into Heaven by Zeus. There Endymion fell in love with Hera. He was then deceived with a shape of cloud and was cast out and went down into Hades. Such is the story. It is surprising to find that

Endymion fell in love with Hera rather than the moon. The story relates, apparently, to a version of the legend which makes Endymion the son of Zeus, and which tells how Zeus allowed him to choose what he would, and he chose to sleep forever, remaining deathless and ageless.

It is impossible to read the last book of *Endymion* without seeing that Keats made an attempt to draw that story into his narrative. If the action of Book IV seems hopelessly confused, we may attribute it to two things: that this particular portion of the myth itself is exceedingly vague; and that having involved his hero with the Indian maid, Keats allowed her to accompany Endymion on his journey to Heaven—a fact which added complexity to vagueness, especially when he had to get rid of the Indian maid.

The story begins at line 330. Mercury appears, touches the ground with his wand, and departs. He is followed by two winged steeds, upon which Endymion and the Indian maid are transported to the sky. The shape of cloud by which, according to the story from Hesiod, Endymion was deceived, is in Keats's poem the shapeless cloud of mist that envelops both Endymion and the maid in the sky. Keats personifies this enfolding cloud as Sleep, journeying to Heaven from his cave in the Cimmerian depths. Sleep has learned that

> a young man,
> Ere a young bat could plump its wintery skin,
> Would at high Jove's empyreal footstool win
> An immortality, and how espouse
> Jove's daughter, and be reckon'd of his house.

The description of the purple mist, in which Sleep is "slow journeying with head on pillow" is excellent:

His litter of smooth semilucent mist,
Diversely ting'd with rose and amethyst,
Puzzled those eyes that for the centre sought;
And scarcely for one moment could be caught
His sluggish form reposing motionless.

The horses with their riders enter the mist and at once all
are overcome with slumber. In the deception of this
slumber Endymion enters Heaven:

Behold! he walks
On heaven's pavement; brotherly he talks
To divine powers: from his hand full fain
Juno's proud birds are pecking pearly grain:
He tries the nerve of Phoebus' golden bow,
And asketh where the golden apples grow,

and so on for a passage of some length. Keats avoids,
however, the incident of Endymion's falling in love with
Hera. Instead, he sees the moon rise and awakens, still
in the cloud of Sleep and still in the company of the Indian
maid. If Keats is to follow the legend he must have Endymion descend to Hades. But first he must get the Indian
maid out of the sky. It takes him some seventy lines, in
which Endymion and the maid travel about the sky on
their horses, conversing, until at last Keats suddenly lets
the Indian maid drop like a hawk to the earth, and that is
the last of her for a while. With the Indian maid out of
the way, the legend may proceed, and it does. Keats turns
at once to a description of the Cave of Quietude. It is the
dwelling place of Sleep, which Hesiod places in Tartarus,
near the hall of Hades. Keats's description rests upon that
of Ovid in the eleventh book of the *Metamorphoses*. To
this cave Keats has conducted Endymion because he must
take him to the lower world and because of the legend

that Endymion, when he had his choice from Zeus, had chosen sleep.

The incidents of the legend are now complete. Endymion has been transported to Heaven, he has been deceived with the shape of cloud, he has descended to Hades, and he has received the gift of sleep.

What will Keats do next? He has to get Endymion out of Hades and proceeds to do so by means of the same winged horse. Then he puts in the pageant in the sky. Then he wakes Endymion, because a sleeping hero will not do as the protagonist of a narrative poem. Endymion encounters the Indian maid, none the worse for her hawk-like descent from the sky, and resumes his amorous attentions to her. He determines to give up the life of dreaming in favor of reality:

> There never liv'd a mortal man, who bent
> His appetite beyond his natural sphere,
> But starv'd and died.

He will devote himself to rural felicity and his love for the Indian maid. He paints for her a picture of the happy life which they will lead, a picture which is an attractive and rather quaint compound of English countryside, Roman pastorals, and images such as Wedgwood loved to raise in chaste white figures on his pottery. The poem now takes an unexpected turn. Instead of yielding to Endymion, the Indian maid, who hitherto has shown no compunctions on that score, addresses an impassioned lament to Love, and then declares that she is unable to be Endymion's love:

> Ah, bitter strife!
> I may not be thy love: I am forbidden—
> Indeed I am—thwarted, affrighted, chidden,

By things I trembled at, and gorgon wrath.
Twice hast thou ask'd whither I went: henceforth
Ask me no more! I may not utter it,
Nor may I be thy love. We might commit
Ourselves at once to vengeance; we might die;
We might embrace and die: voluptuous thought!
Enlarge not to my hunger, or I'm caught
In trammels of perverse deliciousness.
No, no, that shall not be: thee will I bless,
And bid a long adieu.

Up to this time there has been no hint of any such complication. It would seem that Keats is now endeavoring to finish off the moral allegory. Thus far, little has come of the moral meaning. Endymion has, indeed, eschewed the visionary life, but only for a life of earthly delight. The Indian maid, who is shortly to be converted into the chaste goddess Diana, becomes suddenly mindful that Endymion must be spiritualized. Keats's cue is for Endymion to renounce earthly pleasure in favor of good works, and for the Indian maid to devote herself to chastity. This renunciation is made by both, and, had it not been that Keats had determined to make the canto last for a thousand lines, the resolution could have taken place at once. He still has, unfortunately, a hundred lines to go, a space which is consumed with various wanderings, farewells, conversations, and soliloquies. Peona, the sister who appeared in the first book, is reintroduced for no very good reason. At last the contemplated end approaches. The Indian maid is metamorphosed into the moon goddess, who explains:

                                  Drear, drear
Has our delaying been; but foolish fear
Withheld me first and then decrees of fate;

> And then 'twas fit that from this mortal state
> Thou shouldst, my love, by some unlook'd for change
> Be spiritualiz'd.

Keats has completed his thousand lines, with three extra in which Peona goes home through the wood "in wonderment."

There can be no doubt that Keats was thoroughly aware of the faults in his poem. He did not plan ahead with sufficient exactness. The result was that he constantly found himself at the end of an incident in a situation from which it was difficult to extract the narrative. He endeavored to give length to a theme which was unsuited to protraction and significance to a myth which was as light as the moon's kisses. In the end he admitted his mistakes candidly, and hoped to profit from his experience.

The youthful poem reflects the colors of an age which in a few brief years Keats was to adorn with true genius. One sees in it the influence of the rather mushy and over-lush poetry of Hunt. The vivid but strained imagery of Mrs. Tighe is apparent, with a more vigorous sensuousness. One sees the same unmasculine prettiness which Benjamin West gave to his too softly graceful mythological paintings, and the overrich Venetian coloring which Blake so much resented in his English contemporaries. At the worst there is something of the conspicuously amorous but never improper Angelica Kauffmann. Sometimes the flowing images, with their gay and graceful action, catch their spirit from Flaxman's early work for Wedgwood. The classic scenes are of the late Roman rather than of the Greek, pastoral idealizations which remind us of Canova and Winckelmann in a period of taste which preceded the Elgin marbles and the admiration of Greek austerity.

Keats's Titans

I SHOULD like to venture the suggestion that had Keats completed *Hyperion* it would have turned into what might be described as a British epic. Saturn would have made an effort to regain his ancient throne; but after the final overthrow of the Titans, he would have become the ruler of the Isles of the Blest, and those Isles of the Blest would have been the British Isles. A considerable portion of the poem would have been a prophecy delivered as a consolation to Saturn, much as Adam and Eve are consoled by the prophecy and dream in *Paradise Lost*. The prophecy would have concerned the poets, tracing the rise of English poetry from its origin in the songs of the bards among the ancient Druids to the triumph of later times. Saturn's consolation would have been that, though he had lost his ancient kingdom, he should rule over another which in the fullness of time would be greater than that which he had lost.

Since I have had the temerity to suggest a hypothetical end to an unfinished epic, not much additional reproach can be leveled at me if I suggest a hypothetical middle as well as an end.

It will be guesswork, since Keats left no outline of his poem. Nevertheless, it will be plausible guessing, not made altogether out of thin air. And I am convinced that if the reader will suspend his disbelief and indignation long enough to examine the poem with the outline which I suggest in mind, he will find that the written portions of the epic fall into a kind of perspective that clarifies the poem and increases one's enjoyment of it.

To attempt to reconstruct hypothetically an outline of the unfinished action of an epic poem upon a mythological theme is not a wholly indefensible procedure. A poet does not embark upon an epic poem without a plan in his mind. That Keats had a plan we know from remarks on the subject both by Woodhouse and by Haydon. Inevitably some marks of that plan must be left upon whatever part of the poem is written. When a poet deals with a mythological theme, he is in some respect bound to tradition. He may invent, to be sure, but his invention must bear some relation to the myth. In an epic poem, moreover, it is reasonable to assume that the poet will pay some attention to the conventions of epic poetry. My inferences will be drawn from what I regard as intimations of a plan in the finished portion of the poem, from the myths with which Keats was dealing, and from consideration of epic convention. They are supported from what else we know of the poem from other sources. They will have, I believe, this use: they will make it more readily possible to meet and dispose of many of the criticisms which have been leveled against the poem; and they will relieve Keats of the "allegorical" interpretations which have been fastened upon it—interpretations which, I think, would have dismayed and angered him had he foreseen them.

The action of the poem would, in the main, have been subordinate to a broader theme, that of celebrating the progress of poetry, the overthrow of the Titans serving primarily as a means for introducing that theme. I conceive Keats's plan to have been substantially this: Enceladus would have led a final effort against the Olympian gods which would have ended when he was overwhelmed by being buried under Sicily, his heavings and gigantic convulsions turning into the eruptions of Mount Aetna. Hyperion would have lost his brightness to Apollo, the myth of the earlier sun god merging into the myth of the later sun god. Saturn, and those of the Titans whose fates are not otherwise determined by myth, would have been exiled to the far-off island of Britain. Before their departure, Asia, whose destiny was to be a different one, would have taken leave of them in a farewell which would have consisted of a prophecy. Her prophecy would have been of the origin of poetry in the East, and the rise of Asiatic culture. Mnemosyne, the goddess of memory, would have recounted to Apollo, in accordance with the epic tradition, events which had taken place prior to the opening of the action of the poem. To Apollo would then have been given the opportunity to describe the great glory of the arts of Greece which should arise under his inspiration. The Titaness Moneta would have warned Apollo of the passing of Greek supremacy before the rise of Rome and the Latin poets, and she would have consoled Saturn with the prophecy of his happy rule in the Isles of the Blest and the promise of the triumph of English poetry.

The usual story respecting Saturn is that after he had been overthrown he fled to Italy. Vergil describes him as concealing himself in Latium, where at length he civilized the rude inhabitants, establishing the Golden Age and ruling over his people in placid peace. But such is the Roman story. Hesiod imagined Cronus, with whom the Romans associated Saturn, as ruling over the Isles of the Blest at the end of the earth, surrounded by the deep-eddying ocean. Pindar describes the felicities of these isles, where Cronus ruled with mild sway over the heroes who had departed from life. Here too dwelt the Titans after their overthrow, as we may infer from a fragment of Aeschylus in which the chorus of twelve Titans come to Prometheus from the eastern part of Ocean's stream.

In very late myth, however, the Isles of the Blest came to be associated with Britain. Plutarch relates stories to the effect that Cronus lay asleep, guarded by Briareus, in a sacred island near Britannia in the western ocean. Procopius tells a story which is repeated by Tzetzes about the fishermen who dwell on the coast of France, opposite Britain, who ferry mysterious boats containing the souls of the dead across to the British Isles, which have clearly become the dwelling place of the blessed. The name passed into British legendary history, and we find Holinshed describing one Samothes as the "Saturne" or "first ruler" of Britain. Matters of this sort were eagerly taken up by the speculative mythologists of the early nineteenth century. Edward Davies, for instance, in his *Celtic Researches* was much concerned to identify Britain with various legendary places known in Greek myth, and Francis Wilford identified Albion with a variety of legendary places such as the Isles of the Blest, the island of Atlantis, over which Saturn is fabled to have ruled, the White Island of Indian myth, the Aeolian Isles, Elysium, and other happy places and gardens. William Blake, in his remarkable fashion, identified the Druids with the patriarchs, and these in turn with figures from Greek myth.

There is nothing extraordinary, therefore, in supposing that Keats might have struck upon the legendary idea that Saturn after his overthrow ruled over the Isles of the Blest, and that the identification of the Isles of the Blest with Britain suggested an interesting way to turn the epic story. We do not need to suppose that he would have used the legend absurdly. It could be treated in poetry merely as a dim prophecy like those "legends of the first of days" which, Keats tells us, Saturn

> Studied from that old spirit-leaved book
> Which starry Uranus with finger bright
> Sav'd from the shores of darkness, when the waves
> Low-ebb'd still hid it up in shallow gloom.

But it might serve as a hinge on which to turn the epic story toward Britain and thus to join the rather empty classical myth of the Titans, which formed the understructure of the poem, to a far more interesting, perhaps even a patriotic, theme.

The procedure of the story leads us to suspect that Keats was conducting his poem toward the theme of poetry.

The Titans of the poem do not exist at all as characters. They have shapes, distinct and visible; nevertheless, as Coelus describes them, they are

> symbols divine,
> Manifestations of that beauteous life
> Diffus'd unseen throughout eternal space.

When they are overthrown, it is by figures more beautiful than themselves; and the justification for their overthrow is that they have been succeeded by figures of greater beauty. Oceanus defends the succession of divinities from the primal gods to the Olympians on the ground that each successive race is more beautiful than the last,

and he concedes his own defeat to Neptune after he has
seen his successor's beauty:

> Have ye beheld the young God of the Seas,
> My dispossessor? Have ye seen his face?
> Have ye beheld his chariot, foam'd along
> By noble winged creatures he hath made?
> I saw him on the calmed waters scud,
> With such a glow of beauty in his eyes,
> That it enforc'd me to bid sad farewell
> To all my empire.

Clymene describes her realization that the newer race is
superior in beauty and in the capacity to create beauty,
when she tells how she first saw the young Apollo and
heard his music. She had been making melody upon a
"mouthed shell"; but when she heard the music of Apollo,
that "new blissful golden melody," she threw her own
shell away upon the sand. The music that she had made
with her poor skill was melody no more after she had
heard Apollo's. Hyperion, the brightest and most beautiful
of the Titans, is the last to be overcome, and yet we know
that he is no match for Apollo, whose radiance is not
merely that of a rising and setting sun, but rather the
inspiration of forms of beauty superior to those known to
the Titans. The whole emphasis of the poem is upon the
right of the more beautiful to succeed the less beautiful.
And since the action all moves toward the triumph of
Apollo, it is only proper that we should assume that the
action is moving toward what Apollo stands for. Like
the Titans, he is a divine symbol, a manifestation of beauty.
But he is a much more concrete symbol than the Titans.
The vague beauty of the Titans takes in Apollo a definite
form: he is the patron of all the arts, but particularly of

poetry. If the pointing in the story means anything, it means that Keats is leading us to what Apollo would naturally represent in a fable, the poetry of Greece.

So much, I think, may be readily granted. Let us now consider my inference that the poem was to have looked beyond the era of Greek poetry, culminating in a prophecy of the British muse.

It will be convenient to set before the reader a passage from *Endymion* which contains, I believe, the germ of the plan which Keats had in mind for the latter portion of *Hyperion*. The fourth book of *Endymion* commences with the following lines:

> Muse of my native land! loftiest Muse!
> O first-born on the mountains! by the hues
> Of heaven on the spiritual air begot:
> Long didst thou sit alone in northern grot,
> While yet our England was a wolfish den;
> Before our forests heard the talk of men;
> Before the first of Druids was a child;—
> Long didst thou sit amid our regions wild
> Rapt in a deep prophetic solitude.
> There came an eastern voice of solemn mood:—
> Yet wast thou patient. Then sang forth the Nine,
> Apollo's garland:—yet didst thou divine
> Such home-bred glory, that they cry'd in vain,
> "Come hither, Sister of the Island!" Plain
> Spake fair Ausonia; and once more she spake
> A higher summons:—still didst thou betake
> Thee to thy native hopes. O thou hast won
> A full accomplishment! The thing is done,
> Which undone, these our latter days had risen
> On barren souls.

In this piece Keats is imagining, for poetic purposes, that Britain has had a presiding muse, loftiest of them all, and of most ancient birth. He provides her with a parentage from Heaven and Air, much as mythologists like Hyginus describe the earliest generation of the Greek gods as born of abstract natural personifications such as Terra and Aethra. He imagines her biding her time, in prophetic foreknowledge, while the poetic cultures of the ancient world arise: first the poetry of the East, then that of Greece, then that of Italy. At last the fruition of her hopes is accomplished, and the poetry of England comes into being.

Now an examination of *Hyperion* suggests a kind of parallelism that is worth considering. In the passage in *Endymion* Keats seems to regard the succession of cultures as an upward movement. Of the eastern voice he says merely that it speaks in a solemn mood. When the nine Muses of Greece summon the British Muse, she divines such home-bred glory that she does not heed their call. Ausonia speaks "a higher summons," but still the British Muse gives no heed, trusting to her native hopes. At last comes "the full accomplishment" of English poetry. In *Hyperion*, Keats places a clear emphasis upon the idea that there is to be a rising succession of eras, each better than the last. As Oceanus explains the matter to Saturn, there is no defeat for the era which is superseded by its successor, since each era is born of the preceding one, and the parent age should view its offspring's superiority with pride. Saturn and the Titans were born of, and superseded, the elder gods. They in their turn are being superseded by the Olympian gods who are their children. And the Olympian gods will in their turn be superseded by another race:

> As Heaven and Earth are fairer, fairer far
> Than Chaos and blank Darkness, though once chiefs;

And as we show beyond that Heaven and Earth
In form and shape compact and beautiful,
In will, in action free, companionship,
And thousand other signs of purer life;
So on our heels a fresh perfection treads,
A power more strong in beauty, born of us
And fated to excel us, as we pass
In glory that old Darkness: nor are we
Thereby more conquer'd, than by us the rule
Of shapeless Chaos. Say, doth the dull soil
Quarrel with the proud forests it hath fed,
And feedeth still, more comely than itself?
Can it deny the chiefdom of green groves?
Or shall the tree be envious of the dove
Because it cooeth, and hath snowy wings
To wander wherewithal and find its joys?
We are such forest-trees, and our fair boughs
Have bred forth, not pale solitary doves,
But eagles golden-feather'd, who do tower
Above us in their beauty, and must reign
In right thereof; for 'tis the eternal law
That first in beauty should be first in might:
Yea, by that law, another race may drive
Our conquerors to mourn as we do now.

Oceanus is speaking literally in terms of the gods themselves, rather than of the cultural eras which they represent. But one cannot suppose that Keats excluded a larger
meaning for such a passage. Let us consider again the lines
in *Endymion*. The eras of poetic culture which Keats
mentioned were those of the East, of Greece, of Italy,
and of England. May we find any intimations of parallelism in *Hyperion*? I think so, if we perceive that certain
figures among the gods stand for the cultural eras.

Among the Titans whom Keats mentions is one whose
presence is unusual, and whose parentage has often puzzled
readers of the poem:

Asia, born of most enormous Caf,
Who cost her mother Tellus keener pangs,
Though feminine, than any of her sons:
More thought than woe was in her dusky face,
For she was prophesying of her glory;
And in her wide imagination stood
Palm-shaded temples, and high rival fanes,
By Oxus or in Ganges' sacred isles.
Even as Hope upon her anchor leans,
So leant she, not so fair, upon a tusk
Shed from the broadest of her elephants.

Caf, of course, has no place in Greek myth. Keats's intention in having Asia born of Caf is, however, intelligible if we consider that Bailly's *Letters on the Atlantis of Plato* expounded the theory that Asiatic culture took its origin from the vestiges of an Atlantean people who had developed a prehistoric culture in the Caucasus Mountains at the region of the (mythical) mountain Caf. The passage in Keats's poetry is an allusion to Bailly's theory of the origin of Asiatic culture. Keats's Asia is, then, more than a Titaness. She is a Titaness who stands for a cultural era, and we should suppose that any action respecting her in the poem will be significant of the rise of the culture which she represents. In a sense we have a figure in the epic who could be parallel to the first era in the passage in *Endymion*, that of the East. Hers could be the "eastern voice of solemn mood."

Mnemosyne and Apollo obviously are figures in the epic who stand for Greek culture. The Titaness Mnemosyne, as the mother of "the Nine," and Apollo, as the god who is closely associated with the Muses and is the patron of all the arts, are not random choices by Keats for inclusion in the action of the epic.

Mnemosyne is first mentioned in the poem as "straying in the world." She cannot be one of the Titans who is overthrown, since her destiny lies before her. In the third book it is she who appears to the young Apollo on the Isle of Delos, where he first becomes conscious of his powers. She is revealed as having forsaken the elder generation of gods "for the sake of loveliness new born," and we learn that she has appeared to Apollo in his dreams, giving him the lyre

> Whose strings touch'd by thy fingers, all the vast
> Unwearied ear of the whole universe
> Listen'd in pain and pleasure at the birth
> Of such new tuneful wonder.

It is in her face that the young Apollo reads "a wondrous lesson," learning his own divinity and prescience:

> Knowledge enormous makes a God of me.
> Names, deeds, gray legends, dire events, rebellions,
> Majesties, sovran voices, agonies,
> Creations and destroyings, all at once
> Pour into the wide hollows of my brain,
> And deify me.

I think there can be no doubt that the lyre at which "all the vast unwearied ear of the whole universe listen'd," is not merely the lyre of the god Apollo. It is Greek poetry, just as the "names, deeds, gray legends, dire events, rebellions" and so on are the themes of the great poets of Greece. Apollo is not merely a god: he is the poetic culture of Greece which will rise after the "eastern voice of solemn mood."

If *Hyperion* were to have dealt with the successive rise of the eras which produced great poetry, developing in epic form the little outline in *Endymion*, then Asia and

Apollo would presumably be the representatives of the first two eras mentioned in *Endymion*, those of the East and of Greece.

There is no reason to suppose that the lines in *Endymion* were in fact an outline of a plan to be carried out rigidly in *Hyperion*. Even if we suppose that the lines in *Endymion* foreshadow a projected plan for *Hyperion*, we should not have to suppose that the third era mentioned in *Endymion*, that of Ausonia, or Italy, would be included. And yet if we look for a kind of parallelism between the eras mentioned in *Endymion* and figures among the Titans who could represent the eras, it is possible to carry that parallelism still further.

In the reworked form of the poem which Keats published under the title *The Fall of Hyperion: A Dream*, there appears a figure named Moneta. The name is an unusual one, though it was not an invention of Keats. Among Latin writers the name Moneta occasionally appears as the Latin name for the Greek Mnemosyne, and it is thus that Keats uses it, for he definitely identifies Moneta with Mnemosyne. Moneta is mentioned by Hyginus, however, not as Mnemosyne, the mother of the Muses, but merely as one among the very earliest of the Titans who were born of Aethra and Terra. Similarly in Keats's poem she is a Titaness. That is, putting the two together, Keats makes her a Titaness, identified with Mnemosyne, the mother of the Muses, but appearing under her Latin name. Now if in the epic poem Keats had intended to have a figure who should represent the voice of Ausonia—the voice of Latin poetry as distinguished from Greek—what more appropriate name could he have found than that of Moneta, a Titaness who was the muse of Latin poetry?

If Asia was to have been the figure who stood for the poetry of the East, and Apollo for that of the Greeks, then Moneta would have been the figure who stood for Ausonia. Saturn, of course, ruling over Britain, the Isles of the Blest of the legend, would be the Titan to represent the last of the eras mentioned in *Endymion*, that of English poetry.

But how might such representation be accomplished in an epic poem? It is highly significant, I think, that Asia and Apollo are each endowed with prophetic power, and that the name Moneta means "Warning." Prophecy of the future is a conventional epic device, a necessary consequence of the fact that the actual time of an epic poem is confined to a comparatively restricted period. When we find Keats endowing three of his figures with the knowledge of things to come, we may suppose that he intended to use them for conventional epic purposes.

We have already seen that Asia, "prophecying of her glory," possesses the power to look ahead to the time when Asiatic culture would flourish. And we know that Apollo is prescient of his glory to come. Indeed, Keats makes Apollo pointedly declare: "Knowledge enormous makes a god of me." It is the emphasis upon Apollo's foreknowledge which prompted Sir Sidney Colvin to the opinion that Apollo was to have engaged in some sort of prophecy.

Moneta would, on etymological grounds alone, be an apt personage for prophecy. And in this respect Moneta forms an interesting contrast with Mnemosyne, to whom might properly belong the relation of the great events prior to the beginning of the poem, while to Moneta could remain the revelation of things to come. The fact that Moneta, in the reworked form of the poem, is actually associated with Saturn, sole priestess of the temple in which his image stands, suggests that to Moneta would have fallen not only the prophecy concerning Latin poetry, but that relating to Saturn's future rule over the Isles of the Blest, and consequently the prophecy concerning the rise of English poetry.

In pointing to the possible parallelism between *Hyperion* and the passage in *Endymion*, I have shown that the briefly outlined "progress of poetry" in the latter could have been expanded into epic statement in the former. There are at least intimations that such was Keats's intention. Since the poem was never finished, it would be absurd to contend that anything has been *proved*. Nevertheless, if we should now find that at nearly every point in the finished cantos something is illuminated by supposing that we have guessed Keats's working plan, then we shall have arrived at a position that is useful critically.

It has sometimes been offered as an objection to the poem that Keats commenced the action at a time when the war of the Titans was practically over, and that not enough of the war remained with which to continue the story. The observation is correct, but the objection is not valid if we suppose, as I think we rightly should, that the events of the war itself were to have been of secondary importance. Keats is not likely to have got into the difficulty of a war in heaven, with the Titans heaving mountains at Olympus and with gigantic strategies such as had taxed the powers of Milton. It is no accident that at the opening of Book III he leaves the Titans in alternate uproar and sad peace, calling upon his Muse

> O leave them, Muse! O leave them to their woes;
> For thou art weak to sing such tumults dire!

It is more likely that this choice of the end of the war for the beginning of the poem was a quite deliberate one. Only a few incidents of the struggle remained to be told, and once these had been completed, the poem could advance to more important business.

It is interesting to notice how careful Keats has been to complete the war before the action of the poem commences. Although there is frequent mention in ancient myth of the War of the Titans and the later War of the Giants, which came to be confused with it, legend does not associate many names with actual fighting in those wars. Cottus, Gyes (Gyges in Keats), Briareus, Porphyrion, Alcyoneus, Hercules, Typhon, and Enceladus are the names most frequently associated with the actual warfare. Keats, who does not distinguish between the War of the Titans and the War of the Giants, omits altogether Hercules and Alcyoneus from the participants. Cottus, Gyes, Briareus, Porphyrion, and Typhon he describes as already completely overwhelmed. Of the figures whom Keats mentions as yet capable of resistance, Enceladus alone has any real legendary connection with the war. There is no legend whatsoever connecting Hyperion with participation in the fighting. It is clear from the fact that Enceladus in the poem exhorts the remaining Titans to continue the struggle that he was intended for an active part in the poem. Presumably Keats expected to tell the magnificent story of how he was overcome when Athena hurled the whole island of Sicily upon him, and how his groanings and writhings became the eruptions of Mount Aetna. Keats is at his best in converting a mythical figure into a natural phenomenon, and he had probably elected the story of Enceladus as one worth the telling.

As for Hyperion, it is clear that he must be overthrown by Apollo, but since the telling of his story need be predicated in advance by no known set of legendary conditions, Keats was free to accomplish the overthrow in his own fashion. I think that we may see how he proposed to do it. In the last part of the poem, Apollo, as he becomes aware of his own divinity, is passing through a kind of convulsive struggle

> Most like the struggle at the gate of death
> Or liker still to one who should take leave
> Of pale immortal death, and with a pang
> As hot as death's is chill, with fierce convulse
> Die into life.

Was not this fierce and painful struggle through which Apollo died into life already the overthrow of Hyperion? Was it not to have represented the elder god of the sun merging into the younger god of the sun? After all, Hyperion and Apollo were but different legendary embodiments of the same natural phenomenon, and the elder god may be conceived as yielding to the later, not in a struggle, but in the confused merging of the two as legend itself has merged them. I think that, had we encountered Hyperion further in the poem, we should have found that his brightness had already passed into the form of Apollo. The description of Apollo's assumption of deity is not then a description of "an hysterical wife," as a German critic has called Keats's Apollo, but another of those convulsive mergings which Keats had executed so skillfully in *Lamia*. It was the struggle of a dying myth as it passed into a brighter and more beautiful form.

It may be objected that since the title of the epic poem is *Hyperion*, we should expect that the protagonist would

figure more significantly in the action. But *is* Hyperion
the protagonist? When, in *Endymion*, Keats wrote the
line "Thy lute voiced brother will I sing ere long,"
he must have been referring to Apollo, not to Hyperion, as
no legend ever connected Hyperion with a lute voice,
whereas the epithet would be quite applicable to Apollo.
That it was Apollo, rather than Hyperion, whom Keats
regarded as the hero of the poem is implied in a comparison between *Endymion* and *Hyperion* which Keats
made in a letter to Haydon before the poem had been
begun. One great contrast between them would be, he
said, "that the Hero of the written tale being mortal is
led on, like Buonaparte, by circumstance; whereas the
Apollo in *Hyperion* being a fore-seeing God will shape
his actions like one." Hyperion's importance at the beginning of the epic comes from the fact that he is more the
antagonist of Apollo than the protagonist of the epic.
Apollo, the patron of the arts of Greece, was an important personage. His rise signified something great and
beautiful. Hyperion, however, was so obscure a figure that
no body of legend had gathered about his name. Keats
needed a Titan for Apollo to overthrow, and Hyperion
as the Titan god of the sun was his natural antagonist.
But Keats found so little legendary matter connected with
Hyperion that he was obliged to transfer to him the
legendary conceptions that had gathered about Helios,
the son of Hyperion, another god, who was a distinct personage, to be confused neither with Hyperion nor with
Apollo. The eastern and western palaces of Hyperion
in the poem were those which Ovid and others describe
as the palaces of Helios. The movements of Hyperion in
the epic are merely those of the rising and the setting of

the sun, magnificently conceived, to be sure, but not endowed by the poet with intellectual or ethical significance. But if we perceive the position of Hyperion merely as the Titan sun god, a power of nature which must yield to the infinitely superior Apollo, the light of the mind, then we may perceive that the absence of legendary material respecting Hyperion was no real obstacle to Keats in the structure of the action. The relegation of Hyperion to his proper place in the epic removes the emphasis upon the struggle of the Titans and places it where it should belong and where Keats undoubtedly would have placed it—on the significance of the rise of Apollo and the ultimate fate of Saturn.

One very striking characteristic of Keats's Titans may be explained if we suppose that he is preparing them for their abode in the Isles of the Blest. Unlike the ruthless Titans of primitive myth, Keats's Titans are gentle figures who prize tranquillity above all else. The Saturn of legend, for instance, was artful, revengeful, and cruel; he perpetrated a brutal and indecent mutilation upon his unfortunate father, and he devoured his own children. Keats's Saturn is gentle and benign. He regrets that he is

> smother'd up,
> And buried from all godlike exercise
> Of influence benign on planets pale,
> Of admonitions to the winds and seas,
> Of peaceful sway above man's harvesting,
> And all those acts which Deity supreme
> Doth ease its heart of love in.

This is a Saturn fit to be the ruler of a Golden Age. Indeed Keats endows him with the character which the Latin poets attributed to him when he reigned in Latium.

Keats appears to be preparing us for a later, not an earlier, Saturn. If eventually Saturn is to rule over the Isles of the Blest, then Keats's disposition of him will be a happy one. Keats constantly emphasizes the desire of all the Titans for serenity, a serenity which would be more perfectly theirs in the Isles of the Blest than on Olympus. Thea laments "our once serene domain"; Hyperion's anger is at the thought of leaving

> this haven of my rest,
> This cradle of my glory, this soft clime,
> This calm luxuriance of blissful light.

Coelus describes his children as serene creatures:

> Divine ye were created, and divine
> In sad demeanour, solemn, undisturb'd,
> Unruffled, like high Gods, ye liv'd and ruled.

Even the wrathful Enceladus was "once tame and mild as grazing ox unworried in the meads," and in the fury of his wrath, he grieves for the days of calm:

> Much pain have I for more than loss of realms:
> The days of peace and slumberous calm are fled;
> Those days, all innocent of scathing war,
> When all the fair Existences of heaven
> Came open-eyed to guess what we would speak:—
> That was before our brows were taught to frown,
> Before our lips knew else but solemn sounds;
> That was before we knew the winged thing,
> Victory, might be lost, or might be won.

Clymene is gentleness itself, and Oceanus, acquiescing calmly in his overthrow, declares:

> for to bear all naked truths,
> And to envisage circumstance, all calm,
> That is the top of sovereignty.

For such a race of beings, the fiercest of whom laments not his loss of realms, but that the days of peace and slumberous calm have fled, what more satisfactory fate could be in store than the calm of the Isles of the Blest? Even if there were no mythological justification for taking them thither, we should have to suppose that Keats had some calm refuge in mind for them, and since the mythological justification does exist, my inference seems inescapable. The supposition meets a frequent criticism of the poem: that having invited our sympathy for Saturn and the Titans, and having depicted Saturn as an admirably benign deity, Keats was unable to proceed with the creation of another and superior race who should overcome the already satisfactory Titans. But with a British experience ahead of the Titans, we may transfer our sympathy and allegiance temporarily to Apollo, as Clymene, and Oceanus, and Mnemosyne, and Keats did.

Moreover, some of Saturn's words now take on a particular significance. Saturn desires intensely to rule. Not gifted with prophecy, he can at first imagine only a victory by force:

> Saturn must be King.
> Yes, there must be a golden victory;
> There must be Gods thrown down, and trumpets blown
> Of triumph calm, and hymns of festival
> Upon the gold clouds metropolitan,
> Voices of soft proclaim, and silver stir
> Of strings in hollow shells; and there shall be
> Beautiful things made new, for the surprise
> Of the sky-children; I will give command.

We may read into his words both irony and foreshadowing. Saturn will rule, but not by victory. The god who will be thrown down will be Saturn and the Titans

but they will have their triumph calm and their hymns
of festival in the Isles of the Blest. The sky-children will
hear the first stirring of poetic utterance from the bards
whose "voices of soft proclaim and silver stir of strings in
hollow shells" shall indeed make beautiful things anew.
Already Keats's imagination leaps ahead to Britain as, in
the lines which follow, he imagines the aged Titan shaking
"his Druid locks."

But Saturn has no knowledge of his destiny. Another
thought enters his mind. If he cannot overwhelm his
enemies and regain his throne, cannot he create another
realm?

> But cannot I create?
> Cannot I form? Cannot I fashion forth
> Another world, another universe,
> To overbear and crumble this to naught?

Once again there appears to be ironic foreshadowing.
There will be no need for Saturn to shape another world,
though the world which he will rule over will be a very
different one from the world of his ancient power. In
the end it will overbear and crumble the ancient rule to
naught, but not in the sense that Saturn intended. Keats is
shaping the poem with the end in view.

I have already suggested that when Keats described
Saturn's "Druid locks" his imagination was at work on the
metamorphosis of his Greek Titan into the mythical ruler
of ancient Britain. I think that he had an image of the
Druids in his mind also when he speaks of the oaks as
"those green-rob'd senators of mighty woods." And certainly when Keats stood in Fingal's Cave, that impressive
natural cavern which he visited on his walking tour, he
saw an image of the Titans in Britain, for he wrote of it:

"Suppose now the giants who rebelled against Jove had taken a whole mass of black columns and bound them together like bunches of matches—and then with immense axes had made a cavern in the body of these columns—of course the roof and the floor must be composed of the broken ends of these columns—such is Fingal's Cave except that the sea has done the work of excavation and is continually washing there." Keats possessed a copy of Edward Davies' *Celtic Researches*, a book which I have already mentioned as one which dealt with the mythology of Celtic Britain in a highly speculative way and which also was much concerned with the Druids and the early bards. I think it likely that Keats was informing himself about early Britain, the Druids, and the bards with the destiny of Saturn and his Titans in mind.

Woodhouse, who edited Keats's works, tells us: "The poem, if completed, would have treated of the dethronement of Hyperion, the former God of the sun, by Apollo —and incidentally of those of Oceanus by Neptune, of Saturn by Jupiter, etc., and of the war of the Giants for Saturn's reestablishment—with other events, of which we have but very dark hints in the mythological poets of Greece and Rome. In fact, the incidents would have been pure creations of the Poet's brain. How he is qualified for such a task may be seen in a trifling degree by the few mythological glimpses afforded in *Endymion*." In the first part of this statement Woodhouse describes what can be easily inferred from the poem as it stands. The remainder of the statement implies that the action would have been largely invention, but invention based upon dark hints from the mythological poets of Greece and Rome. These I conceive to have been the dark hints which associated

Saturn with the Isles of the Blest and with Britain. If the idea of imposing a Grecian Titan upon Britain seems to us too extraordinary to have appealed to Keats as reasonable poetic invention, we should remember that neither Keats nor others of his generation felt bound by rigid decorum in the use of myth. *Endymion* had been very fanciful. Keats had indeed planned to write *Hyperion* "in a more naked and Grecian Manner" than he had used in *Endymion,* but he would not, I think, have found anything indecorous in taking Saturn to Britain. It is interesting to compare the idea of a British Saturn with a Scandinavian Mithradates, whom Wordsworth once conceived of creating. In *The Prelude* Wordsworth describes some of the themes which he had once considered attempting in verse. Among them is the following:

> Sometimes, more sternly moved, I would relate
> How vanquished Mithradates northward passed,
> And, hidden in the cloud of years, became
> Odin, the Father of a race by whom
> Perished the Roman Empire.

Another plan was to have imagined that the followers of Sertorius fled to the Fortunate Isles, where for fifteen hundred years their descendants kept alive the idea of liberty. If the much more mature Wordsworth could conceive of converting Mithradates into Odin and populating the Fortunate Isles with Romans, we may allow that Keats might imagine exiling Saturn to Britain and peopling the Isles of the Blest with Titans. The latter idea had at least some dark hints in mythology. In January, 1818, Keats saw a good deal of Wordsworth during the older poet's visit to London, and we know from a letter Wordsworth wrote to Haydon that he had taken a liking to Keats.

Shortly after that visit, Keats was intensely interested in his plans for *Hyperion*. Perhaps Wordsworth had some part in shaping them in Keats's mind.

Why did Keats abandon *Hyperion*, after making so promising a beginning? The letter written to Reynolds on September 21, 1819, in which he explains why he has given up *Hyperion*, seems to refer not to the epic but to the later revision of the poem in its form as a dream. He feels that there are "too many Miltonic inversions in it," that Miltonic verse cannot be written but in an artful or rather artist's humor, "that he wishes to give himself up to other sensations," that he cannot distinguish between the parts of the poem which have "a false beauty proceeding from art," and those which have "the true voice of feeling." However much his remarks may explain why he abandoned the *Dream*, they do not explain why he abandoned the epic. Certainly personal reasons had something to do with it. Worry over his failure to hear from his brother in America; the annoyance over Haydon's effort to borrow money from him: both, as he definitely says in his letters, made it difficult for him to go ahead; and there were doubtless other and more serious personal reasons which he does not reveal. Nevertheless, the months following the abandonment of his epic were fruitful poetic ones for Keats and it seems likely that the real reasons were objective rather than personal. On March 8, 1819, Keats wrote to Haydon that he was "in a sort of qui bono temper, not exactly on the road to an epic poem," to which Haydon replied encouragingly: "At any rate finish your great intention of a poem—it is as fine a subject as can be." But despite Haydon's confidence in the project, Keats's mood of diffidence may have been induced by a

sense of the difficulties to be met. Keats was very young.
Milton had brought the experience of a lifetime to *Paradise
Lost*. In the same letter in which Keats described himself
as "not exactly on the road to an epic poem," he wrote:
"I am three and twenty, with little knowledge and mid-
dling intellect. It is true that in the height of enthusiasm
I have been cheated into some fine passages; but that is not
the thing." The writing of an epic poem takes more than
enthusiasm and skill. If Keats had intended to treat the
progress of poetry in a fashion sufficiently elevated for
the epic, he might well have felt his knowledge inadequate. Only two years before, in *Sleep and Poetry*, he had
expressed the need for ten years in which to steep himself
in poetry. In one passage in that poem he impetuously
urges upon himself the need of confidence:

> What though I am not wealthy in the dower
> Of spanning wisdom; though I do not know
> The shiftings of the mighty winds that blow
> Hither and thither all the changing thoughts
> Of man: though no great minist'ring reason sorts
> Out the dark mysteries of human souls
> To clear conceiving: yet there ever rolls
> A vast idea before me, and I glean
> Therefrom my liberty; thence too I've seen
> The end and aim of Poesy.

But a moment later he checks himself with the realization
of what he must accomplish before he can attempt the
loftiest poetic achievement:

> Stay! an inward frown
> Of conscience bids me be more calm awhile.
> An ocean dim, sprinkled with many an isle,
> Spreads awfully before me. How much toil!
> How many days! what desperate turmoil!

> Ere I can have explored its widenesses.
> Ah, what a task!

Perhaps in turning from *Hyperion* to other, and much less ambitious, themes he had merely checked himself again, in the realization that he was not yet ready for an epic accomplishment.

The "desperate turmoil" of Keats's life did not give him surcease. To him the calm for which the Titans yearned was more than a fiction imagined for the argument of a poem. It was an inner necessity of the poet's being, unattained. Like the life of Keats, *Hyperion* is the beginning of an epic poem, beautiful and uncompleted.

Shelley's Prometheus

SHELLEY'S *Prometheus Unbound* has long been esteemed a very fine poem, but it is difficult to read, and one may doubt whether many persons *have* read it with the feeling that they have thoroughly understood what it is about. Nor is the difficulty easily overcome if one attempts to follow the action closely. The drama is built upon the myth of Prometheus, but even one reasonably familiar with that myth may be puzzled by the turns which the action takes. The figure Demogorgon, which plays so important a role in Shelley's play, has no part in the myths connected with Prometheus. The action in which Asia participates is especially difficult to connect with the story. Nor is it easy to see the meaning, or to connect with the fable, the complex and subtle action of the last two acts.

The myth of Prometheus is an attractive one. The story of the Titan who, in defiance of the enmity of Zeus, befriended mankind and suffered a long torment with noble fortitude is one which contains elements capable of lofty treatment. The noble tragedy upon the theme by Aeschylus is one of the finest of ancient times, and the world has lamented the loss of that part of the trilogy in which the myth must have been considered and resolved in ethical terms.

Shelley perceived an opportunity to employ the myth as a vehicle for a tragedy which should be prophetic of the eventual regeneration of mankind through love. We must examine the story to see how this conception could present itself to him.

There was a prophecy, often referred to in Greek myth, that if Zeus should make a certain marriage he should bear a child who should be greater than himself. Prometheus alone knew the name of the woman, or rather the sea nymph, who should bear this child to Zeus. Her name was Thetis. So long as Prometheus kept the secret from Zeus, he held an ultimate power over the lord of Heaven. In the *Prometheus Bound* of Aeschylus, the poet represented Prometheus as tormented by Zeus in order that Zeus might force him to divulge the secret. Prometheus withholds it, despite the fierce torments with which Zeus afflicts him. The end of the trilogy is lost, but it is probable that the mythologist Hyginus preserves the story as Aeschylus told it. In order to escape the punishment upon Caucasus, Prometheus eventually warned Zeus of his danger, in return for which Zeus sent Hercules to release Prometheus. Zeus had come dangerously close to fulfilling the prophecy, for he had fallen in love with Thetis. After the prophecy had been revealed, however, he withdrew from his amour and married Thetis to Peleus. The son born to these two was Achilles, who was greater than his father.

In the Aeschylean drama Prometheus is portrayed as an heroic figure who has endured great sufferings on behalf of mankind. But despite the sympathy which we are invited to feel for his fortitude and his pride in what he has done for the benefit of man, the dramatist pictures him as having sinned in endeavoring to thwart the will of

God by elevating man to dignities which he does not deserve. The punishment of Prometheus is a harsh but merited punishment.

Shelley resented the Aeschylean conception. His belief in the capacities of mankind if they were rightly used led him to reject the idea that Prometheus had sinned in attempting to elevate mankind. Submission to the blind necessity to which in the Aeschylean play Zeus himself was subject seemed to him evil, not good. Man must overcome, not submit. Shelley believed that if man could overcome the evil in his own heart—the resentment against the nature of things, the hate, the fear—then, although still subject to the laws implicit in the nature of things, he would nevertheless be free from an abject slavery to them. His spirit would be free to work in harmony with the will of God, not in opposition to it.

He conceived the idea of having Prometheus refuse to divulge the secret to Zeus, despite his torments upon Caucasus. In ignorance, Zeus would consummate his amour with Thetis, and a child should be born who should be greater than his father and overthrow him. Such a plan would lend itself to a different moral conception from that of the Greek dramatist. Prometheus might be represented as having endured the torments upon Caucasus with a noble fortitude marred only by his hatred of Zeus. Zeus might represent the power of evil—not evil in the universe itself, for the universe was not evil, but evil in the mind of Prometheus and of mankind in general. When Prometheus, through suffering, learned to replace the hatred in his heart with pity and love, then the power of evil would be overcome. The prophecy would be fulfilled indeed in terms of the dramatic action. Zeus would marry Thetis and bear the son who should overcome him. But the prophecy would be fulfilled and evil overthrown only when Prometheus had vanquished the evil within himself.

Shelley's play could begin where the play of Aeschylus left off, allowing a sufficient lapse of time for Prometheus to have learned his lesson. The two plays would be therefore closely united at the beginning. In external respects the Prometheus of Shelley at the beginning of his play would be the same figure as that of Aeschylus.

The Prometheus of Aeschylus is not altogether the same figure which appears in other versions of the myth. Prometheus was not always in Greek myth the admirable figure which Aeschylus wished to make him. Indeed, the story of his quarrel with Zeus reveals him as a sly fellow, deliberately trying to trick the heavenly father. According to the story as Hesiod tells it, the gods were once assembled at Sicyon for the institution of sacrifices. The question arose what part of the sacrifice should be offered to Zeus. Prometheus slew an ox and arranged two separate offerings, of which Zeus was to take his choice. One of the offerings was covered by the stomach, and one by the more appetizing looking fat. Zeus naturally chose the pile covered with fat, only to discover that Prometheus had put under the fat nothing but bones. Zeus pretended to have known all along that there was nothing but bones under the fat, but he was so angry that he determined to punish Prometheus by avenging himself on mankind, whom Prometheus had created from mud and water. He withheld the gift of fire from men. But Prometheus again outwitted him by concealing fire in the pithy center of the fennel stalk. Obviously no such tricky fellow could serve as the protagonist of an ethical drama; hence both Aeschylus and Shelley were forced to elevate his character.

Since in most respects Shelley's play is a departure from that of Aeschylus, it will be convenient, before we proceed to a consideration of the differing action of the play, to set down the long passage in Shelley's *Prometheus* which shows how Shelley's hero is derived from the Prometheus of Aeschylus. When Asia appears before the throne of Demogorgon, she provides him and us with a long exposition of that part of the fable which deals with the original quarrel with Zeus and the subsequent dealing of Zeus and Prometheus with men. With slight variations her account is based upon the play of Aeschylus:

> There was the Heaven and Earth at first,
> And Light and Love; then Saturn, from whose throne
> Time fell, an envious shadow: such the state
> Of the earth's primal spirits beneath his sway,
> As the calm joy of flowers and living leaves
> Before the wind or sun has withered them
> And semivital worms; but he refused
> The birthrights of their being, knowledge, power,
> The skill which wields the elements, the thought
> Which pierces this dim universe like light,
> Self-empire, and the majesty of love;
> For thirst of which they fainted.

Shelley has described briefly the successive overthrow of the primal gods, and the condition of men in the age of Saturn.

> Then Prometheus
> Gave wisdom, which is strength, to Jupiter,
> And with this law alone, "Let man be free,"
> Clothed him with the dominion of wide Heaven.

The idea that Prometheus assisted Zeus with the explicit understanding that man should be free is not taken from Aeschylus. In the Greek tragedy the ingratitude of Zeus is the result of a necessity which he cannot violate. It is because Zeus must conform to that necessity that Prometheus sins in attempting to thwart him. Shelley makes the ingratitude of Zeus a deliberate act. Shelley also goes farther than Aeschylus in making Zeus originally obligated to the favor of Prometheus. There is a story in Apollodorus to the effect that when Zeus was ready to be delivered of Athena, it was Prometheus who solved the obstetrical problem by smashing Zeus' head open with an axe, whereupon Athena emerged. This story doubtless accounts for the fact that here Prometheus gave Zeus not only "the dominion of wide Heaven," but also "wisdom, which is strength." Shelley continues:

> To know nor faith, nor love, nor law; to be
> Omnipotent but friendless is to reign;
> And Jove now reigned; for on the race of man
> First famine, and then toil, and then disease,
> Strife, wounds, and ghastly death unseen before,
> Fell; and the unseasonable seasons drove,
> With alternating shafts of frost and fire,
> Their shelterless, pale tribes to mountain caves:
> And in their desert hearts fierce wants he sent,
> And mad disquietudes, and shadows idle
> Of unreal good, which levied mutual war,
> So ruining the lair wherein they raged.

Here Zeus, following the Aeschylean fable, determines to destroy all men:

> Prometheus saw, and waked the legioned hopes
> Which sleep within folded Elysian flowers,
> Nepenthe, Moly, Amaranth, fadeless blooms,
> That they might hide with thin and rainbow wings
> The shape of Death.

This is Shelley's way of following Aeschylus in making Prometheus replace men's foreknowledge of death with hope. The other gifts of Prometheus are next described, with considerable elaboration from the Aeschylean account. In the Greek tragedy Prometheus is the giver of a wide variety of useful knowledges and skills. Hope and understanding were followed by knowledge of building houses and working in wood; of how to measure the seasons by astronomy; of the use of numbers and letters; of methods of domesticating beasts; of the use of sailing vessels; of medicine; of divination by various processes such as interpreting dreams, oracles, omens, symbols, the flight of birds, entrails, gall, liver, sacrifices, and fire; of the mining of copper, iron, silver, and gold; indeed, says Aeschylus, of all the arts possessed by men. Shelley's list is equally extensive, and more ornate:

> and Love he sent to bind
> The disunited tendrils of that vine
> Which bears the wine of life, the human heart;
> And he tamed fire which, like some beast of prey,
> Most terrible, but lovely, played beneath
> The frown of man; and tortured to his will
> Iron and gold, the slaves and signs of power,
> And gems and poisons, and all subtlest forms
> Hidden beneath the mountains and the waves.
> He gave man speech, and speech created thought,
> Which is the measure of the universe;
> And Science struck the thrones of Earth and Heaven,
> Which shook, but fell not; and the harmonious mind
> Poured itself forth in all-prophetic song;
> And music lifted up the listening spirit
> Until it walked, exempt from mortal care,
> Godlike, o'er the clear billows of sweet sound;
> And human hands first mimicked and then mocked,
> With moulded limbs more lovely than its own,
> The human form, till marble grew divine,

And mothers, gazing, drank the love men see
Reflected in their race,—behold and perish.

In the last lines Shelley is describing the progress of Greek
sculpture from the crude imitation of actual forms to the
development of "ideal beauty," superior to actual forms.
He refers very obliquely to the statue of Niobe, whose
grief expresses the universal love and grief of motherhood.
Shelley's admiration for this statue was unbounded, as is
attested by his brilliant description of it in his *Notices of
Some Sculpture in Florence*.

The account of the gifts of Prometheus continues, now
following Aeschylus more strictly:

He told the hidden power of herbs and springs,
And Disease drank and slept. Death grew like sleep.
He taught the implicated orbits woven
Of the wide-wandering stars; and how the Sun
Changes his lair, and by what secret spell
The pale Moon is transformed, when her broad eye
Gazes not on the interlunar sea:
He taught to rule, as life directs the limbs,
The tempest-wingèd chariots of the Ocean,
And the Celt knew the Indian. Cities then
Were built, and through their snow-like columns flowed
The warm winds, and the azure aether shone,
And the blue sea and shadowy hills were seen.
Such, the alleviations of his state,
Prometheus gave to man,—for which he hangs
Withering in destined pain.

As in the Aeschylean play, Prometheus is man's benefactor
in the gift of a wide diversity of arts and sciences.

Having now examined the expository passage which
Shelley provided for our understanding of the background
of the story, we are better prepared to consider what

Shelley did with the plot. I think we may assume that until
he reached that portion of the play in which it was necessary to turn the fable to his own particular requirements,
no serious structural problem presented itself.

The play had merely to begin with Prometheus as
Aeschylus had left him. He is the same proud and defiant
Prometheus chained to the rock on Caucasus, tormented
by the agents of Jove. He has the same infinite capacity
for enduring suffering, and he is fortified by the same
secret knowledge that he will win his freedom when the
prophecy is at last fulfilled that Jove will marry Thetis
and have a child by her who shall overthrow his father.
A long period of time has elapsed, however, and Prometheus has reached, through suffering, a state in which
he pities rather than hates his enemy. He is anxious to
recall the curse which he had long before uttered in anger
against Jove:

> I speak in grief,
> Not exultation, for I hate no more,
> As then, ere misery made me wise: the Curse
> Once breathed on thee I would recall.

Earth, his mother—the same Earth or Themis who is his
mother in the Aeschylean play—shows him how to recall
the curse, and he does so.

Morally, Prometheus' conquest of the evil in his heart
is complete at this point and the repentant Titan should
be free from his torments, but the ethical problem has not
yet been stated dramatically in terms of the fable. Shelley
manages his mythological material deftly for the purpose.
It was the function of the Furies, in classical myth, to
pursue with torments persons upon whom a curse had
been uttered. In Shelley's play, when the dreadful curse

is repeated, even though it is now recalled, the Furies automatically appear, not to torment Zeus, but to torment Prometheus himself. The moral allegory is that Prometheus, by hating, has, for all the long years of his suffering, been made evil: the torments of the Furies have been called down not upon Zeus, who was cursed, but upon Prometheus, who had done the cursing. Zeus has reigned over Prometheus and persecuted him only because Prometheus, who stands for mankind, has allowed hate (Zeus) to reign in his own heart.

The allegory is carried out in terms of the action. Jove sends Mercury to extract from Prometheus his secret:

> there is a secret known
> To thee, and to none else of living things,
> Which may transfer the sceptre of wide Heaven,
> The fear of which perplexes the Supreme.

Prometheus reproaches Jove for his ingratitude, and refuses to divulge the secret. Reluctantly Mercury imposes new tortures upon Prometheus by means of the Furies: these tortures are in the form of hideous images of the wretchedness which has prevailed in the world because men have not loved their fellow men. Shelley seizes the opportunity to depict the new Prometheus, whose fortitude is unchanged but who has now achieved in his own mind a peaceful serenity which is impervious to pain. He is moved now only by pity:

> I weigh not what ye do, but what ye suffer,
> Being evil. Cruel was the Power which called
> You, or aught else so wretched, into light.

He has become king over himself, ruling the torturing and conflicting throngs within. The Furies depart, having merely strengthened his resolution to endure. Visions o hope begin to appear to him—intimations of the capacities latent in the minds of men. The spirit of love is abroad. The hour of deliverance is at hand, though Prometheus does not know it.

It is now time to consider the structural problems imposed upon Shelley by his plan to alter the Aeschylean plot. The first in importance of these is the projected time of the resolution. Since Shelley is to depict the overthrow of evil in a dramatic prophecy, it is obvious that the time of the resolution cannot be the past.

Ancient writers differed as to the length of time which Prometheus spent chained to the rock, thirty thousand years being the farther limit. He was, at any rate, chained here long enough so that if Shelley chose he could imagine the liberation as taking place, not in the past of a mythological age, but in the future, either remote or immediate. In this fact, I believe, Shelley saw one of the chief conveniences of the legend. His moral drama could be conceived in terms of a Greek myth, and yet it could be pointed at Shelley's own time by having the resolution take place in the immediate future. Shelley conceived Prometheus as having suffered for three thousand years, a time sufficiently distant from what was regarded as the age of myth to bring Prometheus' sufferings to date. Allusions in the play to the French Revolution and a thinly disguised portrayal of contemporary political conditions show that Shelley by no means intended the fiction that the resolution of the play took place in an age of fable, but frankly imagined it as in the near future. It is important to see that the time of the resolution is one of the chief features of the play, for much that is significant in the structure of the drama was dictated by the difficulty of resolving the fable at the time desired.

The advantage was this: Shelley could prophesy the coming of that great new age which he felt was at hand. He could envisage an imminent coming of the time when tyranny and custom would be overthrown, when the hope of man would at last be fulfilled and love and reason prevail. If he should idealize that time, making the regeneration of mankind a more sudden event than the experience of history would promise or calm reason permit, yet in lyrical drama such a vision would not be ridiculous. And Shelley had been inspired by the promise of enlightened political thinking, by events such as the French Revolution, the founding of the American democracy, and the stirring of the desire for freedom in Spain and in the new Greece.

In molding the fable of Prometheus to such an end, the overthrow of Zeus must represent the overturning of the established order, an order which had endured only through the evil in man's nature. Zeus must represent all that Shelley detested: the smugness of false morality, the hypocrisy and spiritual deterioration of institutionalized religion, political tyranny—indeed, all evil established in the world. An enormous weight of meaning would thus be concentrated in one personage of the drama, and yet expressed in terms of action related to the fable. All this could be managed.

But in other respects the moral allegory does not so well adjust itself to the fable. The overthrow of Zeus was to take place by the fulfilling of the prophecy. Zeus was to have a child by Thetis who should be greater than his father, and who should overcome him. Now there is nothing ridiculous in imagining the Titan Prometheus chained on Mount Caucasus for three thousand years. But it i

highly ridiculous to imagine Zeus consummating his
amour with Thetis some time after the French Revolution.
Thetis was a sea nymph whom we are accustomed to think
of as the mother of Achilles. That Zeus had protracted
his love for her with immortal continence from the age of
fable to the early nineteenth century, and then at last
satisfied it, is an idea that is not, to say the least, a very
good one. And yet if Shelley was to resolve the drama in
modern times but still in terms of the fable, he was limited
to this course of action. His ingenious plot was exceedingly vulnerable at the point, and no one, I think, can
come to that portion of the drama in which Shelley deals
with the union of Thetis and Zeus without finding the
plot feeble, if not downright ridiculous. To be sure,
Thetis does not take any part in the drama. She is merely
marked in a stage direction as present among other assembled deities. If one does not know the rather obscure story
about the prophecy—and I suspect that most readers of
Shelley's play have either never heard of it or would fail
to remember it—the reason for Thetis' presence in the
drama is quite obscure. Shelley gets over the matter by
having Jupiter announce the birth of a child to the assembled gods. He addresses himself to Thetis in the following
words:

> And thou
> Ascend beside me, veiled in the light
> Of the desire which makes thee one with me,
> Thetis, bright Image of Eternity!—
> When thou didst cry, "Insufferable might!
> God! Spare me! I sustain not the quick flames,
> The penetrating presence; all my being,
> Like him whom the Numidian seps did thaw
> Into a dew with poison, is dissolved,

> Sinking through its foundations:"—even then
> Two mighty spirits, mingling, made a third
> Mightier than either.

The speed with which Shelley slides over the crisis in the action—and the vagueness of the language employed—leads to the inference that he was well aware that he was in a weak part of the plot.

But the difficulty of managing the belated union of Thetis and Zeus was nothing to the greater difficulty which he faced in the problem of their child. In producing such a child Shelley was really tampering with the myth. There was no such child. Ancient writers had told the story differently. Zeus had withdrawn from the amour when he learned the secret of Prometheus, and had married Thetis to Peleus. The son born to them was Achilles, who was, of course, greater than his father, and consequently the prophecy was fulfilled in him. I have pointed out elsewhere that Goethe probably intended to make use of the story in his *Achilleis* by pretending that although Thetis married Peleus, nevertheless Achilles was the son of Zeus. But Shelley could not proceed in the same fashion, for he could hardly have Achilles, who is generally regarded as having died in the Trojan War, appear in the early nineteenth century as a Christlike Redeemer of mankind. Nor would any other well-known figure with a reputation in Greek myth do for the role. Shelley had to find a figure who would be compatible with the mythological terms in which the drama is expressed, preferably a Greek figure. This figure must be one capable of sustaining a role of immense dignity and moral consequence. And he must be one whose emergence in modern times would not be ridiculous. Shelley's dex-

terity and erudition were not baffled. He produced Demogorgon.

Who was Demogorgon? The name Demogorgon does
not appear in either Greek or Latin literature proper. It is
probable that Demogorgon was born of a mere ortho-
graphical error—the misspelling on the part of a mediaeval
scribe of the word *demiourgon*. In Plato's myth of the
creation in the *Timaeus*, he conceived a figure which he
called Demiourgos. This was a beneficent power, the
artificer of the cosmos, who imposed order upon chaos
and then retired, delegating his power to the gods whom
he had created. In the complex religious systems which
developed after Plato's time, the Demiurge played some
part, having degenerated into a mysterious power, not
necessarily beneficent, whose name was too terrible to
mention, whose home was in the depths, and who had
vague but tremendous powers. Through a misspelling of
the word by mediaeval scholiasts, the already corrupted
Demiurge had his name changed into Demogorgon, who
thus assumed a separate existence. At the end of the Middle
Ages there were apparently extant some documents, now
lost, in which Demogorgon figured. These were probably
documents written by Christian apologists to discredit
pagan myth. In these, Demogorgon was pictured as a
mysterious ancestor of the gods, with attributes associated
with magic, and with fantastic, semiallegorical legends
connected with him. From one of these documents, an
account of Demogorgon passed into Boccaccio's famous
book, *The Genealogies of the Gods*. Renaissance editors
were quick to recognize the relation between Demiourgon
and Demogorgon, and the figure was treated in scholarly
discussions with something of the character both of the

beneficent world artificer of Plato and of the mysterious figure created by the Christian mythographers to discredit pagan myth. So picturesque a figure passed likewise into poetry, and he is frequently referred to by the poets of the Renaissance.

Shelley knew a good deal about Demogorgon. The account of him in Boccaccio he studied carefully. His scholarship on the subject was sufficient also to know that the dreadful and mysterious figure whom Boccaccio depicts was entitled to be regarded as a beneficent power who could impose order upon chaos. For his purposes Demogorgon was well suited. By representing him as the son born of Zeus and Thetis, he would have a figure with legendary associations interesting for dramatic purposes. Demogorgon had sufficient dignity and the proper qualifications to be the power which should reimpose order on a world chaotic with evil. The fact that Demogorgon had existed from eternity was but a slight difficulty, since allegorically one could suppose that the power to shape the good had always existed, but had not operated until the great event of the play—Prometheus' triumph over himself—gave it instigation.

Boccaccio begins his account of the generations of the gods with Demogorgon, devoting several pages to him and to his offspring. Boccaccio professes to be following a fragment (not now extant) of a work by one Theodontius. Theodontius, in turn, was drawing upon a work, otherwise unknown, called the *Protocosmos*. This work he attributed to no less an authority than Pronapides, the tutor of Homer. The Abbé Banier in his *Mythology* gives a paraphrase of the passage in Boccaccio with the statement that he is ashamed to relate such wild tales, and so am I. The wildest of them passed into Diderot's *Encyclopédie*, where they may rest in better company. Matters relevant to our study I shall repeat.

Boccaccio relates that Theodontius names Demogorgon as the primordial ancestor of the gods, and since he finds no reference in any writer to any parents of Demogorgon, he is content to believe that Demogorgon was truly the first of all the gods. He commences his book, therefore, with an imaginary account of Demogorgon. He fancies himself descending into the bowels of the earth through a narrow and rocky defile either in Mount Taenarus or Aetna, passing the Stygian swamps, and arriving at the seat of Demogorgon. Then Demogorgon appears, the ancient father of all the gentile and the pagan gods, surrounded by clouds and vapor, dwelling in the depths of the earth. His very name is horrible. He has a mossy pallor about him, and is clothed by a stale humidity, giving off an earthy, repulsive, and fetid odor.

Boccaccio explains that the belief in Demogorgon did not originate with learned men, but rather with rustic Arcadians who, seeing the vital forces of nature at work in fruits and flowers, her power bringing forth fountains, streams, and rivers, her voice making the earth itself shake in violent convulsions, imagined that nature itself was animated and named the animating spirit Demogorgon. The Abbé Banier, who interprets the name as meaning the "Genius or Intelligence of Earth," expresses the opinion that philosophers had meant no more by it than the vegetative principle, but that "the vulgar fancied it was a real god who resided in the bowels of the earth, to whom they offered sacrifices, especially in Arcadia. We must not forget," he adds, "the opinion of some authors, that

Demogorgon had been a magician so skillful in his art, that he had ghosts and aerial spirits under his command, made them absolutely subject to his will, and severely punished those of them who did not execute his orders."

The materials from which Shelley constructed his Demogorgon are now in our possession, and we may examine the use which he made of them.

First of all we may see that Shelley had a technical difficulty to overcome. According to the myth of Prometheus, the Titan must be liberated by Hercules from his rock in the Caucasus Mountains. The cave of Demogorgon was located in the bowels of the earth with its entrance either through Mount Aetna or through the chasm at Taenarus in Laconia. Shelley needed some intermediary to span the distances involved.

He departs somewhat from the Aeschylean play in introducing a wife of Prometheus named Asia, together with two Oceanid sisters, Ione and Panthea. These he used as the desired intermediaries. Since his inventions concerning the three are difficult to follow, some explanation of them may be useful.

Shelley wished to contend that the state which should be natural for mankind is not a condition of evil, but one in which love prevails. Only in such a natural society can the potentialities of man be fully realized. Only in such a condition can the arts and sciences flourish to produce a true culture. Since Prometheus was the giver of the arts and sciences, Shelley was naturally concerned to work out his social ideas in dramatic terms within the limits of the myth. His inventions concerning Asia are designed for the purpose.

In the Aeschylean play no wife of Prometheus is mentioned. Shelley had discovered, however, that Herodotus mentions Asia as the wife of Prometheus. Elsewhere Asia is mentioned by writers on mythology as one of the Oceanids. These two facts Shelley was able to bring together very ingeniously. In the play of Aeschylus Prometheus is visited by a chorus of friendly Oceanids. To make Asia both an Oceanid and the wife of Prometheus would thus tie the play still closer to the Aeschylean drama, and yet give Prometheus a wife without departing from classical authority. Moreover, to make an Oceanid named Asia the wife of Prometheus would have an additional value. It was commonly believed that the continent Asia was the cradle of civilization. Asia in the play could thus represent the pristine culture, associated with Prometheus, which had prevailed before that culture had been contaminated with evil. She would be the state of love and nature in which civilization could flourish. She is represented at the beginning of the drama as having been exiled to India after the fall of the Titans. Shelley was here presumably recalling Bailly's idea that after the fall of the Atlanteans, or Titans, some vestiges of their culture survived in Asia. Throughout the drama Shelley sustains the idea that Asia is the state of nature and love in which culture flourishes. At one time he pictures her birth in terms borrowed from the myth of Aphrodite rising from the sea. Nature is animated by her presence. These circumstances help us to understand Mary Shelley's comment that Asia was, according to some interpretations, the same as Venus and Nature. I doubt whether anyone other than Shelley had so interpreted the mythological figure, but it is clear that he so interpreted her for the purpose of the drama.

Mindful of the fact that Asia must be not merely a symbol of culture, but likewise a mythological Oceanid, Shelley invents for her two Oceanid sisters, Ione and Panthea. To keep himself in accord with the Aeschylean drama, he has these friendly Oceanids the companions of Prometheus in his suffering. But to give them some genuine function in the play he makes them the intermediaries between Prometheus on his rock and Asia in her Indian vale. They are personages in the drama, but, as Oceanids, they are also bodies of water. Ione is the Ionian sea. Panthea is a combination of the bodies of water which lie at the foot of Caucasus and extend to India. Geographically the idea does not work out very well, because the Ionian sea does not lie at the foot of the Caucasus, nor is there a continuous stretch of water from Prometheus' mountain to India. But poetically the notion works well enough. The sea-green plumes of the sisters are the waves. The illimitable depths of their eyes are appropriate to water figures. The peculiar kind of condensation through which they receive the communications of Prometheus wordlessly, sustains the idea that they are bodies of water at the foot of Prometheus' mountain. They are the intermediaries between Prometheus and Asia because they extend (at least theoretically) from Caucasus to India. The curious fashion in which Panthea carries Ione on her back suggests some topographical arrangement which Shelley must have had in his mind for the juxtaposition of the bodies of water which they represent.

Our knowledge of the Demogorgon myth, together with a perception of the character of Asia and her sisters, now permits us to follow minutely the action of the drama throughout Act II. The hour of Prometheus' deliverance is at hand. Asia has been dwelling alone in exile in a far Indian vale, communicating with Prometheus only through her sisters, the Oceanids. When, however, Prometheus has stifled the evil in his heart by revoking his curse against Zeus, then love becomes the active force in the drama, and the scene changes to the vale where Asia is waiting alone. Panthea and Ione appear to her, informing her of a dream of Prometheus' deliverance. Another Dream then orders Panthea to "Follow! Follow!" and both Asia and Panthea begin to hear the "aërial tongues" of spirits summoning them to follow. These voices, faint as the "farewell of ghosts," are, we may assume, the ghosts and aerial spirits whom Banier described as at the command of Demogorgon. These spirits are sent to summon Panthea and Asia to the cave of Demogorgon, whither they accordingly proceed. A Semichorus of Spirits explains that the musical echoes which the pair are following are indeed the voices which "by Demogorgon's mighty law" draw those who have been summoned to the cave. Shelley next introduces a pair of fauns who have been listening to the voices. They are goatherd fauns who have paused in their milking to question where the spirits live who make such a delightful music in the woods. These, I take it, represent the rustic Arcadians mentioned by Boccaccio, who heard the voices of nature and believed that they proceeded from the earth spirit, Demogorgon. Asia and Panthea arrive at a pinnacle of rock among the mountains, from which they are to enter the realm of Demogorgon. This should be either Mount Aetna or Taenarus, the two places which Boccaccio had mentioned as possible locations of the entrance to the lair of Demogorgon. Uncertain which of the two sites to choose, Shelley seems to have combined the two, giving the place some of the features of Aetna, and some of the cavern at Taenarus, famous as an entrance to the underworld. Shelley's entrance is a "mighty portal like a volcano's meteor-breathing chasm"; on the other hand, unlike Mount Aetna, it is an oracular chasm—a detail supplied, I suppose, because Apollo is believed to have presided over the fissure at Taenarus, and because an oracle of the dead, through which the souls of the dead were led up from the lower world, is mentioned by Plutarch as at the spot. Voices summon Asia and Panthea to descend. They do so and arrive at the throne of Demogorgon. He is at first veiled, but the veil falls, and Panthea describes him as follows:

> I see a mighty Darkness
> Filling the seat of power: and rays of gloom
> Dart round, as light from the meridian sun,
> Ungazed upon and shapeless:—neither limb,
> Nor form, nor outline; yet we feel it is
> A living Spirit.

If this is not point for point the Demogorgon whom Boccaccio imagined, it is as nearly literal as Shelley's style permits.

Demogorgon and Asia engage in conversation in which Asia presses him for an explanation of the origin of evil. From Demogorgon's replies we infer that the creations of God are subject to fate, time, occasion, chance, and change. Love is the great gift which frees man from subjection to these, and evil results from the enslavement of the mind that does not avail itself of the gift of love. Jove has reigned because love has not prevailed. But Jove, serving evil, is subject to fate, time, occasion, chance, and change. The hour of deliverance is at hand because Prometheus, through his long suffering, has at last learned the lesson of love.

The terrible shadow of Demogorgon floats upward from its throne, mounting to heaven. There Jupiter announces to the assembled deities the birth of his child by Thetis:

> Even now have I begotten a strange wonder,
> That fatal child, the terror of the earth,
> Who waits but till the destined Hour arrive,
> Bearing from Demogorgon's vacant throne
> The dreadful might of ever-living limbs
> Which clothed that awful spirit unbeheld,—
> To redescend, and trample out the spark.

The spark is the resisting spirit of mankind.

Jupiter, it appears, is dimly aware that his son is to be greater than himself, although he does not realize that his son will overthrow him. He imagines his fated child to be one who will be the terror of the earth, acquiring great power by overcoming the primordial Demogorgon. The conceit is carried further by Jupiter's announcement to Thetis that their child, mightier than either of them,

> unbodied now,
> Between us floats, felt, although unbeheld,
> Waiting the incarnation, which ascends
> (Hear ye the thunder of the fiery wheels
> Griding the winds?) from Demogorgon's throne.
> Victory! victory! Feel'st thou not, O world!
> The earthquake of his chariot thundering up
> Olympus?

Jupiter supposes that the awful shape which he sees rising is his own son clothed in the form of Demogorgon. He does not realize that his son is Demogorgon himself. As I have previously suggested, the fable is inept at this point.

The son has just been born, but Demogorgon has had a primordial existence. The difficulty is merely technical, and Shelley ignores it. There is no difficulty in the moral significance since the power to overcome evil may be represented as having existed from eternity inoperative until love brings its destined hour.

Demogorgon moves toward the throne of Jupiter, who demands to know what he is. Demogorgon answers:

> Eternity. Demand no direr name.
> Descend, and follow me down the abyss.
> I am thy child, as thou wert Saturn's child;
> Mightier than thee: and we must dwell together
> Henceforth in darkness.

A Titanic struggle ensues in which Jupiter is overcome, falling at last into the abyss. At this point the action respecting Demogorgon is concluded so far as it affects the structure of the play, although his general function as the shaping agent of a new order pervades all the remaining portions of the drama.

During the whole of the action involving the trip to Demogorgon's cave and his ascent to Heaven, we have not been allowed to forget the significance of Asia as representing love. Shelley carries out the allegory by having one of the voices which summon her to Demogorgon explain:

> In the world unknown
> Sleeps a voice unspoken;
> By thy step alone
> Can its rest be broken;
> Child of Ocean!

Love alone could awaken the power of Demogorgon. It is after her arrival at the cave that the destined Hour comes for the overthrow of Zeus. Shelley carries out the idea by having Asia mount the chariot of the Hour and ascend with Demogorgon. As she does so her character as Love is more clearly revealed. It is then that Shelley gives the reader an unmistakable clue to her nature by describing her in terms suggesting the birth of Venus from the sea:

> The Nereids tell
> That on the day when the clear hyaline
> Was cloven at thine uprise, and thou didst stand
> Within a veinèd shell, which floated on
> Over the calm floor of the crystal sea,
> Among the Ægean isles, and by the shores
> Which bear thy name; love, like the atmosphere
> Of the sun's fire filling the living world,
> Burst from thee, and illumined Earth and Heaven
> And the deep Ocean and the sunless caves,
> And all that dwells within them.

The allegory is carried out by having her become increasingly radiant as the fulfillment approaches, and by a profusion of lyric intimations that love is abroad in the world and a diviner day approaching.

With the conclusion of the Demogorgon episode, it remains for Shelley to complete, in accordance with legend, the release of Prometheus by Hercules. This he accomplishes briefly, merely out of deference to the fable, since Hercules has no other function in the play. Hercules points the moral by observing:

> thus does strength
> To wisdom, courage, and long-suffering love
> And thee, who art the form they animate,
> Minister, like a slave.

He then fades from the plot, which, with the deliverance of Prometheus, turns to other matters.

With the foregoing account of the basic structural elements of the play in our minds, the difficulty of reading the drama up to the release of Prometheus in the third act should be removed. It should be possible not only to enjoy and admire the superb moral allegory, but to assimilate the subtle innuendo with which Shelley enriches but sometimes obscures his poetry.

The true movement of the drama is not the fable, but the inner action, which is individual and moral. Man is enchained by his own evil nature, his liver devoured in torment by the eagle of a power which can be overcome by love alone. When man no longer hates, then he is free. Prometheus was destined to be free, but the destiny could be fulfilled only as he met it by fulfilling his own nature. When man lifts his own nature to its highest elevation he becomes no longer enslaved to time, occasion, chance, and change. These are part of the nature of things indeed, but they are bad only if man is made evil by them. With true grandeur Shelley makes his drama of the Titan the drama of the individual man, and the loftiness of the poet's utterance matches the nobility of his theme.

Unfortunately Shelley is often diverted from his best purposes by his inventive ingenuity. Capable of dealing with subtle complexities, he often attempts the unnecessary. The first three acts of *Prometheus Unbound* suffer conspicuously from this fault. For instance, in the first act Shelley found himself dealing with Earth, the mother of Prometheus. He conceived the idea of having Earth speak with "inorganic voice," a kind of murmur of the earth itself. The idea is an attractive one, but for a considerable time the action is bogged down in the question whether Prometheus can or cannot understand what is said to him by his mother. Unable to extricate himself from the simple necessity of having Prometheus and Earth converse in language which everyone can understand, Shelley at last dropped the idea, but not until the main action had been unnecessarily delayed.

Shelley's dexterity in invention led him to bind his play too closely to the Aeschylean tragedy. For example, the chorus in Aeschylus was composed of the Oceanids. At the beginning of the play they commiserate with Prometheus, and subsequently they conduct themselves in the usual fashion of a Greek chorus, pointing and interpreting the action, their questions and comments providing the excuse for Prometheus' speeches. Shelley needed no such interlocutors, since the conversation in the first act takes place between Prometheus and Earth. Nevertheless he invented the two Oceanids, Panthea and Ione, who attend Prometheus. But there was small need for such figures; they had little to do, and Shelley was forced to invent unnecessarily in their behalf. He played on the idea that Prometheus and Asia communicate wordlessly through the agency of the sisters. Their dreams are made to play some part in the action. Asia takes Panthea along with her to the cave of Demogorgon apparently with Ione on Panthea's back. The winged Oceanids of Aeschylus provoked in Shelley some intolerably bad poetry about Panthea:

> hear I not
> The Aeolian music of her sea-green plumes
> Winnowing the crimson dawn?

Indeed they turn out to be vapid creatures who set loose in Shelley a lyric much too aerial for the stern business of the tragedy.

In more felicitous ways the whole fabric of the play is intertwined with that of Aeschylus in a kind of multiple allusiveness. There is some pleasure in identifying the Shelleyan music as Aeschylean echoes, but the pleasure is too refined. Greek tragedies were built upon each other, but they stood as separate structures. Shelley's play is weakened by the constant dependence of its allusions.

The whole of the Demogorgon episode is an example of Shelley's extraordinary dexterity, combined with his tendency to refine too subtly upon particulars. By a very careful study of the structure of the plot it is possible to understand and to defend the use made of Demogorgon. And yet what reader can be expected to carry in his mind sufficient knowledge of the mediaeval Demogorgon to follow the intricacies of the action without extensive study? Even a very learned man can hardly be expected to remember that Boccaccio had described the entrance to Demogorgon's cave as through Mount Aetna or Taenarus. And yet without that knowledge it is impossible to see what Asia is about when she makes the journey which constitutes a considerable part of Act II. The scene with the fauns is pointless if one does not know that Demogorgon controlled airy spirits and that the Arcadians believed in these spirits. And yet few persons can be expected to know Boccaccio's *The Genealogies of the Gods* well enough to get the point. Shelley completely ignores the ordinary limits to learning, and this in drama, where the function of the poet is to communicate rapidly. One does not reproach Shelley with the kind of vanity which one sometimes suspects in Goethe. It was no part of his plan to puzzle the reader with obscure erudition. Such a possibility is alien to Shelley's nature, which would have detested affectation of any sort. It seems rather the fault of an undisciplined delight in ingenuity and a failure to realize that the exuberant and momentary interests of his mind would not be crystal clear to someone who had no clue to those transient interests. And even if one allows the writer of a tragedy the right to suppose that some commentaries and notes will be necessary for the understanding of his work, nevertheless one may feel that the point illuminated is not always worth the long explanation necessary to illuminate it. It is significant too that in the over a hundred years which have passed since Shelley wrote the play, the action involving Asia and Demogorgon has remained obscure because no one has observed how it was built up from Boccaccio's account of Demogorgon.

My own feeling is that the whole second act, involving Asia, is badly proportioned in terms of the whole play. The moral allegory has value, but the long progress of Asia from her Indian vale to the cave of Demogorgon, with her subsequent excursion in the chariot of the Hour, is too long for the amount of dramatic value which it contains. The connection of Asia with Prometheus is, of course, legitimate, but Shelley's identification of her with Love is perplexing and forced in so far as the myth is concerned. Moreover, since Shelley has superimposed the alien Demogorgon upon the Prometheus myth, it is particularly difficult to have the complex Asia also involved. The circumstances of Asia's journey—the voices, the portal of Aetna or Taenarus, the descent into the bowels of the earth—relate to the unfamiliar Demogorgon story rather than to the Prometheus story, and the reader fails to understand either what is happening or why it is happening.

The play is by no means completed with the release of Prometheus. There remain three scenes of the third act and a fourth act. This latter was written some months after the third act was completed, and Shelley describes it as an "afterthought." It is far from being a detached part of the play, however, and Shelley must have been punning on the names of Prometheus and his brother Epimetheus, the one meaning "forethought," and the other "after-thought." The fourth act is a kind of epilogue, but entirely *integral*.

These portions contain some of the finest poetry in the whole drama but they are exceedingly difficult to follow in relation to the plot as a whole. One may say of them generally that their function in the action is this: they depict the uses to which the Promethean gifts will be put after man has been freed from slavery to evil. It will be recalled that in the tragedy of Aeschylus, Prometheus enumerates his gifts to mankind. Similarly in Shelley's play, we are presented, through Asia's words to Demogorgon, with a list of Prometheus' gifts to man. For the most part Shelley follows the list of Aeschylus, but with some alterations. According to Shelley the gifts are as follows: hope, in place of the foreknowledge of death; love; fire; metallurgy; the knowledge of gems, poisons, and materials hidden beneath the mountains and the waves; speech; thought; science; poetry; music; sculpture; medicine; astronomy; sailing ships and navigation; and the art of building. We need not hold Shelley exactly to his list, for it is clear that he intended Prometheus as the giver of the best elements of the mind and of society.

With the overthrow of Zeus, Shelley's problem is to depict the uses to which these gifts may be put, and yet to keep his narrative exposition in terms appropriate to the drama. The problem was a challenge to Shelley's inventive skill, which he met with great subtlety. Let us attempt to follow the turns of his somewhat too elusive invention.

The scene following the overthrow of Zeus consists of a conversation between Ocean and Apollo. Aeschylus introduces Ocean as a character in his play, a fact which presumably suggested to Shelley the idea of using Ocean also. Ocean is represented as reclining near the shore of the mouth of a great river in the island Atlantis. Atlantis has no significance except that, as a visionary isle, it is an appropriate place for the ideal conditions of things to be described and, as an island in the ocean, a fitting scene for Ocean to be personified conveniently and classically as reclining on its shore. Apollo relates to Ocean the fall of Zeus. Ocean then makes a fine speech in which he declares that the sea will now be unstained with blood:

> Blue Proteus and his humid Nymphs shall mark
> The shadow of fair ships, as mortals see
> The floating bark of the light-laden moon
> With that white star, its sightless pilot's crest,
> Borne down the rapid sunset's ebbing sea;
> Tracking their path no more by blood and groans,
> And desolation, and the mingled voice
> Of slavery and command—but by the light
> Of wave-reflected flowers, and floating odours,
> And music soft, and mild, free, gentle voices,
> That sweetest music, such as spirits love.

In other words, the Promethean gift of sailing ships and the art of navigation will no longer be abused by men, but will be turned to good uses. Shelley's language is general, but there is nothing fanciful to see in it a rebuke for the notorious conditions in the British merchant marine.

Thus far the device is a satisfactory one. Shelley wishes to turn the drama toward prophecies of the right uses of the Promethean gifts. One of the Promethean gifts was the art of sailing ships. There is a legitimate excuse for introducing Ocean into the play and Shelley uses Ocean as the agent for prophesying the improved conditions in respect to sailing ships. But it must have been obvious to Shelley that he could not carry such a procedure out in great detail. If he had a scene for each of the gifts, the play would be intolerably long. The gifts must somehow be generalized, so that they may be treated as a group. Apollo's words reveal Shelley's necessity. Instead of mentioning each of the specific gifts over which Apollo might be expected to preside, such as music, poetry, healing, Apollo merely observes in a general fashion:

> And I shall gaze not on the deeds which make
> My mind obscure with sorrow, as eclipse
> Darkens the sphere I guide.

Such a generalization was, of course, too short. Shelley needed a device by which he might represent the enlightened use of the Promethean gifts. He must construct a scene which would be interesting and significant, and of sufficient length to give proportion to the meaning.

He succeeded in working out the problem in an exceedingly ingenious way, and yet his inventions are, without unusually careful study, baffling ones to follow. After Hercules has unbound the Titan, Prometheus addresses Asia with an invitation to dwell with him in a certain cave which he describes in some detail:

> There is a Cave
> All overgrown with trailing odorous plants,
> Which curtain out the day with leaves and flowers,

And paved with veinèd emerald, and a fountain
Leaps in the midst with an awakening sound.
From its curved roof the mountain's frozen tears,
Like snow, or silver, or long diamond spires,
Hang downward, raining forth a doubtful light;
And there is heard the ever-moving air,
Whispering without from tree to tree, and birds,
And bees; and all around are mossy seats,
And the rough walls are clothed with long soft grass;
A simple dwelling, which shall be our own.

At first thought this cave seems to be merely an idyllic
retreat, a figment of Shelley's imagination, which has no
conceivable connection with the myth of Prometheus. But
one's suspicions are aroused when Earth also begins to
talk about a cave where Asia shall dwell. Why all this
talk about a cave? Earth's account of *her* cave seems to
be significant of something:

There is a Cavern where my spirit
Was panted forth in anguish whilst thy pain
Made my heart mad, and those who did inhale it
Became mad too, and built a temple there,
And spoke, and were oracular, and lured
The erring nations round to mutual war,
And faithless faith, such as Jove kept with thee;
Which breath now rises, as amongst tall weeds
A violet's exhalation, and it fills
With a serener light and crimson air
Intense, yet soft, the rocks and woods around;
It feeds the quick growth of the serpent vine,
And the dark linkèd ivy tangling wild,
And budding, blown, or odour-faded blooms
Which star the winds with points of coloured light,
As they rain through them, and bright, golden globes
Of fruit, suspended in their own green Heaven;
And through their veinèd leaves and amber stems,

> The flowers whose purple and translucid bowls
> Stand ever mantling with aërial dew,
> The drink of spirits; and it circles round,
> Like the soft-waving wings of noonday dreams,
> Inspiring calm and happy thoughts, like mine,
> Now thou art thus restored . . . This cave is thine.

One begins to feel that these places described have some particular significance and to watch for the clue with curiosity. Earth summons a spirit, whom she identifies as her torchbearer. She orders the spirit to conduct the assembled company

> beyond the peak
> Of Bacchic Nysa, Mænad-haunted mountain,
> And beyond Indus, and its tribute rivers,
> Trampling the torrent streams and glassy lakes
> With feet unwet, unwearied, undelaying;
> And up the green ravine, across the vale,
> Beside the windless and crystàlline pool,
> Where ever lies, on unerasing waves,
> The image of a temple, built above,
> Distinct with column, arch, and architrave,
> And palm-like capital, and over-wrought,
> And populous with most living imagery,
> Praxitelean shapes, whose marble smiles
> Fill the hushed air with everlasting love.

It would seem to be a Greek temple to which the company is to be transported from the Caucasus Mountains. At last Earth gives us a clue:

> It is deserted now, but once it bore
> Thy name, Prometheus.

Shelley no longer keeps us in doubt about the place to which he has been referring, for he follows with lines which make identification possible:

> there the emulous youths
> Bore to thy honour through the divine gloom
> The lamp which was thine emblem:—even as those
> Who bear the untransmitted torch of hope
> Into the grave, across the night of life,
> As thou hast borne it most triumphantly
> To this far goal of time . . . Depart, farewell.
> Beside that temple is the destined Cave.

The temple must be near Athens, for there the Attic cult of Prometheus celebrated the worship of the Titan in a race known as the Lampadephoria, in which youths raced from the altar of Prometheus in the Academy to the city. They carried lighted torches, and the object of the race was to arrive first at the goal with the torch unextinguished. The temple, then, must have reference to the Academy, the famous grove outside the walls of Athens.

There can be no doubt of our first topographical identification. What of the next? Earth has told Asia that "the destined Cave" is beside that temple. We should expect to find that Shelley has in mind some place near the Academy which was in ancient times associated with Prometheus. That place must be the sacred grove at Colonus, for that spot alone fulfills all the necessary conditions.

There were two places in ancient times connected with the Attic cult of Prometheus: one was his sanctuary in the Academy; the other was the sacred grove at Colonus, a deme outside the walls of Athens, about a mile and a quarter to the northwest, and contiguous with the grove of the Academy. It is the spot where Plato once taught and where the action of Sophocles' tragedy *Oedipus at Colonus* takes place. Within its sacred grove, says the poet, dwells "the fire-fraught god, the Titan Prometheus." And within the sacred grove there was, moreover, a chasm or fissure reputed to lead down to the lower world. This is undoubtedly the cave to which both Prometheus and Earth refer in Shelley's play. In studying Sophocles' play, Shelley had probably learned of the association which Prometheus had with the region, and determined to make use of it in his own.

Outside the walls of Athens, northwest of the Dipylum Gate, was the beautiful walled grove of the Academy, adorned with walks, gardens, and fountains, where Plato loved to teach, and where, under his guidance, was founded the famous Academy, the prototype of the many which have since borne that name. Adjoining the Academy was the grove of Colonus, a spot not less famous for its beauty, which has been described in romantic terms by Sophocles at the beginning of his *Oedipus at Colonus* and in a famous chorus of the play.

The "green ravine across the vale" to which Shelley's characters are directed, would be the "covert of green glades" which Sophocles describes, the low ground of the Academy across the valley of the Cephissus, whose sedgy pools gave the grove its fertility. Shelley's "unerasing waves" upon the "windless and crystàlline pool," echoes Sophocles' description of the "stainless tide" of the Cephissus, and of the bowers "unvexed by wind of any storm."

The temple of Prometheus which Shelley describes with its living imagery of Praxitelean shapes, would be the temple of Prometheus which Shelley supposed to have been within the grove of the Academy. Shelley had authority for his belief that such a temple once existed. Pausanias says that there was an altar of Prometheus in the Academy, and a description of the altar has been preserved by a scholiast on Sophocles. The scholiast quotes a fragment of Apollodorus in which we are told that it stood on an ancient base on which were carved in relief figures of Prometheus and Hephaistos. Some early editors, disputing the reading of the text, insisted that there was, in addition to the altar, a temple to Prometheus. It is from them, presumably, that Shelley derived his temple with its carved ornaments.

The imagery by which Shelley describes the cave and the adjacent grove is not more romantic than that of Sophocles, from whose beautiful description of Colonus, indeed, many of the details are taken. The "mossy seats" which Shelley mentions, recall the seat of unhewn stone on which Oedipus rested. The "wine dark ivy" of Sophocles is Shelley's "dark linkèd ivy tangled wild." The "vine" of Sophocles is Shelley's "serpent vine"; the "laurel" perhaps accounts for Shelley's blooms "Which star the winds with points of coloured light"; and Sophocles' mention of the bowers rich in berries and fruit suggested Shelley's "bright, golden globes of fruit, suspended in their own green Heaven."

Seizing upon the association of Prometheus with the Academy and Colonus, "earth's fairest home," Shelley has decided to transport his character thither. But what is his intention? Surely not merely to include a piece of erudition respecting Prometheus, nor to decorate his poem with reminiscences from Sophocles. He proposes to use the association of Prometheus with the region for dramatic purposes. His concern in the latter portion of the play is to depict the uses to which man may put the Promethean gifts now that evil has been overcome. I pointed out that at the conclusion of the scene in which Ocean appeared, prophesying the good uses to which the gift of sailing ships and navigation might be put, Shelley must have perceived that he could not deal with each of the gifts in a separate scene without dragging out the play to an intolerable length. He must find a device by which to deal with the Promethean gifts in a group.

One of the most enlightened movements of the latter half of the eighteenth and the early decades of the nineteenth centuries was that which led to the formation of the great academies. Everywhere throughout Europe scholars and patrons of the arts and sciences were banding themselves together in academies of music, sculpture, painting, and the sciences. Papers were read, publications encouraged, prizes offered to encourage the young, collections formed, classes established, honorary memberships exchanged between the nations. There was promise indeed of an impartial society devoted to the encouragement of noble efforts, an international fellowship of men of intelligence and good will. The cultivation of an impartial, international spirit, motivated only by the desire for development of the nobler human capacities, was one of the great achievements of the era. It is not to be discounted by the fact that the high hopes entertained of it have not as yet been realized. The same spirit, expressing itself in different forms, remains one of the hopes of the world.

Let us suppose that when Shelley found Prometheus associated with the beautiful grove of the Academy at Athens, and the holy region adjacent to it, he conceived of making use of that fact in a kind of allegorical prophecy of the right uses of the Promethean gifts as those right uses were promised in the spirit of the new academies.

Prometheus invites Asia to dwell with him in the cave. Then, in terms appropriate to the dwelling together of a man and a woman lovingly, in a rustic simplicity, enjoying the virtues of "the cave and place around," Shelley ties his poetry to a deeper meaning. Their life will represent the enjoyment of the Promethean gift of love no longer enslaved to mutability. But it will also represent the cultivation of the capacities of the mind. Asia and Prometheus become symbols of enlightened man developing his capacities. They become, in a sense, the spirit of the Academy as that spirit extends itself in the modern world and into the future, destroying error, developing thought, bringing the mind and human society to their highest fruition. If the language remains appropriate to Prometheus, inviting his wife Asia to dwell with him happily in a cave, the allegory becomes, nevertheless, increasingly transparent:

> We will entangle buds and flowers, and beams
> Which twinkle on the fountain's brim, and make
> Strange combinations out of common things,
> Like human babes in their brief innocence;
> And we will search, with looks and words of love,
> For hidden thoughts, each lovelier than the last,
> Our unexhausted spirits; and like lutes
> Touched by the skill of the enamoured wind,
> Weave harmonies divine, yet ever new,
> From difference sweet where discord cannot be.
> And hither come, sped on the charmed winds,
> Which meet from all the points of Heaven, as bees
> From every flower aëreal Enna feeds,
> At their known island-homes in Himera,
> The echoes of the human world, which tell
> Of the low voice of love, almost unheard,
> And dove-eyed pity's murmured pain, and music,
> Itself the echo of the heart, and all

That tempers or improves man's life, now free;
And lovely apparitions, dim at first,
Then radiant,—as the mind, arising bright
From the embrace of beauty, whence the forms
Of which these are the phantoms, casts on them
The gathered rays which are reality,—
Shall visit us, the progeny immortal
Of Painting, Sculpture, and rapt Poesy,
And arts, though unimagined, yet to be.
Then wandering voices and the shadows these
Of all that man becomes, the mediators
Of that best worship, love, by him and us
Given and returned; swift shapes and sounds, which grow
More fair and soft as man grows wise and kind,
And veil by veil, evil and error fall . . .
Such virtue has the cave and place around.

As always in the subtler poetry of Shelley, one must
attempt to see, before resolving his words into statements
of ideas, the amount of appositeness which the poetry
sustains. Here the words are apposite to a bewildering
number of things. They are apposite to Prometheus as the
benefactor of man; to Asia both as his wife and in her
capacity as Love; to the physical scenery; to the classical
descriptions of the place; to the association of Plato with
the Academy; to the idea of the Promethean gifts; and
to the idea that the Promethean gifts, properly developed,
will elevate and ennoble man and society. Only by taking
account of all these elements may the reader understand
the allegory.

In the invitation to Asia which Prometheus delivers,
Shelley has managed to fulfill his major dramatic object;
that is, to present, in a form appropriate to the drama and
to the myth in which the drama is stated, a prophecy of
the right uses to which the Promethean gifts will be put

in a society in which love has prevailed over man's sub-
servience to the evil in his own nature.

But in availing himself of the dramatically useful association of Prometheus with the site of the Academy,
Shelley has not exhausted the dramatic possibilities of the
situation. He will avail himself of them still further to
reinforce his allegory.

There is, for instance, the matter of the cave. Although
Sophocles says that Prometheus dwelt within the sacred
grove of Colonus, the cave itself and the grove were
especially sacred to the Eumenides. Shelley makes use of
that fact very ingeniously. After Prometheus, Asia, Panthea, and Ione have been transported to the cave, Shelley
introduces a figure whom he calls the Spirit of the Earth.
The spirit is a very gentle, innocent, and tender child.
He describes to the assembled company the happy change
which has come over human society since the fall of Zeus.
I take it that Shelley's point was this: Now that man has
been liberated from the evil of his own nature, the necessity for the Eumenides, that is, the avenging ministers, has
passed. No longer will the cave be sacred to the Furies
whose function it was to punish the sins of men and
whose very name was so dreadful that men dared speak of
them not as the Erinyes, the Furies, but as the Eumenides,
or good spirits. In contrast to these dread figures, Shelley
introduces a figure as opposite as possible to the Eumenides. The Eumenides were the children of Earth. This
new child is likewise a child of Earth, the Spirit of Earth,
and his appearance in the cave once sacred to the more
savage progeny of his mother, marks the alteration in the
order of things. He is the antithesis of what the Furies
represented. Hence the significance of having Earth tell

of the cave. It is inhabited now not by her children the Furies, but by the gentle spirit who will be the friend of Asia.

Having thus bound Earth into the action and the locality, Shelley's invention proceeded still further. Colonus consisted of a grove sloping upward from the low valley of the Cephissus, in which was the garden of the Academy, to a knoll known as Colonus Hippias and to another hill called the hill of Green Demeter. Sophocles speaks of "the hill which was in view, Demeter's hill who guards the tender plants." Demeter, as the Earth Mother, was but one of the many names under which Themis, or Earth, was worshiped. She was the same goddess as Shelley's Earth. Hence the fine speech which Shelley puts into her mouth in the play. Gathering up the associations of the place, and finding Demeter Euchlous (that is, Demeter who makes things fresh and green) associated with Colonus, where the action was taking place, Shelley gave her a speech in which she is represented as the guardian of living things. No longer will she be Earth the destroyer, but in "earth's fairest home" in the new era of love, she will be an earth which nourishes life:

> Henceforth the many children fair
> Folded in my sustaining arms; all plants
> And creeping forms, and insects rainbow-winged,
> And birds, and beasts, and fish, and human shapes,
> Which drew disease and pain from my wan bosom,
> Draining the poison of despair, shall take
> And interchange sweet nutriment.

Shelley has now accomplished his object. He has managed a scene in which he has foreshadowed the felicitous state of man employing the Promethean gifts as they should be used. The drama draws rapidly to a close, or rather to what Shelley originally intended as a close. The Spirit of the Hour, that is, the particular Hour which accomplished the overthrow of Zeus, tells how her chariot and horses have found an honored sanctuary. In one of the finest passages in the play she describes the change which has taken place in the world:

> The loathsome mask has fallen, the Man remains,—
> Sceptreless, free, uncircumscribed,—but man:
> Equal, unclassed, tribeless and nationless,
> Exempt from awe, worship, degree,—the King
> Over himself; just, gentle, wise,—but man:
> Passionless? no: yet free from guilt or pain,
> Which were, for his will made, or suffered them,
> Nor yet exempt, though ruling them like slaves,
> From chance, and death, and mutability,
> The clogs of that which else might oversoar
> The loftiest star of unascended Heaven,
> Pinnacled dim in the intense inane.

The fourth act of *Prometheus Unbound* was added by Shelley several months after he had completed the drama in three acts. Mary Shelley describes it as "a sort of hymn of rejoicing in the fulfillment of the prophecies with regard to Prometheus." Its general relevance to the drama as a whole may best be seen if one keeps in mind while reading it that Shelley is continuing to celebrate the right uses of the Promethean gifts in an age when man has been freed by love from slavery to evil.

The act resolves itself into five pieces of poetic invention, three of which are difficult to understand without careful study. These five inventions I distinguish as follows: the lyric prelude of the Hours and Spirits; the mechanism in which the Spirit of the Earth appears; the

ray of light on the forehead of the Spirit of the Earth,
and the significance of what it reveals; the colloquy between the Spirits of the Earth and Moon; and the final
appearance of Demogorgon.

The first and last of these inventions are easy enough
to discern in their full significance. The lyric prelude to
the act consists of a celebration of the passing of the dead
Hours, that is, the hours of the past in which wretchedness
prevailed; then a celebration and prophecy of the manner
in which the hours of the future will fulfill the hope latent
in them by joining with the capacities of the human mind
to put the Promethean gifts to their best uses:

> And our singing shall build
> In the void's loose field
> A world for the Spirit of Wisdom to wield;
> We will take our plan
> From the new world of man,
> And our work shall be called the Promethean.

The last of the five inventions, the final appearance of
Demogorgon, is merely a recapitulation of the main action
of the fable, the ascendancy of Demogorgon, and a pointing of the spiritual meaning of the play as a whole. The
inspiring stanzas with which the drama closes are in
Shelley's loftiest style and are unquestionably great.

The intervening portions of the act are exceedingly
difficult. When Shelley first introduces his Spirit of the
Earth and the Spirit of the Moon, the reader is puzzled
by the elaborate mechanisms in which they make their
stage appearances. The moon spirit enters in a kind of
chariot which, from the description, we identify as an
image of the moon itself. The apparatus seems more appropriate to a masque than to a serious drama. The mech-

anism in which the Spirit of the Earth enters is much more complex:

> And from the other opening in the wood
> Rushes, with loud and whirlwind harmony,
> A sphere, which is as many thousand spheres,
> Solid as crystal, yet through all its mass
> Flow, as through empty space, music and light:
> Ten thousand orbs involving and involved,
> Purple and azure, white and green and golden,
> Sphere within sphere; and every space between
> Peopled with unimaginable shapes,
> Such as ghosts dream dwell in the lampless deep,
> Yet each inter-transpicuous; and they whirl
> Over each other with a thousand motions,
> Upon a thousand sightless axles spinning,
> And with the force of self destroying swiftness,
> Intensely, slowly, solemnly roll on,
> Kindling with mingled sounds, and many tones,
> Intelligible words and music wild.

Within this mechanism is the Spirit of the Earth. Upon her forehead is a star from which beams of light revolve.

The mechanism is clearly an image of the universe, but what prompted Shelley to introduce so fantastic an apparatus? The thing seems to be a kind of sublimated Orrery, a poetic version of the astronomical apparatus, popular in the eighteenth century, which fashionable persons placed in their gardens or libraries to illustrate the motions of the heavenly bodies.

I think the answer may be this: The setting of the last act is a part of the forest near the cave of Prometheus. The scene is, then, still in the grove of Colonus. We have already seen that Shelley has taken considerable account of the topographical realities of Colonus, together with the associations of the place. A scholiast on Aristophanes' *The*

Birds has a note on Meton, the astronomer. Among other things, he mentions that Callistratus says that there was at Colonus an astronomical toy set up by Meton. May not Shelley, in reading about Colonus, have noticed that piece of information? The thought of the astronomical toy could have given him the idea for his peculiar apparatus. The fact that a knowledge of astronomy was one of the gifts of Prometheus would have fitted in with the idea, and Shelley could adjust the significance of the instrument to his own purposes. The mechanism for introducing the Moon would be merely a parallel invention in order to carry out the device.

Once the Spirit of the Earth has made her somewhat cumbersome appearance, Shelley gets down to the business of significant poetry. A revolving ray of light upon the forehead of the Spirit is described as illuminating the cosmos and the interior of the earth itself. This ray of light we may interpret as the ray of light which the new spirit of inquiry upon the earth will cast upon the universe as man avails himself of the Promethean gifts. Earth in the drama has ceased to be a personage of the Greek fable. The concept has, in the new order, yielded to a new one, the Spirit of the Earth, who assumes combined allegorical roles: first, that of the new spirit in the mind of man which will illuminate the universe by knowledge; and, second, the animating spirit of love which now rejuvenates the earth and, indeed, the whole of creation. It is for the former of these roles that Shelley first makes use of his invention. The revolving ray of light on the forehead of the young Spirit of the Earth reveals the world not as ancient myth conceived it but as the scientific mind conceived it. Hence the ray of light reveals

geological structure. It lights up, moreover, the archaeological and geological evidences with which scientists in
Shelley's time were concerned. As the light turns downward it shows the "cancelled cycles" which we may
recognize as referring to Cuvier's theory of the successive
epochs of the earth. Since Shelley in this part of the play
is engaged in presenting one of his most significant dramatic ideas, we must examine it with some care.

In order to account for the various evidences incompatible with the Biblical account of creation, Cuvier had
developed a theory of four epochs of creation of which
that recounted in the book of Genesis is the last. The
preceding epochs had terminated successively in gigantic
catastrophes which had overwhelmed the earth surfaces
together with their inhabitants. Hence Cuvier had been
able to account for the fossil remains of species unknown
to the historical cycle and for archaeological vestiges anterior to the period of time compatible with Biblical and
other early chronologies. It would seem that Shelley introduces the theory of Cuvier as representing the enlightened
view of earth:

> The beams flash on
> And make appear the melancholy ruins
> Of cancelled cycles; anchors, beaks of ships;
> Planks turned to marble; quivers, helms, and spears,
> And gorgon-headed targes, and the wheels
> Of scythèd chariots, and the emblazonry
> Of trophies, standards, and armorial beasts,
> Round which Death laughed, sepulchred emblems
> Of dead Destruction, ruin within ruin!
> The wrecks beside of many a city vast,
> Whose population which the earth grew over
> Was mortal, but not human; see, they lie,

> Their monstrous works, and uncouth skeletons,
> Their statues, homes, and fanes; prodigious shapes
> Huddled in gray annihilation, split,
> Jammed in the hard, black deep; and over these,
> The anatomies of unknown wingèd things,
> And fishes which were isles of living scale,
> And serpents, bony chains, twisted around
> The iron crags, or within heaps of dust
> To which the tortuous strength of their last pangs
> Had crushed the iron crags;—and over these
> The jaggèd alligator, and the might
> Of earth-convulsing behemoth, which once
> Were monarch beasts, and on the slimy shores,
> And weed-overgrown continents of Earth,
> Increased and multiplied like summer worms
> On an abandoned corpse, till the blue globe
> Wrapt deluge round it like a cloak, and they
> Yelled, gaspt, and were abolished; or some God
> Whose throne was in a comet, passed, and cried—
> Be not!—and like my words they were no more.

The long passage unmistakably refers to the evidences by which archaeologists and geologists were attempting to arrive at a true estimate of the earth's history as opposed to the Biblical fable. With Shelley's hostility to conventional religious belief, which he regarded as superstition, we can well imagine that the new science would particularly recommend itself to him as overthrowing superstition. Since science was one of the Promethean gifts, Shelley could select that aspect of science which most clearly promised the overthrow of the religious beliefs to which he was hostile. The picture of the cycles as Cuvier stated them thus becomes a closely integrated part of Shelley's scheme to celebrate the liberation of the mind through the Promethean gifts. The ray of light from the

Spirit of the Earth adduces support for a scientific hypothesis which Shelley believes will overthrow religious superstition and fable.

It is difficult to reconcile Shelley's statement that the last act of *Prometheus* was an afterthought, with the obvious preparation for it which one finds in the preceding act. In the last scene of Act III, when Asia and the Spirit of the Earth are engaged in conversation, Asia declares that they two will never part

> till thy chaste sister,
> Who guides the frozen and inconstant moon,
> Will look on thy more warm and equal light
> Till her heart thaw like flakes of April snow,
> And love thee.

The Spirit of the Earth exclaims:

> What! as Asia loves Prometheus?

Asia answers:

> Peace, wanton! thou art yet not old enough.
> Think ye by gazing on each other's eyes
> To multiply your lovely selves, and fill
> With spherèd fires the interlunar air?

The Spirit answers, disappointedly:

> Nay, Mother, while my sister trims her lamp
> 'Tis hard I should go darkling.

With this revelation of the adolescent but distinctly amorous instincts of the Spirit of the Earth for his sister, the Moon, the conversation turns to other matters. The incident is clearly a preparation for that portion of Act IV in which the Spirit of the Earth engaged in a kind of love colloquy with the Spirit of the Moon, revitalizing the moon by his love. Presumably Shelley inserted the passage in Act III after he had added Act IV.

At any rate, the wooing of the moon does take place. Shelley pictures the moon as an inert and frozen satellite of the earth. But the new vitality of the earth impregnates the moon with its own life. A spirit is darted from the earth which penetrates the frozen frame of the moon, warming the cold body, melting the snow upon its lifeless mountains, uncongealing its solid oceans, and bringing forth on the moon's surface vegetation and living inhabitants. In this allegory both moon and earth are mere personifications of physical bodies. They are not mythological personages.

The agency which vitalizes the moon is, of course, love, which Shelley imagines for the purposes of this planetary wooing as an interpenetrating spirit which passes into everything: the granite mass of the earth, the growing things upon the earth, the atmosphere around it, and the frozen body of the moon. The wooing of the moon by the earth is merely an allegory designed to express the idea that love is the power which, interfusing all things, distinguishes cosmos from chaos. Shelley is more concerned with man than with the moon. The new spirit of love which is the gift of Prometheus flows into the mind of man, when hate departs, removing the stagnant chaos of thought which has kept man from using the Promethean gifts of knowledge and of skill. As earth feels itself vitalized by the interpenetrating spirit of love, man is healed, like a leprous child, of the disease of hate and fear and pain. No longer are men disunited. Mankind, united by love, learns to control his will, to turn it to good purposes, and to make use of the capacities of his mind.

It is interesting to reflect that while Shelley's personification of earth and moon as lovers is eminently a poetic idea, such as has been used by poets from time immemorial, it was not wholly at variance with conceptions which passed current in scientific thought in his time. Cuvier, in his *Theory of the Earth,* passes in review some of the systems of contemporary geologists which he rejects in favor of his own. Among these he describes several which he regards as more imaginative than scientific. Apparently the popular pantheism of the day had found expression in geological theory as well as in philosophy. Cuvier describes a fantastic system in which the earth is regarded as an animated body, with a complete set of vital faculties, instincts, and volitions. The mountains are the respiratory organs, the schists its organs of secretion, the volcanoes its organs of excretion. Veins are carious sores, abscesses of the mineral kingdom, and metals are the product of rottenness and disease, which is the reason that most of them have a bad smell. (Keats's "Savor of poisonous brass and metal sick," and Shelley's "vegetable silver," may have emanated from such a notion.) Every particle of the earth is alive, with a vital fluid circulating in it, and the processes of assimilation take place as they do in other animated bodies.

Shelley's earth interfused by an animating love which is the divine principle of the universe as well as the fructifying power in life and thought is not far removed from this sort of geological pantheism. From the beginning of the play to the end Shelley has personified the earth as "a living spirit," with "stony veins," whose springs were breasts, whose atmosphere was breath, whose nerves were marble, and so on. Then in the last act the old and withered frame of earth is rejuvenated by the interfusing and universal spirit of love, which is definitely pantheistic in its character. Perhaps in the metaphor of geological pantheism Shelley found some inspiration. Within that metaphor earth, represented as an animate body, might move either as a mythological figure in a fable or as a link in the chain of being from God to matter.

One must at last attempt to estimate the value of what Shelley has done. The complexity of the play stands in startling contrast to the simplicity of that of Aeschylus. Nor can it be denied that Shelley suffers in that contrast. The intricate structure of the play makes an exhausting demand upon the reader, and the reward which he obtains from comprehending the action is often insufficient recompense for the effort involved. I have already suggested certain criticisms of the play up to the point at which Jove is overthrown. Criticism of the remaining portion of the play must be similar in kind. The refinements of allegorical meaning which rest upon the association of Prometheus with the cave at Colonus and the Academy are too erudite and arcane to be clearly communicated. Shelley's invention becomes at times so elaborately ingenious as to border upon the absurd, as it does in the astronomical instrument in which the Spirit of the Earth appears. Advancing scientific thought has left the incident respecting the "cancelled cycles" obsolete. The colloquy between Earth and Moon is an obviously inferior poetic invention.

Morally the play attains a high elevation. In the Aeschylean conception man attains the degree of freedom allowed him by a blind submission to the limitations imposed by the necessity implicit in the nature of things.

Prometheus' pride in his revolt must end in humility and acceptance of the will of God. The moral of the Aeschylean play is that of the book of Job. The moral of Shelley's play does not, it appears to me, differ from that of Aeschylus so radically as Shelley imagined. Man attains a limited freedom by eradicating from his nature its worse elements and being guided by the will of God, which is love. The essential difference is that Shelley allots to man a higher capacity for achievement within the limits of necessity than that envisaged by the Greek poet, an optimistic hope which may or may not be justified by events.

Shelley's Adonais

SHELLEY'S *Adonais* is the most complex poem based on a mythological theme produced by any poet of the Romantic generation. So complex, indeed, is the mythological understructure of the poem that its true character has been scarcely observed.

Adonais is based upon the legend of Aphrodite and Adonis, a legend which is adapted throughout the entire length of the poem. The reason why that fact is not more apparent is that Shelley so generalized the myth in order to make it fit his purposes, and availed himself of such a loose and diversified application, that the presence of the myth in the structure of the poem has been nearly obscured.

Adonais is a poem in which a mythological theme is made to be the vehicle of certain related purposes. As in poems fashionable in the Renaissance, the poem follows the general outlines of a myth, with different levels of application. Thus in *Adonais* there is a mythological level of the poem which rests upon the story of Aphrodite and Adonis. There is a literal level in which that legend is made to apply to the death of John Keats. There is what may be described as a polemical level, in which the myth becomes the vehicle for an attack upon the element of conservative society to which Shelley and his friends were hostile. And there is a philosophical level. In this the myth supports Shelley's statement that the only escape from the evil of the world is for the soul to free itself by death from the limitations of the world and, like Keats, to achieve participation in the Divine Love. Thus the poem proceeds at four parallel but disparate levels of thought, all developed simultaneously. In the dexterity with which Shelley sustains and integrates these levels of meaning, one may see why Shelley described *Adonais* as a "highly wrought piece of art." In the recognition of the difficulties which the poet encountered and the manner in which he met them, a proper criticism of the poem may commence.

The recognition of the fable, the story of Aphrodite and Adonis, is the key to the understanding of *Adonais*. It is the linking theme; in its implications all the meanings are folded. Yet Shelley deliberately veiled the most obvious clues by which we should recognize the fable. The name Adonis has been lengthened to Adonais. Aphrodite appears under the title Urania, an epithet meaning "heavenly," which properly belongs to her but which is not ordinarily associated with the fable. The boar of the legend has been generalized to a symbol of evil, the "unpastured dragon" of the poem. These alterations may appear. at first thought so striking as to cause the reader to doubt that Shelley had the fable of Aphrodite and Adonis in mind at all. But the details of the fable are followed too closely to sustain that doubt. The alterations were deliberately introduced in order to generalize and to apply the theme.

There is no single treatment of the Adonis myth in Greek or Latin literature which tells the full story. The outlines of the whole legend must be put together from a number of sources. Relevant portions of the story are as follows. Adonis was a beautiful young shepherd who was very fond of hunting. Aphrodite, the goddess of love and beauty, fell in love with him and persuaded him to become her lover. Fearful that he might be killed in the hunt, she tried to dissuade him from the pursuit of savage beasts. But one day, when Aphrodite was absent, presiding over ceremonies in her honor, Adonis returned to the hunt, and was mortally injured by a wild boar. Some say that Ares, jealous of Aphrodite's love for the shepherd boy, instigated this disaster. Informed of the injury to her lover, Aphrodite returned to his side, lamenting his fate and grieving that she could not die with him. Her companions mourned with her. At her caresses Adonis revived slightly, and she implored him for a last kiss. According to some, Aphrodite turned his dead body into an anemone. According to others, she followed him to the lower world, where Persephone fell in love with him and refused to give him up. Aphrodite pleaded with Zeus for his return, and at last, with the consent of Hades, Adonis was allowed to return to earth for six months of each year, during the spring and summer. This time he spent with Aphrodite. The return of Adonis was celebrated in an Adonis festival. Annually a song was sung embodying the lament of Aphrodite, and a day of mourning was followed by a day of rejoicing at his revival.

In Shelley's poem no such simple narrative as this is told, but all of its elements may be detected, even though the poet's wing merely brushes them with light allusiveness. Adonais is a beautiful young shepherd whose flocks are, figuratively, Keats's poetic thoughts. The Aphrodite who is in love with him is Urania, the celestial goddess of love and beauty, the Aphrodite Ourania of the Greeks. She appears as an actual goddess, with a distinct and visible form, but in the latter part of the poem she becomes progressively less individual until, at the end, she is not a goddess with the conventional attributes and companions of Aphrodite, but Divine Love, abstractly conceived. Aphrodite's warning to the young shepherd is transposed to her lament, after the injury, that Adonais had not been dissuaded from his boldness in hunting. As in the myth, the injury to Adonais takes place while Urania is absent, presiding over ceremonies in her honor. In this poem she is listening, in her secret paradise, to a young poet read aloud the poems which he had composed under the inspiration of love and beauty. The allusion is probably to Kirke White, whose fate had been somewhat similar to that of Keats. Adonais has, in the meanwhile, been mortally wounded by a beast in the hunt, but has not yet died. When Urania is informed of the injury, she returns to his side, lamenting his fate and grieving that she cannot die with him. The various personifications which mourn for the wounded Adonais are, under English names, the conventional companions of Aphrodite. Adonais revives slightly. She implores him for a last kiss, after which he dies. The legend that Adonis was turned into an anemone is alluded to obscurely, in a fashion which I shall describe later, as are also the descent into the lower world and the refusal of Persephone to give him up.

In the earlier portion of the poem the following of the Adonis myth is fairly clear. In the latter portion the connection is not so readily observed but it is nevertheless sustained. Shelley links the return of Adonis with the survival of the poet's influence after death. The fable is thus continued, as the return of Adonais to the world is imagined and his union with Urania, or Aphrodite, takes place. But since Keats does not return annually for a six-month residence on earth, the fable takes on a symbolic character, developing the theme that the poet's thoughts survive in the world as a quickening influence. For this purpose Shelley had recourse to interpretations of the myth, both ancient and modern.

Ancient writers had recognized in the fable of Adonis a nature myth symbolizing the reawakening of life in the springtime. Macrobius, for instance, had interpreted Adonis as the sun, the boar as the killing winter, Aphrodite as the earth abandoned by the warmth of the sun in the wintertime, and the revival of Adonis as the return of the sun to the earth in the spring and summer. The union of Adonis and Aphrodite thus symbolized the uniting of earth and sunlight to bring forth life. The little baskets of spring flowers, comparable to our May Day baskets, which women carried in the ancient Adonis festival, were in honor of Adonis as the symbol of quick-growing vegetation.

Mythologists of Shelley's time had developed this interpretation of the myth somewhat extravagantly. Hancarville and Knight had read the fable as merely one version of a myth which frequently recurs in the mythology of all countries. Enumerating various pairs of mythical lovers, Hancarville had declared that they were all twofold representations of the generative god, the active and the passive elements of the generative act, or the male and female aspects of the single act of generation. Richard Payne Knight had developed Hancarville's thesis extensively. "The allegorical tales of the loves and misfortunes of Isis and Osiris," he declared, "are an exact counterpart of those of Venus and Adonis (Astarte and Baal); which signify the alternate exertion of the generative and destructive attributes. Adonis, or Adonai was an Oriental (Phoenician and Hebrew) title of the Sun, signifying Lord; and the boar, supposed to have killed him, was the emblem of Winter; during which the productive powers of nature being suspended, Venus was said to lament the loss of Adonis until he was again restored to life."

The boar, which Knight explained as a symbol of "the destroying or anti-generative attribute," he linked to the monster Typhon, whose dismemberment of Osiris had the same meaning as the boar's slaying of Adonis. The Aphrodite who represents the passive generative power is the Mother-Goddess, the Venus–Urania, personified as goddess of love or desire.

The myth of Aphrodite and Adonis was then, according to Knight, a myth in which Aphrodite, the Venus Urania, represented the passive principle of generation, Adonis represented the active principle, and the boar was the destructive principle. Knight believed that the ancients conceived of "female or passive powers of production supposed to be inherent in matter." When the passive power which pervaded earth was joined to the active principle, the united force produced vegetation.

By seizing hold of the idea that Adonis was a symbol of fertility, Shelley was able to make that aspect of the myth serve his celebration of the poet's continued influence after death. Without departing from the story, he attempted, as the poem progressively unfolded, to continue the application of the myth to Keats. The return of Adonis, or Adonais, and his union with Aphrodite, Shelley imagined in language appropriate to the resurgence of life in the springtime, when the warm sunlight operates upon the earth to produce vegetation. But since the object of the poem was to celebrate not the annual return of spring-time, but the perpetually vitalizing influence of Keats's poetry, the imagery was broadened to sustain the additional burden. As Adonis, Adonais represents the fructifying power without which nature is inanimate, but as Keats, Adonais represents the fructifying power of poetry in the world, surviving the death of the poet.

Shelley does not desert the legend even when he has finished his statement of the immortal influence of the poet's thought. The understructure of the myth is sustained to the end of the poem. As Adonais has, by his death, achieved union with Aphrodite, so the spirit of like-minded persons (such as Shelley himself) may, through the death of the body, unite with that high love of which the Uranian Aphrodite is an emblem. "No more let Life divide what Death can join together," is the final message of the poem, but it is still stated in terms of the fable. Urania, divested now of her nature symbolism and her individuality, becomes an allegorized personification of that divine love in which the soul desires to participate. As Shelley, in the prophetic image of the shipwreck, looks forward to the final divestiture of the spirit from its mortal body, the soul of Adonais, which has already attained its union with the divine love, is the guiding beacon.

We may perceive, then, that what I have described as the mythological level of the poem is maintained in one form or another from beginning to end.

On the literal level, the application of the fable to Keats is readily apparent. The shepherd youth, slain in the hunt by the wild boar, is Keats, mortally wounded, as Shelley supposed him to have been, by the savage criticism of *Endymion*. The hostile critic is the savage beast of the legend. The interval elapsing between the criticism of *Endymion* and the death of Keats in Rome is the interval between the wounding of Adonis and the return of Aphrodite to his side to witness his death. The promise of immortality for Keats's name and poetry are figured, as I have already said, under the fiction of the resurgence of Adonais.

It is a familiar fact that Keats and Shelley were not close friends—that, indeed, Shelley had not greatly admired Keats's poetry before reading *Hyperion*. His admiration for Keats was carefully qualified in his prose statements, and even after he had written *Adonais* he admitted to Byron that he felt that he had overpraised Keats in the poem. To Shelley, Keats was a symbol of the just man persecuted by the unjust. The theme of justice is nearly as significant in the poem as the theme of immortality. Shelley believed, and rightly, that Keats suffered at the hands of the reviewers more because of association with Leigh Hunt than because of his poetry. "The offense of this poor victim," he wrote, "seems to have consisted solely in his intimacy with Leigh Hunt, Mr. Hazlitt, and some other enemies of despotism and superstition." When Keats died, Shelley indignantly seized upon the fact of his death —and its supposed cause in the harshness of the *Quarterly Review*—as an occasion for some pointed observations. The reviews of the time were politically controlled, and Shelley had spent a lifetime in revolt against the Tory state of mind, if not the actual Tory party which controlled them. He had himself suffered intensely from the injustice of the representatives of the established powers. Personal abuse of Shelley, calumny, willful distortion, and vilification were flung across the pages of *Blackwood's*, and this vilification had been constantly on the increase.

Shelley probably would have refrained from taking issue with his enemies had not his friends and principles been at stake, and had not the whole affair culminated in the death of Keats. It should be remembered that Shelley himself had been linked in *Blackwood's Magazine* with the "Cockney School," of which school Keats and Hunt were the most condemned, and it is doubly significant that *Blackwood's* had pointed out that Keats belonged to "the Cockney School of Politics as well as to the Cockney School of Poetry." Keats had committed himself to this school with his sonnet "Written on the Day That Mr. Leigh Hunt Left Prison," in which he had charged that Hunt was shut in prison "for showing truth to flatter'd state." In reality Shelley belonged to no school, but he admired Hunt and was indebted to him for that appreciation of his own ideas and poems which Hunt had long publicly shown in the *Examiner*. Shelley was otherwise involved with the reformers of his day. His adventures in Irish reform in his youth, his "Declaration of Rights," his Marlow pamphlets, his connection with Godwin, his acquaintance with the minor reformers Richard Carlile, Francis Place, the Irish radicals Peter Finnerty, Daniel Isaac Eaton, Robert Owen, and his connection with General Sir Ronald Cranford Ferguson, had not left him in an isolated position. While his interest in reform was mainly philosophical, it was not wholly so.

The curious tactics of *Blackwood's* had put him in a position in which it was difficult to act. *Blackwood's* had all along insisted that Shelley was a gentleman, a scholar, and a poet of great ability. Under cover of these compliments, his character, poetry, and convictions had nevertheless been assailed even more savagely than those of Keats. This difficult situation in respect to *Blackwood's* was probably the reason why he selected the review of Keats in the *Quarterly*, rather than the more savage one in *Blackwood's*, for his special attack, although he had ample personal reason for feeling that both the *Quarterly* and *Blackwood's* deserved rebuke.

It appears to have been Shelley's original intention to stress the polemical purpose of his poem. But cancelled passages of the preface and cancelled stanzas reveal that he toned down this aspect of his work. He deleted from the preface important passages relating to himself. He cut out such passages as the following: "Persecution, contumely, and calumny, have been heaped upon me in profuse measure; and domestic conspiracy and legal oppression have violated in my person the most sacred rights of nature and humanity." From the poem itself he struck out a revolutionary passage in which he speaks of those who keep

> A record of the wrongs which, though they sleep,
> Die not, but dream of retribution.

But much of the polemical remains. *Blackwood's* had warned Shelley to seek better companions than Leigh Hunt and "Johnny Keats." In *Adonais* Shelley not only declares an admiration for Keats but says that he will follow Keats's soul as a beacon. *Blackwood's* had, in a nasty passage, compared Shelley to Hunt in contemptuous fashion: "But of Mr. Shelley much may be said with truth,

which we not long since said of his friend and leader Mr.
Hunt: he has not, indeed, all that is odious and contemptible in the character of that person; so far as we have seen
he has never exhibited the bustling vulgarity, the ludicrous
affectation, the factious flippancy, or the selfish heartless-
ness, which it is hard for our feelings to treat with the
mere contempt they merit." In *Adonais* Shelley avows his
admiration for Hunt:

> What softer voice is hushed over the dead?
> Athwart what brow is that dark mantle thrown?
> What form leans sadly o'er the white death-bed,
> In mockery of monumental stone,—
> The heavy heart heaving without a moan?
> If it be He, who, gentlest of the wise,
> Taught, soothed, loved, honoured the departed one,
> Let me not vex, with inharmonious sighs
> The silence of that heart's accepted sacrifice.

It is idle to say, as some critics have said, that this praise
might better have been applied to Joseph Severn. *Adonais*
without reference to Leigh Hunt would not have fulfilled
Shelley's intention. It is similarly pointless to say that
Shelley makes poets mourn for Keats who did not actually
mourn for him. Shelley's mourning poets are not so much
friends of Keats as common allies in the cause of justice.
Thus the Pilgrim of Eternity mourns at the tomb of Keats,
not as a personal friend, but as one who, like Keats, had
been attacked as the champion of liberal causes, and who
had, like Keats, been followed by

> the mingled howl
> Of Northern Wolves, that still in darkness prowl;
> A coward Brood, which mangles as they prey,
> By hellish instinct, all that cross their way.

Nor was it friendship for Keats that led the Tom Moore of the poem to mourn at the tomb of Keats, but the fact that he was "the sweetest lyrist" of Ireland's "saddest wrong."

Of the dead poets who welcomed Keats in the Unapparent, Chatterton was selected not alone because Keats had admired him, but because he was, as Keats had believed, the victim of "base detraction" in an "ingrate world." Sidney is pictured as welcoming Keats because Sidney was the defender of poetry from the attacks of the Puritan *School of Abuse*. Lucan, "by his death approved," who had conspired to kill the tyrant Nero when Nero had oppressed the poets by refusing them the right of free speech, likewise appears as a champion of liberty. Thus each of these men was not only a poet who, like Keats, had died young, but each was a man who, like Keats, had dared "the unpastured dragon in his den." *Blackwood's* had warned Shelley that if he did not turn from his present practices he would "sink like lead to the bottom" and be forgotten. Shelley replied that those who have "waged contention with their time's decay" are among "the kings of thought . . . and of the past are all that cannot pass away." To *Blackwood's* condemnation of his "proud spirit" he defiantly replied with a description of himself as "A pardlike Spirit beautiful and swift."

The polemical character of the poem, then, cannot be ignored. The preface, even without the cancelled passages, is a flaming and angry invective. The poem begins with an appeal to Justice to declare the wrong which has been done and to make of Keats's sad fate an echo and a light unto eternity. Milton is at once introduced as a man who, despite the enmity of his contemporaries, had in the justice of time come to rule over the thoughts of men because he had dared to oppose the tyrannies of his day and champion the cause of human liberty. Keats is pictured as one who was destroyed because he dared the unpastured dragon in his den. Those living poets who are the champions of noble causes mourn his fate, and Shelley in particular weeps his own fate in that of Keats. Defiantly Shelley praises that in Keats's poetry which has been condemned by the critics. He boldly associates himself with those who had been outcast by society, scorning the advice of the critics. Although he privately detested the poetry of Hunt, he singles out Hunt for special praise in defiance of the prevailing hatred of him. He makes the dead champions of great causes welcome Keats in the Unapparent. And he points out that ultimately the influence of those who have fought for the right prevails. So much for the polemical level of the poem.

On the philosophical level, the poem passes beyond any mere celebration of the greatness of Keats and of the ultimate triumph of his influence in the world. Nor does it rest with the idea that those who have waged contention with their time's decay will survive those who have opposed reform. Neither the beauty of the world nor the thought of the ultimate triumph of causes which Shelley held dear could finally compensate for the inadequacy and impermanence of earthly things. Shelley had ample cause in his own life to be weary of the world, and in the contemplation of the pure Being of which all earthly things are but an imperfect shadow, he yearned to be rid of the body which kept his soul from participation in unchanging essence. In imagining the soul of Keats freed at last from the limitations of its earthly dwelling, Shelley offered one more pertinent reflection as his final message. If death is all that keeps us from what we seek, why linger when by dying we may attain it? Shelley was not the first nor the last to reach that great conviction, but his expression of it is one of the noblest utterances of English poetry. He did not have long to wait before his desire for death was fulfilled. He did not take his own life, but it is strange to remember how very closely the circumstances of his death resemble the imagined scene of the closing lines of *Adonais*.

It would perhaps not be fanciful to compare the fourfold structure of *Adonais* with that of a musical composition for four instruments, in which the theme is now sustained by one, now by another, or by two or more in harmony, and in which variations of the theme may be explored without loss of unity. Shelley is often dexterous in making the imagery fit the various themes. He does not, indeed, attempt to force a fourfold allusiveness upon each line, but rarely is any passage limited to a single meaning. An instance in which the imagery brilliantly coincides with three of the themes occurs at the beginning of the poem. Shelley, announcing his lament for *Adonais*, addresses himself to one of the Hours, with the *h* capitalized:

> And thou, sad Hour, selected from all years
> To mourn our loss, rouse thy obscure compeers,
> And teach them thine own sorrow.

Here in a literal sense the sad Hour is the hour in which Keats had died, and the obscure compeers the hours which had not been distinguished by such an event as the death of Keats. But the Hours are mythological personages, Dike, Eunomia, and Eirene, who, as the companions of Aphrodite, always accompany her in her lament for Adonis, and it is appropriate that Shelley should call upon them on this occasion. A polemical significance may be equally discerned. We may suppose the "sad Hour" to have been Dike (Justice), whose function it was to inform the gods when an injustice had been done. Her "obscure compeers" would be Eunomia and Eirene (Harmony and Peace), whose obscurity in the world Shelley deplored. It was their duty to superintend the moral world of human life. Shelley calls upon them to make "an echo and a light unto eternity" out of the injustice done to Keats by his politically inspired enemies.

In other instances the myth and the facts are not so congruent. Keats died in February, while the lamentation for Adonis took place later in the springtime, a convention which Shelley followed in the poem. Rossetti notes that: "This introduction of Spring may be taken as implying that Shelley supposed Keats to have died in the Spring: but in fact he died in the Winter—February 23." It is more likely that Shelley merely could not adjust the fable to the fact at this point. A more striking instance of the stubbornness of the material is shown in the incident of the final kiss. It is difficult to imagine that this portion of the story could be applied to Keats, but Shelley attempted to make use of it. By imagining that the interval between the wounding of Adonis and the return of Aphrodite for the final kiss could be compared to the interval between Keats's wounding by the critic of *Endymion* and his death in Rome, Shelley attempted to fit the disparate themes together. But since he had already begun, in conventional elegiac fashion, to lament the death of Adonis, he was forced rather awkwardly to imagine Adonis merely as lying under the vault of the blue Italian sky, as though in sleep, while death and corruption dared

not deface him. The analogy between Keats dying of
tuberculosis in Rome and Adonais awaiting the shadow of
"white Death," is plausible but faint. Then, upon Urania's
return, demanding the final kiss, Shelley declares:

> In the death-chamber for a moment Death
> Shamed by the presence of that living Might,
> Blushed to annihilation, and the breath
> Revisited those lips, and life's pale light
> Flashed through those limbs, so late her dear delight.

There was no analogous incident at the death of Keats.

In other ways Shelley encountered difficulties in applying the details of the fable to the poet. In order to make
later use of the symbolism of the return of Adonis, it was
necessary at least to allude to the descent of Adonis into
the underworld, where Persephone became enamored of
him and refused to give him up. Since the application of
that portion of the fable to Keats was pointless, Shelley
was forced to say vaguely:

> For he is gone, where all things wise and fair
> Descend;—oh, dream not that the amorous Deep
> Will yet restore him to the vital air;
> Death feeds on his mute voice, and laughs at our despair.

Adonis in the fable was a shepherd. In order to use this
detail, Shelley availed himself of the conceit that the poetic
thoughts of Keats were his flocks:

> The quick Dreams,
> The passion-wingèd Ministers of thought,
> Who were his flocks, whom near the living streams
> Of his young spirit he fed, and whom he taught
> The love which was its music, wander not,—
> Wander no more, from kindling brain to brain,
> But droop there, whence they sprung; and mourn their lot

Round the cold heart, where, after their sweet pain,
They ne'er will gather strength, or find a home again.

To preserve the convention that the companions of
Aphrodite mourned over Adonais, Shelley struck upon the
device of selecting the conventional companions of Aphrodite whose names, translated into English, might be taken
as descriptive of Keats's poetic inventions. Thus Aphrodite in Greek myth is conventionally attended by the
Desires and Loves: Eros and Anteros, Himeros and
Potheros. These become the Desires and Adorations which
mourn for the dead poet. Her companions Aglaia (Splendor) and Peitho (Persuasion) become the Splendours and
the Persuasions of the poem. The activities of these
mourners are developed elaborately from the seventh
stanza of Bion's *Lament for Adonis*. The device is ingenious but not wholly satisfactory as a description of the
poetic qualities of Keats.

The incident of the conversion of the dead body of
Adonis into an anemone, mentioned by Bion, suggested
the lines:

> The leprous corpse touched by this spirit tender
> Exhales itself in flowers of gentle breath;
> Like incarnations of the stars, when splendour
> Is changed to fragrance, they illumine death
> And mock the merry worm that wakes beneath.

The "flowers of gentle breath" are from the Greek
anemone (windflower), from *anemos* (wind or breath).
The star shape of the anemone, or Adonis flower as it is
still called, suggested the "incarnations of the stars." But
the delicate allusiveness of the passage is not readily detected, since the incident is not narrated. It is merely
touched upon in this almost hidden fashion.

A recent critic has objected, reasonably enough, to the comparison of Keats to so many fragile things. Keats was made of sterner stuff than the "pale flower," the "bloom, whose petals nipped before they blew," or the "broken lily." Shelley was recalling the association of Adonis with the delicate springtime vegetation, such as was carried in the Adonis baskets in the ancient festival, but the idea was not a felicitous one if we consider it in terms of Keats's character. Much of the language of the poem is appropriate not to Shelley or Keats but to Aphrodite, "most musical of mourners." The amorous character of the language in which Shelley mourned for Keats led a psycho-analytically minded critic to interpret the passages as an indication that Shelley was homosexual. Pointing to the fact that in *Adonais* Shelley was "portraying and glorifying a *Man*" (the italics are his), he asks: "Yet how are the love-expressions in it to be taken? Are they to be put aside as amiable but rather meaningless enthusiasms, or are they to be interpreted directly and candidly, as *meaning what they say?*" The critic was doubtless thinking of such a line as that echoed from Bion's *Lament*: "Kiss me, so long but as a kiss may live." He did not realize that Shelley was speaking in terms appropriate to Aphrodite mourning for her lover. He had missed the mythological element of the poem altogether, or had mistaken it as those critics do who interpret Urania as the Muse of Astronomy. But his comment points to conspicuous flaws in the poem: the awkwardness in which the elaborate device involved Shelley, and the inappropriateness of parts of the poem to Keats.

When one considers also that Keats was not killed by the wound of the critic, as Shelley supposed, the application of the legend to Keats loses its chief justification. Shelley learned the true facts about the death of Keats after *Adonais* had been written, but obviously he could not correct his error without destroying the whole scheme of the poem.

On what I have described as the literal level of the poem, the application of the myth to John Keats, the device proved, then, not very successful. In order to make it work at all, Shelley had to be so vague that the details of the fable were all but lost, and the picture of Keats which it was intended to give was faulty at the time and still more obviously faulty once the character of Keats and the facts of his life and death were better known. The best passages dealing with Keats are those which were not tied down to the fable: allusions to his poetry; the magnificent lines,

> To that high Capital, where kingly Death
> Keeps his pale court in beauty and decay,
> He came; and bought with price of purest breath
> A grave among the eternal . . .

the beautiful description of his grave in the Protestant cemetery at Rome near the pyramid of Cestius; and the very fine stanzas that Shelley developed from Keats's own sonnet "To Chatterton."

The polemical element of the poem was adjusted to the basic myth with less distortion than was necessary in the narrative of the death of Keats. The chief difficulty which the modern reader finds in this whole aspect of the poem lies, however, in the fact that we do not regard Keats as Shelley regarded him. Keats was not slain by the critic; Shelley exaggerated Keats's role as the daring champion of liberal causes; and the immortality of his poetry had practically nothing to do with his having waged contention against his time's decay—in any political sense, at least. Moreover, much that the critics had said of Keats's poetry was true, as Keats himself recognized.

It was in exploring the symbolism of the Adonis myth and in attempting to adapt it to the philosophical affirmations at the end of the poem that Shelley employed himself most subtly. One cannot avoid the feeling, however, that the poem becomes too subtle, and it is certainly in the latter part of the elegy that one most easily loses the meaning. Shelley's problem was to find and sustain an analogy between the annual return of Adonis and the survival of Keats's poetry. By exploiting the fable as a nature myth—taking Adonis as the sunlight and Aphrodite as the "abandoned earth," he imagined the return of Adonis as bringing the resurgence of springtime. This conception was made applicable to Keats by identifying the voice of Keats —that is, his poetry—with the music of reanimated nature. By drawing upon the symbolic interpretation of Hancarville and Knight, Shelley made Adonis, or Adonais, represent the active aspect of the creative spirit, an idea which was, of course, applicable to the influence of the creative spirit of Keats in the world after his physical death. In the imagery which sustains this motif, Aphrodite becomes the passive element of the creative spirit, on which the active spirit operates. The union of Adonis and Urania thus produces the "one Spirit," that is, the twofold principle of fertility. Hence the intricate imagery in which Adonis becomes the "plastic stress" of the "one Spirit." The weakness of the poetic idea is that in attempting to amalgamate the nature myth and Keats, Shelley made nothing very clear of either one. Keats does not revive annually in the springtime, as Adonis did. Nor does his poetry produce vegetation. Adonais is neither wholly Adonis nor wholly Keats. The symbolic character attached to him does not perfectly fit either the idea of sunlight bringing the vegetation to life or the creative spirit of a poet vitalizing the world of thought after his death. Furthermore, it is difficult to follow the manner in which Adonais and Urania lose their individuality, fading from distinct and visible personages into nature myths.

This difficulty is the more marked as Shelley advances to the concept of Urania not merely as a personage of a fable nor merely as a principle in a nature myth, but as a philosophical abstraction. Urania becomes the Divine Love, the Platonic One; she is the permanent and unchanging essence, participation in which constitutes the final refuge of the soul. We are thus faced with an extraordinary number of guises in which Urania appears in the poem. In the first place it is a little difficult to recognize Urania as the Aphrodite of the myth at all, for Shelley does not confine her to a single mythological form. She is the goddess who is in love with Adonis; she is also what that goddess stands for—love and beauty as the object of the poet's desire. But Shelley shifts her into other aspects of Aphrodite. For instance, in virtue of her role in myth as Venus Genetrix, the mother of all forms, Shelley makes her "the mighty Mother," and Adonais is temporarily her son, instead of her lover. Shelley speaks of her as in her widowhood which would seem to be an allegory based on the idea that love and beauty are widowed in the modern world. She becomes the earth abandoned by the sunlight in the wintertime. She becomes a principle of fertility. And she becomes the unchanging essence of which all earthy thing are an imperfect image. It is hard to keep one's grasp upon her as she passes through these Protean changes, and one may well wonder whether her intricacies are worth the trouble.

Because Adonais contains many echoes of the language of the classical elegies and because Shelley has borrowed from the elegies many of their conventional devices, the elegies of Bion and Moschus, together with some of the pastoral verses of Theocritus, are commonly spoken of as Shelley's models or sources. No more mistaken notion could be expressed in a criticism of the poem. Adonais is highly original, both in form and conception. The imitation of the language and conventions of the classical elegies was a deliberate device intended to impart a traditional character to the poem. But to describe the classical elegies as models for Adonais does Shelley's poem no service. Shelley must have supposed the capacity to perceive these borrowings as the elementary equipment necessary to read the poem at all. The very originality of Adonais consists of the fact that intentionally recognizable elegiac conventions have been made to subserve a novel and subtle purpose. It is quite likely that as Shelley devised, "in the accents of an unknown land," a new lament for the "most musical of mourners," he had studied the whole literature of Adonis laments, including the many Italian versions of the theme. In many instances Shelley's language, even when he is closest to the fable, more nearly resembles the ornate style of the Italians than the simpler one of the Greeks. The "secret Paradise" of Urania is reminiscent of the garden of love in which the goddess resides in Girolamo Parabosco's *Favole d'Adone*. In at least one case a borrowing from the Italian may be clearly detected. In Marino's

L'Adone, just before Venus is aroused to return to her
dying Adonis, the poet writes:

> L'Aurora intanto che dal suo balcona
> Gli humidi lumi abbassa a la campagna
> Vede anelante e moribondo Adone.

Shelley's lines are:

> Morning sought
> Her eastern watch-tower, and her hair unbound,
> Wet with the tears which should adorn the ground,
> Dimmed the aërial eyes that kindle day.

Here the phrase "eastern watch-tower" is a literal translation of the word *balcona,* which is derived from the
Arabic *bala,* "look-out place," and was used in early
Italian for the "sky," or the "East," or as "window of
Heaven." Considering the common theme of the two
poems and the similar position of the incident in the
parallel fables, Shelley's use of the phrase must indicate
that he had his eye upon the famous Italian poem. In a
letter dated November 9, 1815, Shelley had ordered from
Lackington, Allen and Co., "an Italian poem by Marino
called L'Adone"—a fact which would seem to indicate
an early interest in the Adonis fable. But we should regard
the Italian poems no more than the Greek as Shelley's
models. The epithet "most musical of mourners" which
Shelley applies to Urania shows that he is aware of the
many poets who have composed laments for Aphrodite on
the death of Adonis. We are to understand that Shelley's
poem is operating upon a long mythological and literary
tradition, and our consciousness of the fact is requisite to
a perception of the composite character of the poem.

Adonais is brilliant but not always clear. Despite the fact
that Shelley's finest powers were employed in it, and that

it contains some of his noblest verse, one feels that he has not overcome the immense difficulties which he laid in his own way. For Shelley's attempt to carry a complicated device throughout the poem, a dexterity and superficial brilliance were needed, alien to a great poetic conception. The myth which constituted the enfolding theme of the poem had to be generalized until it was obscured and in the manifold applications weakened until it meant no single thing. The figure Adonais became so diaphanous that it did not emerge wholly either as Keats or as Adonis. Shelley so involved himself in the intricacies of his medium that, despite an ingenuity of which no other poet of his generation was capable, he did not effect a clear-cut poetic conception.

Goethe's Helena

No MORE remarkable or fantastic use of mythological material was made during the entire course of the Romantic period than the Helena story which Goethe wove through the episodic *Second Part of Faust*.

Although much of the play has generally been regarded as incomprehensible, admirers of Goethe have continued and will continue to read it because of the eminent place which Goethe occupies in the world of letters and because the very incomprehensibility of the play becomes a kind of challenge to one's critical powers.

The following essay is addressed to readers whose curiosity has been aroused by Goethe's intricate manipulation of the Helena theme. Hitherto, I believe, no commentary has revealed what a thing of shreds and patches the story is. Yet an examination of its character is interesting, not as an exposure of the failing powers of a great poet in his last work, but as a study of the manner in which a subtle poetic mind strove to use the myths of an ancient civilization as a vehicle for modern expression. In Goethe's struggles to bring Helen of Troy and Faust into intelligible relation to each other there is a salutary poetic lesson.

In the old *Faust Book* which was Goethe's chief source for the legend of the famous German magus, there were two incidents involving Helen of Troy. Among the prankish escapades attributed to Faust was the story that at the request of a company of students, Faust conjured up an image of Helen, displaying her beauty for the admiration of the crowd. It is further related that many years later, remembering the beauty of Helen, he called her again into existence, married her, and had a son by her whom he named Justus Faustus.

In the *First Part of Faust*, Goethe paid no attention to these stories, but during the many years that his mind was at work upon the Faust story, he was constantly fascinated by the possibility of making some use of them in a projected *Second Part*. From time to time, and over the course of many years, he formed plans and wrote out scenes or the beginnings of scenes. A version of the story involving Helen, later rejected, was read aloud by Goethe to some of his friends as early as 1780. He commenced the recomposition of it in 1800, mentioning it frequently in his correspondence with Schiller, but he laid it aside again in the autumn of that year and did not resume work upon the subject until twenty-five years had elapsed. At last, in 1827, it was published as a separate work under the title *Helena: A Classic Romantic Phantasmagoria*. Finally, only a few months before his death, Goethe completed the whole *Second Part of Faust*, having worked out the scenes involving Helen of Troy to his own satisfaction. Needless to say, during the long evolution of the play, plans in respect to it had been frequently altered.

As the play now stands, the Helena theme, incorporated into the labyrinthine windings of the plot, admittedly is an almost disparate part of the play. Not unlike some of the secondary actions of the Shakespearian plays, it is at times intertwined with the main action but remains an essentially separate thing. Goethe was content to allow the episodic character of the *Second Part of Faust*, permitting the various elements to bear only a general relation to the play as a whole.

As the legend dictated, Helen of Troy appears in the action twice. Once an image of her is conjured up for the admiration of the court, and again the incident of Faust's marriage to her, with the birth of a son to the pair, is elaborated into the complex Helena episode which constitutes the whole of the long third act. In addition to the actual appearances of Helen, there are incidents and scenes which form the preparatory machinery. The most notable of these are the scene with the Mothers, and the famous Classical Walpurgis Night, both of which are devised primarily as the means by which Helen of Troy is produced for the required action.

The greatest difficulty which the modern reader of the *Second Part of Faust* encounters is not the difficulty of understanding what Goethe wrote, but the difficulty of understanding what prompted him to write it. It must be at once apparent that the relations between a magus of the German Renaissance and the classical Helen of Troy are bound in the nature of things to be incongruous. In the Faust story they are acceptable as a species of Till Eulenspiegel prank. Marlowe, in his *Faustus*, accepted the appearance of Helen as a mere trick. He attempted to give it little significance beyond its mere indication of Faust's power. Goethe, however, undertook to endow the two incidents with significance of a more serious sort. One cannot help feeling that Goethe's judgment must at times have rebelled against a situation which his poetic vitality nevertheless accepted as a challenge.

We know that he accepted the challenge of the Helen story. He declared that, the story relating to Helen having been a part of the Faust legend and even of the puppet play of Faust, it had become his duty to deal with the theme. In order therefore to understand the amazing workings of the *Second Part of Faust*, it is necessary to consider the nature of the task which Goethe undertook.

It is obvious that the task would strain the resources of the most inventive mind. Goethe must have regarded his problem as threefold. The elements of the original stories relating to Faust and Helen must be included in the action in recognizable form; that is, they must not be distorted so far as to lose all resemblance to the original. The treatment of the stories must be interwoven harmoniously into the treatment of the legend as a whole. Lastly, the stories must be endowed with some superior significance of sufficient dignity to warrant their inclusion in a play which would convert the life of Faust into a drama of the development of man's soul. The problems which these necessities raised, and the intricate solutions which Goethe found for them, account for many elements in the completed play which are difficult to understand.

The first and greatest difficulty which Goethe had to surmount must have been the selection of a proper significance for the introduction of Helen of Troy into the sort of spiritualized treatment of the Faust legend which he had undertaken. Helen was, of course, famous for her beauty. Goethe could seize hold of that indisputable fact, and we know that he did so. But the difficulty lay not in the fact of Helen's beauty, but in the nature of it. The beauty of Helen was a physical beauty. It was a beauty which called out the love, the jealousy, the indulgence, the gallantry of men. But no matter how chivalrously the poets had treated her, no one had ever suggested that Helen's beauty was a force for good, a high influence upon the soul. Yet Goethe desired to convert her into a spiritual influence upon Faust, and by extension, into a symbol of the refining influence of the passion for beauty in the soul of man.

If Goethe had been successful in converting the wily Iphigenia of Euripides into a figure whose devotion to the good had overcome evil, might he not also elevate the character of Helen of Troy? If anyone could have accomplished such a transfiguration, Goethe would have done it in the *Second Part of Faust*, for he counted the plan among his major projects over a period of fifty years. But in the last analysis one must conclude that the effort was unsuccessful, and that Goethe, like many another poet who contrived too subtly with classical myth, was entrapped in the meshes of his own invention.

The two successive appearances of Helen demanded by the legend gave the poet an opportunity to present Helen first as a mere vision of beauty which should inspire the restless Faust with a yearning which his soul had not known before and secondly as an embodiment of that which his soul had sought and at last possessed.

The first of the two appearances was more manageable than the second. Goethe elected to show Helen, not merely as a beautiful woman, but as the model form of beauty in woman. She represented, indeed, the ideal beauty of the Winckelmann aesthetic. The portrayal of the incident is shaped somewhat by the circumstances of the preceding scenes. Faust is at the palace of the Emperor. In the original legend, Faust had evoked Helen of Troy at his own house at the request of a group of students who had assembled there. These students, having come uninvited to Faust's house on a certain Sunday, and having provided themselves with meat and drink, fell into conversation about the beauty of women. One expressed the desire to see Helen of Troy, so famous for her beauty. Faust, ordering them to remain silent and seated, left the hall, returning with Helen gowned in velvet. After the students had admired her, he led her out of the hall, and the students saw no more of her. This incident had, however, been preceded by an earlier incident at the court of the Emperor very similar to it. The Emperor had requested Faust to make Alexander the Great and his paramour, famous for her beauty, appear before them, and Faust had done so. Since in Goethe's play Faust was already at the court of the Emperor, Goethe apparently decided to telescope the two incidents, producing, not Alexander the Great and his beautiful paramour, but Paris Alexander and Helen of Troy.

The Emperor has demanded that Faust instantly produce Paris and Helen, distinctly shown in their ancient shape and bearing. They represent, we are told, the model forms of man and woman. Here is the first indication that Goethe is to endow Helen with particular significance. In the legend she is famous simply for her beauty. In the play she is the ideal beauty.

Mephistopheles disclaims the power to evoke the images desired, probably because, since he is a later and northern myth, he has no knowledge of the Greek myths and no power over them. He sends Faust to the realm of the much too mysterious Mothers. Scholars have certainly made too much of the Mothers. Goethe has himself explained that the Mothers were an invention of his own, based on some hints from Plutarch. It is obvious that Goethe needed an interesting device by which Faust could summon up a myth in visible form. He had remembered some mysterious goddesses mentioned by Plutarch as being called the Mothers, and he had remembered likewise from Plutarch a sort of Neoplatonic realm in which subsisted "the causes, shapes and primitive images of all things which have ever existed and which shall exist." Such a realm, presided over by the convenient Mothers, was an eminently suitable place from which a mythical person might be evoked, and thither Mephistopheles sends Faust.

The court assembles, and after some dramatic elaborations, Faust produces first a Greek temple, and then, with the temple as a stage setting, a moving tableau or dumb show, in which Helen and Paris appear. Goethe has encountered a difficulty which he resolves in a somewhat incongruous fashion. He has elected to present Paris and Helen as model forms. Unfortunately for his purpose, although both Paris and Helen were famous in antiquity for their beauty, neither painters nor sculptors had established any tradition in the plastic arts of representing either Paris or Helen as a model form. It would have been convenient had there been some famous picture or sculptured group for Goethe to imitate in his tableau. He met the situation by borrowing from antique gems the conventional picture of Endymion receiving a kiss from Artemis. With disarming frankness Goethe at once confesses his theft by making one of the court ladies declare that the image is like "Endymion and Luna—as they're drawn!" and the Poet agrees with her.

Dramatically the incident provides Faust with his opportunity to see perfect beauty for the first time, and

Goethe does not fail to make clear, in an excited speech by Faust, that the experience has made a profound impression.

Otherwise the scene is unimportant in the structure of the play. Goethe seizes the opportunity to allow his mind to play over the scene with a light and amusing sarcasm. The object is to poke fun at the vulgar attitudes of polite society in the presence of a beauty which that society has not the capacity to understand. He has his fun with a variety of characters who were, probably, real persons.

In order to understand the action which follows, it is necessary to remember that that portion of the play which deals with the second evocation of Helen had been finished and published before the play as a whole was completed. At the time when *Helena: A Classic Romantic Phantasmagoria* was first published, Goethe had expressly stated that he was not ready to reveal how Helena had been brought back from Orcus into life. She stepped forth upon the stage, but the occasion and the method of her sudden appearance had not been explained. The problem of over-arching this difficulty Goethe felt as a challenge to his ingenuity.

Much of the poetry of the Romantic generation is marred by the poets' admiration for complicated devices through which to conduct the action. This trait of a poetic period is nowhere more astonishingly demonstrated than in the elaborate sequence of devices by which Goethe felt it desirable to evoke Helen for her place in the action of the drama.

For the first appearance of Helen, Goethe had invented the Mothers as a means for restoring a mythical person to temporary existence. For the second appearance, he considered a number of possibilities. Various of his notes and written plans give us some hint of rejected or partially rejected plans. But it is to the play itself, not to the rejected fragments or to the rejected plans, that we must turn for insight into the complex procedure of his invention. Actually he appears to have altered his plans in a very confusing fashion while he was writing, without taking the pains to remove inconsistencies brought about by the changes.

At the time of the composition of the *Helena*, it would appear that he had decided upon two devices, involving first a visit to the Graeae by Mephistopheles, and secondly an expedition on the part of Mephistopheles and Faust into Thessaly to obtain the aid of the Haemonian women.

In the Helena episode of the third act, the reader is somewhat puzzled to find Mephistopheles engaged in a twofold masquerade. He retains his own character but it is oddly superimposed upon the role of a stewardess of the house of Menelaus. Her appearance and name indicate that she has some connection with the three daughters of Phorkys, those obscure mythological women who shared amongst them but one eye and one tooth, and who were known to myth as the Graeae or the Phorkyads. Mephistopheles masquerades as a huge and hideous woman called Phorkyas. She has but a single eye and a single tooth, and the chorus at once recognize her resemblance to the fabulous Gray Women. The point of the masquerade is by no means clear. If we suppose, however, that Goethe had had intentions respecting the Graeae which were never fulfilled, the appearance of Mephistopheles in the guise of Phorkyas will be explained.

There is a legend recorded by Apollodorus that when Perseus went in search of the Gorgons, he first went to the Graeae. He persuaded them to give him the eye and the tooth, and, when he had obtained possession of these indispensable objects, he refused to return them until the Graeae divulged the way to certain nymphs who armed him to meet Medusa. It is likely that Goethe originally intended to have Mephistopheles visit the Graeae for information as to how he might obtain the power to summon Helen of Troy up from the realm of the shades. By cajolery and flattery he would obtain possession of the eye and the tooth, which, like Perseus, he would then refuse to return until the Graeae granted his request. Apparently he was to have retained the eye and the tooth, assuming himself the actual appearance of one of the Gray Sisters, Enyo, whom Goethe mentions in his notes. Then he would have continued in the masquerade until Helen returned to Hades. At any rate, at the time the *Helena* was published, clearly Mephistopheles was so masquerading, and there must have been some reason for it. But by the time Goethe came to the composition of the anterior parts of the play his plans had changed. The original function of the Graeae had been dropped. But rather than change the already published third act, which would have been the logical thing to do, Goethe attempted lamely to patch up the inconsistent parts. Some incident was necessary to lead up to the otherwise inexplicable appearance of Phorkyas in the succeeding act. Goethe took refuge in the unsatisfactory device of having Mephistopheles encounter the Graeae during the events of the Classical Walpurgis Night. Their cavern had, perforce, to be shifted to Thessaly, where it had no business to be. The cajolery and flattery with which Mephistopheles was to have approached the Gray Sisters is retained, probably from lines already written. But since the Graeae were no longer needed as instruments in the obtaining of Helen, the incident ends vaguely, without Mephistopheles' obtaining possession of the eye and tooth, or even asking for it. Mephistopheles is satisfied merely to imitate the appearance of the sisters. With this inadequate piece of patching Goethe prepares us for the now meaningless masquerade of Mephistopheles in the third act.

The actual agents for the raising of Helen from Hades were not, however, to have been the Phorkyads. Goethe had a more ingenious device in store—the power of the Haemonian women. The Haemonian or Thessalian women were hags—witches, in short—who were very famous in antiquity. From remote times Thessaly had been famous for the magic practiced there, and until late Roman times the sinister doings of the disreputable hags of Thessaly had continued to attract the attention of the poets.

For Goethe's purpose the Haemonian women were admirably suited, because they were particularly noted for their power to bring back the dead to life. Not only could they revive the bodies of recently dead persons, calling back their spirits to answer questions, but they rivaled the powers of the blind Teiresias in calling up shades from the underworld. Indeed it was claimed for one of their number, Manto, the Thessalian sibyl, that she was a descendant of Teiresias. They had, moreover, the power utterly to subvert the laws of nature, and even to force the most powerful gods to do their will. Obviously such creatures were eminently suitable agents to bring Helen of Troy up from the realm of the shades and to endow her with the life necessary for her reappearance in the drama of Faust's life.

At the time of the composition of the Helena episode, Goethe had already determined to employ the agency of the Haemonian women in the evocation of Helen and her companions. Thus in the third act, after Helen returns to Hades, Penthalis, the leader of Helen's companions, informs the others that they are now rid of the power of the Thessalian hag. It seems likely, however, that Goethe had intended to keep his story parallel to the Perseus story. Just as the Graeae, after Perseus had obtained the eye and the tooth, sent him to the intermediary nymphs before he reached the Gorgons, so in this story the Graeae were to send Mephistopheles to the Haemonian women. Equipped with the eye and the tooth and the dread appearance of Enyo, Mephistopheles could force the hags to do his bidding.

But during the composition of the anterior portions of the play, Goethe appears to have struck upon an invention more to his fancy. He wished to preserve the conceit that Mephistopheles was a northern and mediaeval myth who could not be expected to know much of such antique figures as the Graeae and the Thessalian witches. He needed an intermediary agent to bridge the gap lying between his mediaeval and his classical figures. For that purpose he dropped the Graeae from their projected role, and substituted for them a new creation, Homunculus. Goethe describes Homunculus as a *daemon*. He is also a mediaeval creation, brought into being according to the Paracelsian formula for the making of an homunculus. As a Paracelsian homunculus he is sufficiently mediaeval, as a daemon sufficiently classical, to make a convenient bridge between the mediaeval and the ancient cultures. Homunculus knows about the Thessalian witches. It is he who proposes to

Mephistopheles that they conduct Faust to Thessaly in order that he may enter upon his quest for Helen. Thus the dramatic function of the Graeae was, in the process of Goethe's composition, replaced by that of Homunculus.

Having hit upon so unusual a device for linking the mediaeval and the antique worlds, it pleased Goethe to endow Homunculus with more than merely a technical role. Homunculus, one infers, is the inventive spirit of the poet himself. The craving to come into being, which characterizes Homunculus, is a whimsical statement of the poet's desire to bring his poetic invention into being. When the invention is finally completed, that is, when the liaison between the mediaeval and the antique is actually accomplished and the German magus is given possession of the classical Helen, Homunculus is no longer necessary. Goethe shatters him to get rid of him. But it is no accident that he shatters him at the end of the second act, for when Goethe finally completed the linking of his Helena episode with the other portions of the action at that point, it was the last exercise of his poetic invention. The play was finished. There was nothing more to come into being. The Homunculus might be shattered, the light extinguished.

In the second scene of Act II, Goethe commences to prepare us for the introduction of the second of Helen's appearances. According to the *Faust Book*, when Faust was in his twenty-third year the desire to possess Helen took hold of him. We are told that this ambition came into his mind "after he had slept his first sleep."

Faithful to the legend, Goethe introduces the matter in this fashion. In the midst of the scene in which Homunculus is created, a stage direction tells us that a side door opens showing Faust stretched out upon a couch. He is sleeping the "first sleep" required by the legend. The phial containing Homunculus slips out of Wagner's hands and hovers over Faust, shining upon him; Homunculus, by his occult power, interprets for the audience the dream which is passing through Faust's mind. This dream is of the conception of Helen. The graceful picture which Goethe paints for us seems to have been inspired by one of the many famous paintings of Leda and the swan, perhaps that of Correggio. Against a background of fair scenery, with waters moving in forest shadows, the figures of women undressing emerge. The picture becomes clearer. Leda, who is to become the mother of Helen, is bathing. Her beauty splendidly expresses her descent from the gods or high heroic races. The swans appear. The maidens fly. Only Leda, proudly composed, awaits the coming of the swan prince, Jupiter. The picture fades, and Homunculus tells us no more of Faust's dreaming. Although there has been no mention of Helen, we know that Faust's desire for her beauty has been awakened, and, as Homunculus explains, that Faust will no longer be satisfied with his northern and gothic surroundings. We feel the first intimations in Homunculus' words that the approaching experience with Helen is to signify the awakening of the northern consciousness to classical beauty. Mephistopheles, and heretofore Faust, have belonged to a northern, mediaeval, and "Romantic" world. Helen is to be a symbol of classical culture.

Homunculus has a plan to satisfy the new yearning in Faust's mind. This plan is nothing less than to obtain Helen for Faust. Homunculus does not at once reveal that plan nor tell how Helen is to be obtained, but we may infer that the plan is nevertheless complete in his mind. Faust is to be transported to Thessaly, where the Haemonian witches will be called upon to evoke Helen by their magic powers. Homunculus is very mysterious about the plan. He suggests that there is a region to the southwest, unknown to Mephistopheles. It is the great plain through which Peneus flows, where Pharsalus is situated. These indirect references to Thessaly mean nothing to Mephistopheles, who is puzzled and disinterested. But Homunculus rouses his interest by mentioning the Thessalian witches. Mephistopheles recalls having made some inquiries long ago concerning these creatures, and he agrees to "descend to the Peneus." As the act closes we understand that Mephistopheles and Homunculus will transport Faust to the great plain of Thessaly.

In discussing the matter with Mephistopheles, Homunculus has recalled that it is Classical Walpurgis Night. But the fact that it is Classical Walpurgis Night is merely incidental to the plan. The real object of Homunculus is to get Faust in touch with the Thessalian witches, who will procure Helen of Troy for him.

The primary concern of the second act is to conduct the action from the moment of Faust's arrival upon Thessalian soil to the point at which the Helena story of the third act commences. Goethe had originally intended to divide this action into two parts. The first was to have comprised the incidents attendant upon Faust's arrival in Thessaly, his quest for the Haemonian hag whose power he should employ, and his eventual success in enlisting the aid of Manto, an obscure Thessalian sibyl, descendant of Teiresias, of whose legendary existence Goethe had learned through the *Lexicon* of Suidas. The second part of the action was to have comprised an account of a descent into Hades. Goethe's plans for the descent into Hades were ambitious ones. Manto, Faust, and presumably Mephistopheles, were to have descended to the lower world through a cavern which led downward below the hollow foot of Mount Olympus. They were to have presented themselves before Persephone, to have pleaded for the return of Helen, citing the precedent of other shades who had revisited the world above. Eventually, through the power of Manto, Persephone was to have yielded Helen upon certain conditions compatible with the account of her visit to the earth already printed in the third act.

As the play actually was completed, the original design was both obscured and altered. The action of the first part of the plan concerning the events that take place upon Thessalian soil was obscured by the subordination of the main action to the incidents of the Classical Walpurgis Night. The action of the second part of the plan, the descent into Hades, was omitted altogether.

It is not difficult to understand why Goethe altered his plans in respect to the descent into Hades. It is likely that in his extreme old age he was reluctant to attempt something which he felt he could not finish with credit. The theme of a descent into Hades has been treated with the noblest distinction by the very greatest poets. Doubtless Goethe was reluctant about attempting to emulate such world-famous accomplishments, uncertain whether age and death would spare him the requisite energy and time. Unfortunately, however, he was unwilling to relinquish all of the plans that he had made. Portions of the descent into Hades had been written before the project as a whole was abandoned. In the effort to salvage these already written portions, he made the unhappy decision to recast and utilize them as portions of a Classical Walpurgis Night.

I think that it was in reading the *Pharsalia* of Lucan that Goethe hit upon the idea of having a Classical Walpurgis Night which would make an amusing and interesting counterpart of the Walpurgis Night on the Brocken. In the preparation of his plan to conduct Faust to Thessaly, where he might encounter a Thessalian witch, Goethe must naturally have turned to the *Pharsalia* for Lucan's account of the battle of Pharsalia, the most notable historical event which had taken place upon Thessalian soil. And Lucan, too, would be called to his mind because of the famous description of Erichtho, the Thessalian witch.

Lucan tells us that after the battle of Pharsalia, such was the rage of Caesar as he surveyed the bloody scene of Pharsalia's plain, covered with dead bodies, that he would allow no burial for the dead. The bodies of the slain were left for the birds and beasts of prey, and for time. The Pharsalian plain, with its unburied dead, became a "field of ghosts." Goethe's imagination must have seized hold of the idea that upon the visit of Faust to Thessaly some effective use could be made of this ghost-haunted plain. Then, enlarging upon the idea, he saw that he could introduce, not merely the ghosts of the unburied soldiers of the Roman armies, but "the legion of the Hellenic legends," the "fabulous forms of ancient days." In the quest of Helen, who was herself a myth, Faust and his companions could encounter mythical personages who were somehow connected with the region through which they were passing. Encounters with these personages could be blended into the action, but, better still, they could be turned to satirical purpose. The ingenuity of the scene would lie, not merely in the fact that in such a fashion the progress of Faust through Thessaly could be enlivened by classical reminiscence, but in that the various figures of such a Classical Walpurgis Night could be given a modern application, turned for a whimsical, or semiserious, or profoundly telling thrust.

It seems likely that Goethe's original intention was to confine himself, in his Walpurgis Night, to figures native to the Thessalian scene. There was enough legend connected with Thessaly to supply him the material necessary to carry out such a project. But when he gave up his plan to write an account of Faust's descent into Hades, he had on his hands various portions, partially completed, of *that* unfinished project. What he actually did was to transfer his cherished fragments of the uncompleted descent into Hades into the Thessalian Walpurgis Night, hoping that the loose form demanded of the Walpurgis Night would accommodate various scraps of invention intended for another purpose. The result is an altogether disjointed and haphazard structure, the central portion of which is overwhelmed by a profusion of unconnected parts, many of them composed in Goethe's best style and no one of them without merit had it retained its original function.

Undoubtedly in his extreme old age Goethe's judgment had failed him, and in the effort to bring together his long projected play he considered that he might save treasured portions of his plans by lumping them in a form which would make few demands upon his shortening period of life. As a bewildered but forgiving reader attempts to follow the poet through the play, it is still possible to discern the materials which had been shaped for a superior building.

The action as originally devised in Goethe's mind had by no means been lacking in form. The peculiar geographical features of the great Thessalian plain and the rich historical and mythological associations of the region were well adapted to the dramatic action planned. Goethe had taken the trouble to equip himself with a great deal of information useful for the development and enrichment of his theme. Thessaly, as recent events have recalled to us, is an area bounded on all four sides and entirely enclosed by mountains. At the west is the great central range of the Pindus Mountains. At the north, running straight across to the Aegean Sea, are the Cambunian Mountains, terminating at the east, on the Aegean, in Mount Olympus, the loftiest of the mountains of Greece. From north to south, all along the Aegean coast, are mountains of which famous Ossa and Pelion are the chief, and below them are the rocky and cavernous shores of the Aegean. At the south, extending from the Pindus range to the Aegean, are the Othrys Mountains, which reach the sea between the Malian and Pagasaean gulfs. The most celebrated of the few openings to this great enclosed square is the famous Vale of Tempe, at the northeast corner, separating Olympus from Ossa. The great plain itself is divided in two parts, separated by a range of hills which run north and south through its center. These two parts are known as Upper and Lower Thessaly, both parts being drained by the River Peneus and its tributaries, their combined waters finding an outlet to the sea through the gorge of the Vale of Tempe.

The action takes place on various parts of this great

plain and its adjacent seacoast of the Aegean. Thus Goethe avails himself of the peculiar geographical conformation of Thessaly as a mighty stage for the drama, in which the scene shifts rapidly from one varied part to another, without losing the encircling unity of a single location.

Myth and history had made this mountain-inscribed plain famous. The poet who intended to move his creations across so famous a land would find ample matter with which to enrich his theme. The Thessalian plain had, for instance, been the scene, not alone of the great battle of Pharsalia, where Caesar had defeated Pompey in one of the most famous battles of antiquity, but also of various battles in which the last Philip of Macedon and his son Perseus had fought a losing war with Rome, in which the power of Macedonia was broken and the independence of Greece was lost. These historical facts might serve as the subject for reflective comment as the figures of the drama were carried by the shifting action to different parts of the plain. Thessaly had been the ancient home of Jason; there the Argonauts had assembled, and there had built and launched their famous ship. Mount Pelion had been the home of the centaurs, and on that mountain had been the cave of the great teacher Chiron, who had instructed Jason, Hercules, Achilles, and all the heroes of the elder generation. The poet could hardly fail to make some reminiscent use of associations so famous. And there was much more to attract his attention: the temple of Aesculapius at Tricca, the largest and most famous of the shrines devoted to the art of healing; the medicinal herbs with which the centaur Chiron had become famous as a healer, and which the Thessalian women had used in their enchantments; the legend of the great earthquake which had

rent Ossa from Pelion; the famous witch Erichtho, of
whom Lucan has left so horrible a picture; Manto, the
Thessalian sibyl; the strange reputation of the witches
for their power to bring down to earth the heavenly
bodies, even the moon itself; the piling of Ossa on Pelion
in the war with the giants; and much more, too—enough
to tax the allusive powers of the most dexterous poet.
If the associations of the land alone were not sufficient,
there was the Aegean Sea where Nereus had his cave—
not far distant from the Vale of Tempe, if we may trust
Lucan's statement that Nereus heard the sound of the
earthquake that rent the Vale of Tempe. And almost in
sight of the Thessalian shore was the island of Samothrace,
where dwelt those mysterious Cabiri who had excited so
much controversy among the German mythologists.

Had Goethe not tampered with his plans, the value of
the locality as a stage for the action would have been
great. The wandering of the strange triad, Faust, Mephistopheles, and Homunculus, in quest of the mythical Helen
through a mediaeval Thessaly in which the ghosts of
antiquity haunted the regions which history and myth
had made famous, should have made an excellent device
for the operation of Goethe's poetic invention—an invention so adept in turning to account the possibilities attendant upon a dramatic situation. But as the play finally stands,
the result of so many compromises and alterations, the
peculiar value of the locality is lost. Many—indeed, most—
of the monstrous figures encountered in the Classical
Walpurgis Night have no connection whatsoever with
Thessaly. The careful division of the scenes into various
portions of Thessaly—the Pharsalian plains, with the River
Enipeus in the background, the various parts of the Peneus

River, and the rocky seacoast of the Aegean—loses most of its point since few of the figures which appear in those scenes have a necessary connection with the locality.

To a certain extent the original design is carried out. At the suggestion of Homunculus, he and Mephistopheles conduct Faust through the air to Thessaly, where they alight upon a plain not far from the Pharsalian fields. Here in a magnificent passage Goethe's design grows apparent. Pharsalia is haunted with its ghosts. Goethe seizes hold of the situation to give it a modern, and an eternal, application. Pharsalia reënacted in an "after vision." . . . How often will it be repeated! It will forever be reënacted. The ghosts which haunt the battlefield of Pharsalia are the ghosts which haunt a Europe devastated by Napoleon and haunt a frightened world today. The empty struggle for power is continued by men who, unable to rule themselves, attempt to impose their will upon others, and force opposes force. Goethe, like Lucan before him, had seen the monstrous folly of the Pharsalias of the world and wept the loss of freedom which was the price of all the squandered blood.

Goethe's reflections are put into the mouth of Erichtho, who, sitting in the darkness, broods over her evil reputation and watches the flickering campfires of the ghostly Pharsalia. She is the first of the mythological figures whom we encounter in Thessaly, and her presence is eminently appropriate, since she is the most famous of the Thessalian witches. In the *Pharsalia* Lucan has given an extensive and lurid account of her tremendous powers. It was natural that she should appear near the field of Pharsalia, since according to Lucan that was the region in which she was accustomed to operate. Goethe had, perhaps, encountered a difficulty in the handling of Erichtho, since, as the most famous of the Thessalian witches, she might well be the one chosen to guide Faust to the underworld. But the action would have been thus terminated too quickly. Goethe had in mind another witch for his purpose. Moreover, the sinister Erichtho had been given so notable a literary life by Lucan that there was little left to say of her without mere borrowing from the Roman. Goethe had at one time planned to engage in a little satire on philological speculations concerning the etymological and symbolic relationship between Erichtho and Erichthonius, but he abandoned the plan, contenting himself with a glance at the "superfluous slander" heaped upon Erichtho by Ovid, Lucan, and perhaps Lucan's scholiasts.

To have selected the ghost-haunted battlefield of Pharsalia as the scene of the initial action was well considered, since the transition from the field haunted by the dead to wider areas haunted by myths might be accomplished naturally.

Erichtho calls attention to the legion of Hellenic myths which gather at this night's awful festival, and the airy travelers from the north scatter, each in pursuit of his own adventures. Faust enters upon the quest of Helen. Goethe at once reveals the spiritual nature of Faust's quest—a quest which involves the desire to escape from the limitations of the mediaeval and northern tradition into the broader and freer culture of the Greeks—by showing the influence which the mere arrival upon Greek soil has upon Faust:

> Here, on Grecian land!
> I felt at once the earth whereon I stand.

Through me, the sleeper, fresher spirit stealing,
I rise refreshed, Antaeus in my feeling.
(Taylor's translation)

The refreshment which Faust feels is not merely the influence upon Faust of the first contact with Greece, nor is it the Renaissance in Germany speaking through Faust. It is rather the new awakening, the spirit of Greek art speaking through Winckelmann, and Lessing, and Schiller, and Goethe himself. It is in Germany the second and the greater Renaissance, the influence of the Greek expanding and arousing the provincial German culture to the lofty and generous internationalism which marked the highest achievement of the German mind.

In the first scene Faust takes little part, merely inquiring for Helen. The sight of various figures reminiscent of ancient times comforts him with the feeling that he is on the right way. He is informed by a sphinx that Chiron will lead him to Helen. In the second scene Faust approaches the Peneus River, where is enacted a graceful scene of the approach of the swan to Leda, again reminding us of the birth of Helen. Chiron the centaur arrives, becoming Faust's guide. The appearance of Chiron, who is, by legendary right, native to Thessaly, allows Goethe to introduce matters proper to the Thessalian scene. A conversation ensues in which Goethe turns his classical erudition into pointed banter at the arts of pedagogy and of healing. Chiron gives us a splendid reminiscence, in glowing and heroic verse, of the great heroes of the Argonauts whom he has taught. It leads to his tribute to Hercules, here regarded as the model of masculine beauty. Talk of the most beautiful man leads Faust to inquire about the most beautiful woman, and Goethe invents for Chiron an imaginary incident concerning Helen. This allows him, in lieu of a legendary connection between the two, to talk about Helen. There is a discussion of her age, with a thrust at the disputes of modern philologists on that vexed question. Faust suggests that she should be timeless, thus preparing for the actual appearance of Helen in the next act, when she does indeed escape the limitations of age and time. Chiron offers to take Faust to Manto, who is the personage whom Goethe reserved as the agent for obtaining Helen. His choice had fallen upon Manto because Suidas had described her as a Thessalian sibyl, and her connection with Thessaly thus made her useful. Goethe makes her a priestess of Aesculapius, perhaps recalling that there had been a famous shrine of Aesculapius at Tricca, in Thessaly. Goethe's geography becomes a little uneasy at this point in the play. Chiron transports Faust to Manto's dwelling, which, we are informed, is near the Peneus River and at the foot of Mount Olympus. He seems also to identify the place as the site of the battle of Pydna, though no such geographical combination is possible except on the stage. Chiron's conversation with Manto may be intended as a slur at the rash experiments of the allopathic practice fashionable in the medicine of Goethe's time, and perhaps at the growing fashion for hydropathy, the water cure. Manto inquires what Faust desires, and, when she learns that he wishes Helen of Troy, she replies that she loves persons who are lured by the impossible. In this remark she speaks well in the Thessalian tradition, for Lucan says of the Thessalian women that "they practice all that is judged impossible." With little ado, Manto at once starts with Faust through a cavern which leads down to Hades through the hollow foot of Olympus. She tells Faust that it was she who smuggled Orpheus into Hades, but that is a detail invented by Goethe. At this point the narration respecting Faust abruptly ends.

The remainder of the action in the Classical Walpurgis Night has nothing to do with Faust or his quest for Helen. It is concerned, instead, with the disposal of parts of the originally projected descent into Hades, with the solution of the altered and abandoned visit to the Phorkyads, and with the disposal of Homunculus after he is no longer needed.

As the play now stands, there are two disjointed and cumbersome pieces of satire, dismembered and scattered through the maze of the Classical Walpurgis Night. One of these is part of a projected satire against the Plutonist-Neptunist controversy; the other is part of a satire directed against the doctrine of economic mercantilism.

In Goethe's time geologists were agitated over a controversy concerning the formation of the earth's surface. There were two schools of thought, the Plutonists and the Neptunists. The Neptunists, after Lehmann and Werner, assumed that the earth had at first wholly been covered by water, which had held in solution the materials of all rocks. From this aqueous solution, granite, gneiss, and other crystalline formations were first precipitated. Other formations were deposited later, in layers designated as transition, secondary, and alluvium. "This arbitrary hypothesis," says Lyell, "rejected all intervention of igneous agency, volcanoes being regarded as partial and superficial accidents, of trifling account among the great causes which have modified the external structure of the globe." The popularity of the Neptunian hypothesis waned when Hutton taught that granite, as well as trap, was of igneous

origin. The theory of igneous origin was extended to
account for the origin of all stony substances, and mountains themselves were regarded as the result of great
igneous upheavals. Those who advocated the igneous interpretation were known as the Plutonists. Goethe clung to
the Neptunian hypothesis because it was more in harmony
with the idea of an orderly, slow, but progressive development. As he hated violence in society or art, so he opposed
the doctrine of violent upheaval in nature. He perceived
clearly, however, that the Neptunian theory was being
displaced by the superior evidence adduced in support of
the Plutonian.

It would appear that for the *Second Part of Faust* he
had planned an amusing satire in which the Plutonists
would be victorious, but their victory a victory gained in
Hell. He planned this satire to be a portion of the drama
which would unfold as Faust and his companions descended into Hades. In the realm of shades, two ancient
Greek philosophers were to be represented as disputing
over the very controversy then agitating modern Germany. For his purpose he had found two primitive Greek
philosophers about whom not a great deal is known, but
who advanced theories which, with a little distortion,
could be made applicable to the controversy. These two
were Thales and Anaxagoras, the former representing the
Neptunists, the latter the Plutonists. It is probable that
both Pluto and Neptune themselves were to have figured
in the dispute.

In abandoning the descent into Hades, Goethe was
unwilling to relinquish the project altogether, particularly
since he had already written portions of it. These portions
he transferred to the Classical Walpurgis Night, with

little or no effort to adjust them to their altered location.
Had the satire been written as an incident of Faust's
incursion into the realm of Pluto, the application to the
Plutonists would have been deft and the victory of the
Plutonists in Hell would have been amusingly satirical.
Had Thales and Anaxagoras been encountered among the
shades of the dead, rather than among the ghosts of
Thessaly, their excuse for being and their part in the satire
would have been plausible and artistically connected. In
the play as it stands, much of the satirical element is introduced through the agency of a figure called Seismos, who
gives various demonstrations of his power of upheaval
and boasts of earthquakes he has caused in Thessaly and
elsewhere. Seismos is the only personification in the Classical Walpurgis Night; he is not a mythological figure. It
seems very likely that the role which he plays in the
drama was originally intended for Pluto himself, and that
in the transfer of the action from Hades to Thessaly,
where the fire god of the underworld would be inappropriate, Seismos was invented to take his place as the champion of violent upheaval. In Claudian's *Rape of Proserpine*
there is a fine passage in which the poet describes the
movements of Pluto as producing violent upheavals as he
threads his way through the labyrinth of the underworld.
The movements of Pluto were such as the modern Pluto-
ists attributed to earthquakes produced by subterranean
force. Goethe, we may imagine, had intended to depict
Pluto as demonstrating his power in a similar fashion.
Seismos, as a substitute for the god himself, has little point
in the satire. How Neptune was to have been introduced
I do not know, but one may suspect that both he and certain of his marine attendants were somehow to have been

included and that those portions of the Classical Walpurgis Night which involve Thales and Anaxagoras with various marine figures are leftover portions of the Neptunist side of the controversy.

In abandoning the descent into Hades, Goethe may have seen some color of an excuse for transferring the Neptunist controversy to Thessalian soil. Ancient geographers believed that at one time Thessaly was wholly covered by water and that a great earthquake had split Mount Ossa from Mount Olympus creating the Vale of Tempe and providing an outlet for what had previously been an inland sea. Legend attributed this work either to Hercules or to Neptune, the earthshaker. During the Plutonist-Neptunist controversy, Thessaly had been examined with considerable interest by travelers to the great plain and the Vale of Tempe. Sir Henry Holland had examined the geological structure of the remarkable rocks of Meteora in Thessaly, finding indications which might be regarded as support for either side of the Neptunist-Plutonist controversy; but at Tempe he had inclined to the belief that some convulsion of nature had indeed opened its narrow passage. When we recall that in Goethe's play Seismos boasts about his activities in Thessaly, that various upheavals occur, and that the controversy later involves certain marine myths we cannot avoid the feeling that Goethe had definite plans about Thessaly which were neither completed nor abandoned and that the geography of Thessaly and the Plutonist-Neptunist controversy had some connection with them. But in the final form of the drama the whole matter is unsatisfactory.

There is another set of figures in the Classical Walpurgis Night which has a very obscure connection with th action as a whole. These are the Gryphons, the Giant Ants, the Arimaspians, the Dactyls, the Pygmies, the Pygmy Elders, and the Emmets. None of these figures has any mythological connection with Thessaly. All, however, have two things in common: they are monsters, and they are concerned with the procuring, guarding, or use of metals which are taken from under the earth—mainly gold. In the first act of the play Goethe had directed his satire against the extension of paper credit. The Emperor is persuaded to issue paper credit against the security of un-mined gold. It seems not improbable that Goethe had intended his satire against the prevailing economic mercan-ilism of the day, exposing the fallacy that gold consti-utes real wealth. If we assume that he intended to develop his satire in that portion of the play dealing with the descent into Hades, the various figures which I have listed may be fitted into a pattern. The gold hoarders, the ex-ponents of economic mercantilism, would have been the monsters of Hell; their underground activities—grubbing gold out of the crevices of the earth and hoarding it in caverns—would have been appropriate to an action involv-ing a descent through a cavern into the bowels of the earth.

Throughout the composite parts of the Classical Wal-purgis Night, Goethe's characters wind a labyrinthine way. Faust pursues his quest for Helen, and at last disappears on his way to the lower world. Mephistopheles is momen-tarily free from the exigencies of the plot. The visit to the Graeae, now unnecessary except to excuse Goethe's pre-vious commitments, is the only office which he must perform. Homunculus has no further connection with the Helena story and must be disposed of. On both these figures Goethe may hang the looser elements of his garbled plans, and they become the racks to which are attached the pieces of the anti-mercantilist satire and the geological satire, as well as other scraps no longer related to the main action.

Mephistopheles is used mainly as the interlocutor of the various mythological figures who appear, serving merely as a device to allow the myths to give themselves utterance. Homunculus is relegated to the Anaxagoras-Thales fragments. He expresses a desire to listen to the talk of the philosophers, and Goethe's conceit that Homunculus desires to come into being permits Homunculus to fit into the Plutonist-Neptunist controversy as it involved the processes not only of inorganic, but of organic, creation. He continues to function as a guide, taking less and less part in the action, until at the end of the act Goethe shatters him, partly to get rid of him and partly to indicate that his own poetic invention no longer had any need to come into being, since this scene was the last written to complete the play.

Throughout the whole affair, Goethe's wit scintillates in so brilliant a fashion that it does much to compensate for the gross lack of continuity and even of fundamental meaning. The stray observations of Mephistopheles are often amusing and trenchant. Goethe's ingenuity is at its most acute in turning the chances of the moment into piquant satire of a hit-or-miss variety. Mephistopheles, accustomed to the gruesome North, finds himself unexpectedly at home in the equally gruesome South. He professes to be shocked at the amount of nakedness which he perceives when he mingles with the figures of the classical world. He reflects:

Indecency, 'tis true, is our ideal,
But the Antique is too alive and real;
One must with modern thought the thing bemaster,
And in the fashion variously o'erplaster.

(Taylor's translation)

He pokes fun at British travelers who are so fond of staring

at battle fields, historic traces,
Cascades, old walls, and classic dreary places.

He gets the Gryphons involved in a tirade against the etymologists. They are offended by all the unpleasant words associated etymologically with their name, and as the ancient monsters show their contempt for modern philology a highly entertaining interlude is set in motion. When Homunculus desires to listen to the talk of the ancient philosophers, Mephistopheles observes:

For here, where spectres from their hell come
Is the philosopher also welcome.

And so, wittily and sarcastically, Mephistopheles weaves an aimless way through the composed pieces which Goethe had elected to rescue by this device of a Classical Walpurgis Night.

We come at length to the most important portion of the play, the third act, which consists of the so-called Helena episode. After the bewildering maze of procedure which has led up to the appearance of Helen of Troy, the reader is anxious for a clear and significant piece of dramatic action. Helen, we have been given to understand, will represent the ideal of the classically beautiful. Here, in the classical portion of the play, when the northern mind is to be elevated by the influence of the Greek spirit, we are prepared to expect a clarity of design which will convey a definite meaning.

But the reader soon finds that in attempting the third act he has entered upon a difficult experience. The act begins in the manner of a Greek tragedy, with a remarkably fine approximation of the classic meters and a dignity and beauty of style that reveal the poet at his very best. We are prepared to expect, as Goethe leads us to the actual union of Helen of Troy with the mediaeval Faust, that some extraordinary developments will have to take place in the plot. And we are prepared to accept them as fundamentally symbolic in character.

But we are by no means prepared for the extraordinary action which is, in fact, set in motion. The masquerade of Mephistopheles in the guise of Phorkyas is exceedingly puzzling. The reader does not know that the original reason for the masquerade can no longer explain it. In abandoning his original plan to send Mephistopheles to the Graeae, from whom he was to obtain the eye and the tooth, forcing them to direct him to Helen, Goethe had completely obscured the dramatic function of Phorkyas. The retention of the role, its significance removed, is bewildering enough. But that is the least of the puzzling features of the action. No very good reason is apparent why anything happens as it does. Why, for instance, in presenting Helen as resurrected into mediaeval life, does Goethe choose to show her at the moment of returning from Troy? The episodes of Helen's life were many. Why was this one selected, and what particular appositeness has it for the drama in hand? Why does Lynceus, who has a definite resemblance to the Argonaut, suddenly figure in the action? Why, when Helen has been raised with such great difficulty from the dead, should Menelaus be announced as having followed Helen to Faust's castle?

No Thessalian sibyl raised *him* from the dead. Why does the Justus Faustus of the legend, the son of Faust and Helen, become transformed into Euphorion, who is the son of Achilles and Helen, according to some obscure myths? Indeed, one is forced to ask why at every point, and the answers which scholars have given seem never wholly adequate.

There is, however, an explanation of the problem which, while it may at first sound wholly preposterous, may be the right one: that the whole third act was written by Goethe originally as the end of an epic poem concerning Achilles and was subsequently made over—and very badly made over—to serve as the central episode for the drama about Faust.

About 1796 Goethe became intensely interested in a project for an epic poem of which Achilles was to be the central figure. One canto of this poem was actually written before Goethe abandoned the project, and this first canto was published as the *Achilleis*. It has been generally believed that the classical material aroused Goethe's interest anew in the story of Helen of Troy in connection with Faust and that he abandoned the epic in favor of a return to his earlier project. We know, at any rate, that in 1800 he actually composed a considerable portion of the *Helena*.

Although Goethe drew up several plans for portions of the epic, we have no knowledge of how he intended to end it. Let us speculate on what his intentions were.

The story of Achilles is rich with legendary material, only a small portion of which was used by Homer. Not the least interesting of the many legends gathered about the name of Achilles are those dealing with his posthumous career. Of these one of the most fascinating is that which links him with Helen of Troy in a marriage which took place on Leuke, the Island of the Blest, after his death and after Helen's return from Troy.

These stories have been preserved only in a very fragmentary form, by late and little-read authors and their scholiasts. Piecing together a number of fragmentary items, however, one receives the impression that there was once a widely known story to the effect that Achilles and Helen were ultimately destined for each other, the perfect hero to be united with the most beautiful woman in another world of bliss.

Hints as to the existence of a story connecting Achilles and Helen may be found in the following circumstances. A fragment of the Cyprian poems preserved by Proclus tells us that once Achilles asked to be allowed to look upon Helen of Troy, and that his mother, Thetis, and her mother, Aphrodite (according to that poem), arranged the meeting. There is a prophecy reported in Lykophron, in that most obscure of all poems, the *Alexandra*, that Helen would appear to Achilles in his dreams, making him pine upon his bed, distracted by her phantom face. Quintus Smyrnaeus records a prophecy that after the death of Achilles the hero should dwell in bliss upon a holy island in the Euxine Sea; the prophecy reveals the Elysian life which he should there enjoy, dwelling with gods and honored by the tribes that dwelt near by. Lykophron makes Cassandra prophesy that Achilles would be the fifth husband of Helen. And Pausanias heard a story among the Cronians that one Leonymus, being sent on a mission to the white island, Leuke, saw Achilles and other heroes, and saw Helen there, married to Achilles. Ptolemy Chennus says that Helen had a son by Achilles in the Island of the Blest, born with wings, whom on account of the fertility of the region they named Euphorion. (*Euphoria* means "power of bearing.") Jove fell in love with Euphorion, but, unsuccessful in his suit, struck the youth by lightning while Euphorion was fleeing in the isle of Melos, and turned into green frogs the nymphs who buried him.

Let us suppose that Goethe's mind operated upon these stories, devising an end for his epic poem. We know, from his various notes on the poem, that he wished to deal with events subsequent to the war with Troy, involving the return of the heroes, and that Achilles, who is generally regarded as having died in the war itself, was the central figure of the projected epic. Since the poem was to deal with the return of the heroes, certainly the return of such an important figure as Menelaus with Helen would be a probable theme. And if Achilles was to be connected with events subsequent to his death, how was that difficulty to be overcome? Obviously the stories which I have just repeated would give him an opportunity to link the return of Helen with the final destiny of Achilles on Leuke.

In the following paragraphs I shall set down hypothetically the story which I believe Goethe actually to have written as the last book of the *Achilleis*, and I shall assume that the reader will observe that in effect it follows minutely the action of the Helena episode of *Faust*.

I conceive the epic poem to have proceeded nearly to its end. Achilles has been slain, but his posthumous career has not yet been told. Goethe has been dealing with the return of the heroes from Troy and now intends to round out the story by combining a narrative of the return of

Helen to Sparta with that legend which makes her ultimately become the wife of Achilles on the island of Leuke.

Helen, accompanied by a group of captive Trojan women, among whom is Penthalis, is, after the destruction of Troy, taken home to Sparta by Menelaus. The ships have touched the shore of Sparta, having crossed the estuary of Eurotas. Menelaus disembarks, lingering on the shore with his warriors. He orders Helen and her women to go up the Eurotas by boat, and thence overland to his palace. He orders that when she arrives she shall present herself before the wise old stewardess and the maidens whom he had put in charge of the palace and its treasures when he departed for the war with Troy. There she shall examine the household, which she will find in good order, and she shall prepare the materials for a sacrifice, including a sharp sword. Helen, during the long trip home from Troy, has been uncertain what the attitude of Menelaus is toward her. She does not know that the materials of the sacrifice and the sharp blade that she is to prepare are intended for herself.

Obedient to the order of her husband she does as she is told, with the encouragement of her women. She first encounters the stewardess, who, let us suppose, is an invention of Goethe. She is a slave woman whom Menelaus had captured as a part of his booty in a Cretan expedition; after Helen's elopement with Paris, she had been put in charge of the household. She is a loyal servant to Menelaus, cordially detesting Helen and all Trojans. The stewardess reproaches Helen in the bitterest terms, thus giving Helen a chance to explain away the charges leveled against her character. The other servants of the house express their contempt likewise, not to Helen directly, but to her women. They reply in kind, in a series of bitter verbal exchanges.

The stewardess mentions, among other things, some of the strange rumors attached to Helen's name. She mentions the rumor that Helen did not actually go to Troy, but that she had been in Egypt, merely an image of her appearing at Troy. This, of course, would refer to the famous variant of the Helen legend, employed by Euripides in his drama, *Helena*. She mentions likewise the legend that Achilles long ago, despite the decree of fate, loved Helen. The stewardess has heard, moreover, that Helen appeared to him in his dreams.

Helen instructs the stewardess to prepare the sacrifice. The stewardess, who has already received her orders from Menelaus and knows that Helen and her women are to be the victims, now has the pleasure of revealing that fact and taunting them with it, to the dismay of the victims. But it is not the destiny of Helen to die in the sacrifice.

On Mount Taygetus, the fabled Lynceus keeps his watch, overlooking the valley of the Eurotas and, indeed, observing with his sharp eyes the events which take place over the whole ancient world. Perceiving the danger which threatens Helen, he becomes her rescuer. Presenting himself to her, he informs her that on the island of Leuke dwells the fair-haired Achilles for whom she is ultimately destined. Helen, who has learned her destiny from the prophecies of Cassandra, reluctantly consents to accompany him thither. Her maidens are not so reluctant. Lynceus calls upon Hermes, who becomes their guide, transporting them to the isle.

Thus far in transposing the story from the Helena episode of *Faust* to a hypothetical end for the *Achilleis*, only very slight alterations have been necessary.

Before I continue, I must explain why I conceive Lynceus to have been involved in the story. Lynceus was the helmsman of the Argonauts; there is no immediately obvious reason why he should be involved in a story concerning Helen and Achilles on Leuke. But since in the Helena episode in *Faust* there is actually a person named Lynceus, and since he bears a very evident resemblance to Lynceus the Argonaut, the connection must be considered. The point is probably this: Lynceus had an excellent reason for going to the rescue of Helen. Many men had loved her, but of these Lynceus had been the first. In Helen's childhood, Lynceus, aided by his brother Idas, had abducted her, carried her away from home, but yielded her to the charge of Theseus. This story was told about Lynceus by admirers of Theseus. It seems that there is a rather disreputable story that Theseus once abducted Helen when she was a child. Persons wishing to protect the reputation of Theseus, presumably invented the story that Lynceus was the real abductor and that Theseus became her gallant protector. At any rate, in such a story lies the connection between Lynceus and Helen. I imagine Goethe to have known the story and to have conceived the idea of having Lynceus rescue Helen by way of making amends for his past wrong.

If the reader will follow me in my rather elaborate assumptions about Lynceus, he will perceive that the whole garbled and confused action concerning Lynceus in the Faust play may now be reduced to a very clear and orderly story about him in the epic—hypothetically reconstructed, it is true, but deduced from the incidents involving him in the drama.

To judge from the published canto of the *Achilleis* and the extant plans for the *Achilleis* which Goethe wrote out, he planned, like other epic poets, on introducing figures whose narratives would form interesting elaborations of the theme and serve for various significant uses. Lynceus presumably was to have been such a figure. He was an interesting person about whom many legends had gathered. So sharp-eyed was he that many stories had been told of his remarkable vision. He could observe phenomena in the sky which were visible to no other man. As watchman for the Argonauts, he had guided the ship even on cloudy nights, for his vision could penetrate the clouds. He could see the rich ores which lay below the surface of the earth, whence had arisen the legend that he was the first to undertake the operations of mining. And there is the story, alluded to by Pindar, that he kept his watch upon Mount Taygetus. Together with his brother Idas, he had been associated with Castor and Pollux, the brothers of Helen, in many of their adventures. His name is remembered for his part in the expedition of the Argonauts, the slaying of the Caledonian boar, the seduction of Helen, a famous incident involving the theft of a herd of oxen, and many other adventures.

Goethe actually alludes to all these matters concerning Lynceus in the drama, and the resemblance of his metamorphosed Lynceus to the Lynceus of antiquity has been often noticed, but no one has perceived why such a classical Lynceus has become involved with the mediaeval Faust. We are now, I think, in a position to resolve the incidents concerning him into their original order.

Working backward from the Lynceus incidents in the
Faust play, I reconstruct the action as follows. When
Lynceus presents himself before Helen, he apologizes for
his part in her original abduction, thus giving Helen the
opportunity to forgive him. She does so on the ground
that it has been her unhappy fate, because of her beauty,
to seduce the hearts of men, bringing endless woe as a
consequence. (Helen's speech of forgiveness, the reader
will observe, has been transposed by Goethe. I shall point
out subsequently just how Goethe's modifications were
made.) As expiation for his sin, Lynceus lays at her feet
the vast treasures which he, by virtue of his wonderful
eyesight, has mined from the ores of the earth. He tells
her the story of his life, a narrative which allows Goethe
to weave into his discourse an account of the many famous
events of antiquity with which the name of Lynceus was
associated. His speech perhaps would be similar to the
prophecy which Valerius Flaccus, in the *Argonautica*, put
into the mouth of Zeus—a prophecy in which the story
of the Argonauts became an allegory of the rise of Greek
culture and its eventual culmination in the supremacy of
Rome. Goethe would have pointed the prophecy not to
Rome, but to the rise of the culture of the North.

Helen and her companions arrive at Leuke, where she
is greeted by Achilles, who dwells, surrounded by some
of his heroic companions, loved and venerated by all
about him. Helen is presented to the hero as he sits upon
his throne, surrounded by golden-haired boys. These boys
are similar to the golden-haired boys who surround the
throne of Zeus in the published canto of the *Achilleis*.
Constructed artificially by Hephaestus, they are endowed
with life by the Hours, and serve as the attendants of

Achilles. Achilles offers Helen his love; Helen, who has known her ultimate destiny, accepts the offer; they dwell together in Leuke for some time in bliss.

In the meanwhile, Menelaus, arriving at his palace in Sparta, learns from the stewardess that Helen has departed for Leuke. Ever adventurous, he sets out a second time in pursuit of her, this time with the futile object of compelling her return from the Island of the Blest. His approach is seen, Achilles assembles his warriors, and Menelaus is vanquished.

Achilles and Helen dwell together in the happy isle, secluded from the world. Their child, Euphorion, is born, the winged offspring of the perfect hero and the most beautiful woman. His career, as it is outlined by Ptolemy Chennus, constitutes the closing portion of the poem, ending with his death when he is struck down by the lightning of the jealous Zeus.

Goethe was not in the habit of telling a story simply for the story's sake. He liked to elevate character, to endow the persons and events with significance. It is unlikely, then, if he were to construct a story such as I have outlined, that he would confine himself to mere narrative. It is not difficult to imagine that he could endow such a tale with rich and varied significance, nor will it be difficult to imagine what sort of character he would give it.

We know from Goethe's discussion of some reconstructions of the lost paintings of Polygnotus that he had in his mind a conception of Helen as one whose beauty was so transcendently great that her mere presence was compensation for the trouble which had dogged those who loved her. Man rejoiced in her as in the highest earthly good. She represented a perfect beauty, more to be desired than power, gold, and wisdom. From the finished canto of the *Achilleis* we know something of Goethe's conception of the character of Achilles. He was the perfect hero, "the best of the Greeks, the worthiest favorite of the gods." Athena laments that he must die because, she declares, the world is in need of a princely man like him who could turn the youthful rage, the craving for destruction, into a mightier and creative purpose. Achilles was one who, had it not been for the doom of death, might have brought order into the world; he might have been a model after which man could govern himself. He would not, meditated Athena, have been a warlike figure, but one who would have turned to the arts of peace; building towns, not destroying them; building colonies; improving the conditions of the world.

May we not suppose then, that in uniting these two persons in Leuke, and giving them a winged child, whose name, Euphorion, signified "fertility," Goethe intended to work out an allegory? Euphorion, the winged child, would be the poetic spirit, born of beauty and of noble capacity for action. He would represent perfected man. If at last he were to be struck down by the envious lightning of Zeus, the garments in which his spirit had been clothed, the forms in which the poetic spirit had expressed itself, would remain for man.

In the *Achilleis*, there is an indication that in order to develop his allegory, Goethe had intended to make an ingenious use of a very famous legend. The reader will recall that when Prometheus was chained to his rock in Caucasus, he refused to divulge a secret which he alone knew. The secret was that by Thetis, Zeus would become the father of a child greater than himself. The common legend is that eventually Prometheus revealed the secret to Zeus. Zeus had loved Thetis, but now, realizing his danger, he withdrew from his amour and arranged that she should become the bride of Peleus. Achilles was the child of that union. In the *Achilleis* Goethe intimates that Achilles was actually the child of Zeus and Thetis, despite the marriage of Thetis to Peleus. When Thetis complains to Zeus of the approaching death of Achilles, Zeus replies in a speech which holds out to Thetis the hope that Achilles may escape the destiny of death. His promise is a veiled one, but it clearly looks forward to some existence after death for Achilles. To this utterance is linked an ambiguous statement that the gods, even Hera, the principal goddess, do not know who is fated to return home from Troy. Goethe seems to be pointing to the fact that Helen will later be connected with Achilles. When Hera, listening to Zeus' promise to Thetis, angrily reproaches Zeus, reminding him that Achilles is fated to die, she also reminds him that the gods cannot alter the decrees of fate. She recalls the prophecy that Zeus will at last succumb to the Titans. Zeus gaily answers that perhaps the day of the Titans is not far off. He shows no regret at the prospect of this event. Considering the fact that according to legend Euphorion was to be the beloved of Zeus, is it not likely that Goethe intended to have the ancient prophecy that Zeus would have a son greater than himself fulfilled in Euphorion? If so, the symbolism of Euphorion would be clear. He would represent the poetic spirit born of active power and of perfect beauty, perfected man rising above the older order of things, not with revolution and hate, but with the benevolent love of Zeus himself.

At a great many points, inference supports the hy-

pothetical reconstruction of the end of the *Achilleis* which
I have just outlined. It remains for me to point out that
the wholly preposterous idea occurred to Goethe of transferring the whole thing to the story of Helen and Faust
in the Middle Ages, translating the fair-haired Achilles
into the fair-haired German magus. With the somewhat
tragic recognition, most of the difficulties which the reader
of the third act encounters are resolved in an unexpected
fashion.

Even the meter of the *Achilleis* is retained, except in
passages where the plot had to be modified. And the most
remarkable thing about the whole affair is that one cannot
charge the failing judgment of Goethe's old age with the
responsibility for such a fantastic procedure, since the
fragment of 1800 shows that the idea of transferring the
plot of the *Achilleis* to the Faust story had been conceived
and partly worked out in the period of Goethe's greatest
powers.

It has often been said that some of the poetry in the
Helena act represents Goethe at his best. This undoubted
fact is the reason why critics have been reluctant to admit
the very great weakness of the conception as a whole. It
has been difficult to reconcile the excellence of the poetry
with the at times almost meaningless content. The dignity
of Helen in the opening passages, the wonderful skill and
clear beauty displayed in the classical meter, the overtones
suggestive of profound and controlled meaning, belong,
not to the *Helena* printed as a phantasmagoria in 1827, but
to the unfinished *Achilleis* of 1796.

Only one critic has come near to seeing what the true
situation is. Eugene Oswald, in his *The Legend of Fair
Helen*, has a chapter on Goethe's use of Helen. When, in

outlining the narrative, he comes to the birth of Euphorion,
he asks the question: "Has Faust become Achilles?" "Apparently," is the only answer he was able to give to this
question. If he had phrased his question in reverse, "Has
Achilles become Faust?" the cat would have been out of
the bag.

The imposition of the plot of the *Achilleis* upon the
Faust story is, of course, incongruous. The actual analogies
in the two stories which might justify such a process of
transformation are only too slight. Faust is to be united to
Helen, a son is to be born to them, who, in the Faust
legend, should be Justus Faustus; Faust and Helen are to
live together, and eventually Helen and the son are to disappear. Certainly the basic analogies are slight, yet Goethe
appears to have considered them sufficient.

As the Helena play stands, the reconstructed outline
which I have given is the opening of the act as it proceeds
until Helen enters her palace. There Helen encounters
Phorkyas who still retains the role of a stewardess brought
from Crete, and retains it despite the fact that Goethe has
imposed upon her character that of Mephistopheles disguised as the now meaningless Phorkyas. What we have is
a threefold impersonation, in which the outlines of the role
of the original stewardess are still evident. The other
servants, whom Helen had been instructed to assemble, do
not appear, having been absorbed into the character of
Phorkyas. The speeches of Phorkyas are far more appropriate to the hostile stewardess than to Mephistopheles,
and indeed Goethe appears to have made them over
scarcely at all. Although Phorkyas is alone in the house,
she continues to speak of the "other servants," all of whom,
however, have disappeared from the play. The reciprocal

taunting which I have supposed to have taken place between the other servants and different women among
Helen's attendants, takes place now only between Phorkyas
and the attendants. It was, of course, necessary for Goethe
to rid himself of the other servants, since the appearance
of Phorkyas among them would have been incomprehensible to them. Some slight changes must have been
made in the dialogue, to make the insults appropriate to
Trojan women come from Hell rather than merely from
Troy. Little change was necessary until the time came for
the rescue of Helen. Instead of having Lynceus come down
from his watch upon Taygetus, Goethe makes Phorkyas,
who but a moment before has been gloating over the imminent death of Helen, herself inform the women of a means
of escape. She does not, of course, tell them of Leuke
and the fair-haired Achilles, but of a bold and virile race
of Germans, whose castle, instead of the watchtower, is
located upon Taygetus. Helen and her women are transported to the castle not by Hermes but by Phorkyas,
although a reminiscence of the original plan is retained
in the words of the Chorus, who ask whether Hermes'
form hovers in front, his golden staff gleaming. Helen is
presented not to a golden-haired Achilles but to the blond
Faust, who is surrounded not by his golden boys but by
beautiful blond German youths. Phorkyas disappears temporarily from the action, but, astonishingly enough,
Lynceus now appears in the role of watchman for Faust.
Goethe could not fit the speeches and actions of the
classical Lynceus into his new role. Nevertheless, instead
of abandoning Lynceus altogether, Goethe retained him,
making over the story in a hopelessly garbled fashion.

Faust charges Lynceus with having failed to notify him

of the approach of Helen, and, in lieu of a welcome for Helen, turns Lynceus over to her for judgment. Lynceus pleads that the coming of Helen so dazzled him that he forgot his duty. Helen now makes her speech of forgiveness. In my opinion, according to the original plan Lynceus was to plead for Helen's forgiveness, not on the trivial charge now leveled against him, but on the more serious charge of having abducted her in her youth. Helen's beautiful and dignified reply would be more pertinent to such a charge. She declares that she dares not punish the evil she has wrought, that it has been her evil destiny to corrupt men:

> Now plundering,
> Seducing, fighting, hurried to and fro,
> Heroes and Demigods, Gods, Daemons even,
> Hither and thither led me, sore perplexed.
> (Taylor's translation)

Lynceus replies in a curious kind of ballad, the subject matter of which appears to have been taken over from the long narrative in which he was to have told the story of his life. In the ballad as it now stands, one may perceive vestiges of the original discourse which are comprehensible only if one regards them as the garbled remains of a narrative relating to the classical Lynceus, his brother, and his companions.

Faust now makes his suit to Helen, who accepts him. The first incident of their new life of bliss consists of Helen's lesson in the art of using modern rhyme.

Not even Menelaus is dropped from the story, even though his appearance in the Middle Ages is as unexpected as it is remarkable. Phorkyas announces that Menelaus has arrived to avenge the theft of Helen. Faust assembles his leaders, instructs them to defeat Menelaus, and, when they report that they have been victorious, assigns the conquest of the Greek world by northern arms during the Middle Ages to leaders representing various cultures, reserving Arcadia for himself. The passage is very obscure. Scholars have professed to see in it some sort of symbol of the conquest of the Greek world by northern arms during the Middle Ages. It seems likely that this passage, and the speeches of Lynceus, are very sketchily reworked from passages in the *Achilleis* in which Goethe showed in prospect the conquest of the Greek world in the Middle Ages and the subsequent triumph of Greek culture in Europe.

Helen and Faust live together blissfully, not in Leuke, which Goethe could hardly make their place of residence without giving himself away, but in an idealized Arcadia. There Euphorion, properly the son of Achilles and Helen, is born to them. It was necessary for Goethe to modify the story considerably in dealing with Euphorion. Indeed, the whole symbolic meaning had to be altered from that originally projected. In the *Achilleis*, Helen was to have represented beauty—not classical beauty, but beauty uncircumscribed by historical definition. Achilles was to have represented the active man—not a Greek man, but man himself. In bringing together two figures from widely disparate cultures, an ancient Greek and a German of the late Middle Ages, Goethe had a different problem on his hands. This he solved, or tried to solve, by having Helen represent classical beauty and Faust represent the Romantic spirit. It seems to me that nothing clear was achieved by this solution, as one fails to discern in Helen anything which does really represent a concept of classical beauty. One is willing to regard Faust as the embodiment of a

restless spirit which, without argument, may be accepted
as Romantic, but what is to be achieved by the union of
the two? What is Euphorion to represent? He can no
longer be the fulfillment of the Promethean prophecy.
The solution which Goethe struck upon was to retain the
idea that the winged child would represent the creative
spirit. No longer could he be perfected man. He had,
rather, to represent the blending of the classical and
Romantic spirits, for better or worse. The character of
Euphorion merges, as the drama proceeds, into that of
Lord Byron. The choice was inevitable. Byron was a creative spirit, the product of elements that might be regarded
as both classical and Romantic. Byron's travels in Greece,
his attachment to the land and its cause, his death at
Missolonghi, the rich store of "classical" allusion in his
works (his classical knowledge was not profound but was
by no means contemptible) led Goethe to conceive of
Byron as a fit exemplar of the significance of Euphorion.
If the choice seems rather absurd to us, it was certainly
not so to Goethe. Goethe himself would have been a
better exemplar of the product of Romantic and classical
influences, but he could hardly have identified himself
openly with Euphorion without appearing pretentious.

The outlines of Euphorion's life and death as depicted
in the play must be regarded as an adjustment, an unsatisfactory compromise, of the threefold character which he is
forced to sustain: he is the mythological figure, made over
from the story of Achilles and Helen so as to fit the story
of Faust and Helen; he is the symbol of the union of the
classical and Romantic spirits; and he is the English poet
whom Goethe had selected as the exemplar of the symbol.
It was inevitable that such a complex poetic creation would

result in something partly incongruous, partly incomprehensible. Not even Goethe's dexterity could succeed in making a blend of such composites satisfactory for dramatic purposes.

Consider, for instance, the fate of the son of Helen and Faust. In accordance with the Faust story, Justus Faustus must disappear. According to the classical myth, Euphorion must be struck down by the lightning of Zeus. According to history, Byron must die at Missolonghi. Goethe's problem was to thread his way through this set of complexities. He must, moreover, remember that the son of Helen and Faust symbolizes the creative spirit and the union of the classical and Romantic spirits. Some symbolic meaning should therefore be attached to the vaguely described death of the boy. But from such a situation nothing clear could or did emerge.

With the disappearance of Helen, the situation was simpler. Helen returns to Persephone, leaving behind her the garments, the outer forms in which the classical beauty had been enfolded. These forms remain for the inspiration of Faust and the use of successive generations of men.

Penthalis and the chorus remain to be disposed of. Penthalis returns with Helen, reassuming a merely mythical existence. The Trojan women, who have been nameless, refuse to return to their original obscurity. They are myths loose in the modern world. Amusingly enough, Goethe follows the trend of contemporary mythology, allowing them to become nature myths, merging themselves with the elements.

So ends the Helena episode, and so, I think, should end the notion that the *Second Part of Faust* is a truly great work of art. I feel sure that the intricate play has so far yielded to critical analysis as to reveal weaknesses inexcusable on any ground other than the extreme old age of the poet. And yet, as we have seen, old age was not wholly responsible for the grossest of them. An element of vanity in the exploitation of obscure classical learning; a willingness to deal mysteriously with that erudition; an admiration for vague symbolism and allegory; endless energy wastefully expended in minor inventions; a taste for ornate elaboration inappropriately applied to Greek themes; a disregard for form, proportion, clarity, and good sense—these were not merely the faults of Goethe's old age. They were, rather, the faults of a generation of poets who attempted to apply the product of antique culture to objects incapable of bearing the burden imposed upon them. Greek myth, eagerly sought as the vehicle for poetic expression in an alien age, confounded those who made use of it.

Selected Bibliography

Albinus, Peter.   *See* Grotius.

Anthon, Charles.   A Classical Dictionary. New York, 1863.

Apollodorus.   The Library, with an English Translation by Sir James George Frazer. 2 vols. London, 1921.

Apollonius of Rhodes.   Apollonii Rhodii Argonautica ex recensione et cum notis Rich. Fr. Phil. Brunckii . . . accedunt scolia Graece, Vol. II. Leipzig, 1813.

Aristophanes.   Scholia Aristophanica . . . Arranged, Emended, and Translated by William G. Rutherford. 3 vols. London, 1896-1905.

Bailly, Jean Sylvain.   Histoire de l'astronomic ancienne, depuis son origine, jusqu'à l'établissement de l'école d'Alexandrie. London and Paris, 1775.

——Letters sur l'Atlantide de Platon et sur l'ancienne histoire de l'Asie. London and Paris, 1779.

——Lettres sur l'origine des sciences, et sur celle des peuples de l'Asie. Paris, 1777.

Banier, Antoine.   La Mythologie et les fables expliquées par l'histoire. 3 vols. Paris, 1738-40.

——The Mythology and Fables of the Ancients, Explain'd from History . . . Translated from the Original French. 4 vols. London, 1739-40.

Barlow, Joel.   The Vision of Columbus; a Poem. Hartford, 1787.

Bayle, Peter.   The Dictionary, Historical and Critical, of Mr. Peter Bayle. 2d ed. London, 1734.

Beauford, William.   "Druidism Revived" in Charles Vallancey, Collectanea, Vol. II, No. 7 (1781).

Beaufort, Francis.   Karamania; or, A Brief Description of the South Coast of Asia Minor. London, 1817.

Blake, William.   Poetry and Prose of William Blake, Edited by Geoffrey Keynes. London, 1927.

Boccaccio, Giovanni.   Joannis Bocatii: Περι γενεαλογιας deorum, libri quindecim cum annotationibus Jacobi Mycylli. Basel, 1532.

Bochart, Samuel.   Samuelis Bocharti geographia sacra. Leiden, 1707.

——Samuelis Bocharti opera omnia; hoc est Phaleg, Chanaan, et Hierozoicon. Leiden, 1712.

Boudinot, Elias.   A Star in the West; or, A Humble Attempt to Discover the Long Lost Ten Tribes of Israel, Preparatory to Their Return to Their Beloved City, Jerusalem. Trenton, N. J., 1816.

Brothers, Richard.   A Correct Account of the Invasion and Conquest of This Island by the Saxons &c., Necessary to Be Known by the English Nation, the Descendants of the Ten Tribes. N.p., 1822.

——A Description of Jerusalem: Its Houses and Streets . . . with the Garden of Eden in the Centre, as Laid Down in the Last Chapters of Ezekiel. With plans. London, 1801 [1802].

——A Revealed Knowledge, of the Prophecies & Times. . . . Wrote under the Direction of the Lord God, and Published by His Sacred Command. London, 1794.

Bryant, Jacob.   A New System; or, An Analysis of Ancient Mythology: Wherein an Attempt Is Made to Divest Tradition of Fable; and to Reduce the Truth to Its Original Purity. 3 vols. London, 1774-76.

Buffon, Comte de.   "Epoques de la nature" in the 1778 supplement to Œuvres complètes de M. Le Cte. de Buffon (90 vols. Paris, 1770-88).

Bush, Douglas.   Mythology and the Romantic Tradition in English Poetry. Cambridge, Mass., 1937.

[Carli, Gian Rinaldo.]   Delle lettere americane. Nuova edizione corretta ed ampliata colla aggiunta delle parte III ora per la prima volta impresa [anon.]. Cremona, 1781-83. (First published anonymously at Florence, in 2 vols., 1780. French translation published at Boston, 1788.)

Claudianus, Claudius. Claudian, with an English Translation by Maurice Platnauer. 2 vols. London, 1922.

Colvin, Sir Sidney. John Keats: His Life and Poetry, His Friends, Critics, and After-Fame. New York, 1917.

Conradus de Mure. [Repertorium vocabulorum]. Berthold Ruppel, n.p., n.d. [before 1471]. (Copy in Newberry Library).

Creuzer, Georg Friedrich. Symbolik und Mythologie der alten Völker, besonders der Griechen. 6 vols. Leipzig and Darmstadt, 1810-23.

Cuvier, Baron de. Essay on the Theory of the Earth, Translated from the French by R. Kerr, with Minerological Notes [etc.] by Professor Jamieson. Edinburgh, 1813.

Davies, Edward. Celtic Researches, on the Origin, Traditions, and Language of the Ancient Britons, with Introductory Sketches on Primitive Society. London, 1804.

———The Mythology and Rites of the British Druids. London, 1809.

Delafield, John, Jr. An Inquiry into the Origin of the Antiquities of America. New York, 1839.

Dupuis, Charles François. Memoire sur l'origine des constellations et sur l'explication de la fable par la moyen de l'astronomie, in Vol. IV of the 3d ed. of Joseph Jérôme Le Français de Lalande, Astronomie (Paris, 1781-92).

Evans, John Henry. Joseph Smith, an American Prophet. New York, 1933.

Faber, George Stanley. A Dissertation on the Mysteries of the Cabiri; or the Great Gods of Phenicia, Samothrace, Egypt, Troas, Greece, Italy, and Crete; Being an Attempt to Deduce the Several Orgies of Isis, Ceres, Mithras, Bacchus, Rhea, Adonis, and Hecate, from an Union of the Rites Commemorative of the Deluge with the Adoration of the Host of Heaven. 2 vols. Oxford, 1803.

Frazer, Sir James G. Adonis, Attis, Osiris. 2d ed. London, 1907.

Freneau, Philip Morin. The Poems of Philip Freneau, Poet of the American Revolution, Edited by Fred Lewis Pattee. 3 vols. Princeton, 1902-7.

[Gale, Thomas.] Historiae poeticae scriptores antiqui: Apollodorus Atheniensis; Conon Grammaticus; Ptolemaeus Hephaest.; F. Parthenius Nicaensis; Antoninus Liberalis–Graece et Latine. London, 1676.

Goethe, Johann Wolfgang von. "Achilleis," in Goethes Werke: Festausgabe, Vierter Band, Epen. Leipzig, 1926.

——"Achilleid," in Goethe's Reineke Fox [etc.], Translated in the Original Metres by Alexander Rogers. London, 1890.

——Goethes Faust, herausgegeben von Georg Witkowski. 2 vols. 3d ed. Leiden, 1936.

——Faust, Parts One and Two, Translated from the German by George Madison Priest. New York, 1932.

——Faust: a Tragedy . . . the Second Part, Translated in the Original Metres by Bayard Taylor. Boston, 1871.

Grotius, Hugo. On the Origin of the Native Races of America: a Dissertation by Hugo Grotius; to Which Is Added a Treatise on Foreign Languages and Unknown Islands, by Peter Albinus; Translated from the Latin . . . by Edmund Goldsmid. Edinburgh, 1884.

Hancarville. See Hugues.

Herbelot, Barthélemy d'. Bibliothèque orientale, ou dictionaire universel, contenant tout ce que fait connôitre les peuples de l'Orient. 2d ed., 4 vols. La Haye, 1777-79.

Herbert, Algernon. An Essay on the Neodruidic Heresy in Britannia. Part the First [no more published]. London, 1838.

Hesiod. Hesiod, the Homeric Hymns, and Homerica, with an English Translation by Hugh G. Evelyn-White. London, 1929.

Holinshed, Raphael. Chronicles of England, Scotland, and Ireland. 6 vols. London, 1807-8.

Holland, Sir Henry. Travels in the Ionian Isles, Albania, Thessaly, Macedonia . . . during the Years 1812 and 1813. London, 1815.

Hugues, Pierre François, called d'Hancarville. Collection of

Etruscan, Greek, and Roman Antiquities from the Cabinet of the Hon. W. Hamilton. 4 vols. Naples, 1766-67.

——Recherches sur l'origine . . . des arts de la Grèce. 2 vols. London, 1785.

Hyginus, Gaius J. Auctores mythographi Latini: Cajus Julius Hyginus; Fab. Planciad. Fulgentius; Lactantius Placidus; Albricus Philosophus—cum integris commentariis Jacobi Micylli, Joannis Schefferi, et Thomae Munckeri, quibus adcedunt Thomae Wopkensii emendationes ac conjecturae. Leiden, 1742.

——C. Iulii Hyginus Augusti Liberti fabularum liber . . . ; eiusdem poeticon astronomicon libri quatuor, quibus accesserunt similis argumenti: Palaephati de fabulosis narrationibus liber I; F. Fulgentii Placiadis episcopi Cartaginensis mythologiarum libri III; eiusdem de vocum antiquarum interpretatione liber I; Phurnuti de natura deorum, sive poeticarum fabularum allegoriis, speculatio; Albrici Philosophi de deorum imaginibus liber; Arati phaenomenon fragmentum . . . ; eiusdem phaenomena Graecè . . . ; Procli de sphera libellus. Basel, 1570.

Jacobs, Joseph. "Anglo-Israelism," in The Jewish Encyclopedia, Vol. I. New York, 1901.

Jamieson, John. Hermes Scythicus; or, The Radical Affinities of the Greek and Latin Languages to the Gothic . . . to Which Is Prefixed, a Dissertation on the Historical Proofs of the Scythian Origin of the Greeks. Edinburgh, 1814.

Jones, Sir William. The Works of Sir William Jones [Edited by Anna Maria Jones, with a discourse on the life and writings of Sir William Jones by Lord Teignmouth]. 6 vols. London, 1799.

Keats, John. The Letters of John Keats, Edited by Maurice Buxton Forman. 2d ed. Oxford, 1935.

——The Poetical Works of John Keats, Edited by H. W. Garrod. Oxford, 1939.

Keightley, Thomas. The Mythology of Ancient Greece and Italy . . . for the Use of Students at the University. 3d ed. New York, 1866.

Knight, Richard Payne. A Discourse on the Worship of Priapus, and Its Connection with the Mystic Theology of the Ancients. New ed., privately printed. London, 1865. (A reprint of the privately printed edition of 1786, which was withdrawn from circulation.)

——An Inquiry into the Symbolical Language of Ancient Art and Mythology. London, 1818.

Lucan. M. Annaei Lucani belli civilis libri decem; editorum in usum edidit A. E. Housman. 2d impression. Oxford, 1927.

——Marci Annaei Lucani Pharsalia . . . [edidit] Carol Fred. Weber . . . volumen tertium continens scolaiastas. Leipzig, 1831.

Lyell, Sir Charles. Elements of Geology. Philadelphia, 1839.

Lykophron. Callimachus and Lycophron with an English Translation by A. W. Mair; Aratus with an English Translation by G. R. Mair. London, 1921.

Macrobius, Ambrosius. Macrobius, Franciscus Eyssenhardt iterum recognovit. Leipzig, 1893.

Marino, Giovanni Ambrogio. L'Adone. Venice [1623].

Marsham, Sir John. Chronicus canon Aegyptiacus, Ebraicus, Graecus, et disquisitiones. London, 1672.

Meek, Harold George. Johann Faust, the Man and the Myth. London, 1930.

Mela, Pomponius. Pomponii Melae de situ orbis libri III . . . curante Abrahamo Gronovio. Leiden, 1722.

Mueller, Karl Otfried. Prolegomena zu einer wissenschaftlichen Mythologie. Göttingen, 1825.

Newton, Sir Isaac. The Chronology of Antient Kingdoms Amended. London, 1728.

Nonnus. Nonni Panopolitani Dionysiaca recensuit Arthurus Ludwich. 2 vols. Leipzig, 1909-11.

——Les Dionysiacques; ou, Les Voyages, les amours, et les conquetes de Bachus aux Indes, traduit du Grec de Nonnus Panopolitain. Paris, 1625.

Oswald, Eugene. The Legend of Fair Helen as Told by Homer, Goethe, and Others. London, 1905.

Palaephatus. Palaephati de incredibilibus Graece [edidit] Ioh. Frider. Fischerus. Leipzig, 1789.

Parabosco, Girolamo. Lettere amorose. Venice, 1545.

Pauly, August Friedrich von. Paulys Real-encyclopädie der classischen Altertums-wissenschaft . . . herausgegeben von Georg Wissowa. Stuttgart, 1894-.

Pausanias. Description of Greece, Translated with a Commentary by J. G. Frazer. 6 vols. London, 1898.

Pernety, Antoine Joseph. Les Fables egyptiennes et grecques dévoilées et réduits au même principe. 2 vols. Paris, 1758.

Philostratus, Flavius. Philostratus, Imagines; Callistratus, Descriptiones; with an English Translation by Arthur Fairbanks. London, 1931.

Pluche, Noël Antoine. Histoire du Ciel, considéré selon les idées des poëtes, des philosophes, et de Moise. Paris, 1739-41.

Plutarch. Selected Essays of Plutarch, Translated with Introduction by A. O. Prickard. Oxford, 1918.

Priest, Josiah. American Antiquities, and Discoveries in the West. 2d ed., rev. Albany, 1833.

Procopius. Procopius, with an English Translation by H. B. Dewing. 7 vols. London, 1914-40.

Ptolemy Chennus, or Hephaestion. Ptolemæi Hephæstionis novarum historiarum ad variam eruditionem pertinentium excerpta . . . edidit Jos. Imm. Gisl. Roulez . . . praefatus est Fredericus Creuzerus. Leipzig, 1834.

[Pughe,] William Owen. The Cambrian Biography; or, Historical Notices of Celebrated Men among the Ancient Britons. London, 1803.

Quintus Smyrnaeus. The Fall of Troy, with an English Translation by Arthur S. Way. London, 1913.

Rossetti, William Michael. Adonais, Edited with Introduction and Notes by William Michael Rossetti. London, 1891.

Saurat, Denis. "Blake et les Celtomanes," Modern Philology, XXII (Nov., 1925), 175-88.

Savary, Claude Étienne. Lettres sur la Grèce, faisant suite de celles sur l'Égypte. Paris, 1788.

Savary, Claude Etienne. Letters on Greece, Translated from the French. Dublin, 1788. (Translation of item above.)

Shelley, Percy Bysshe. The Complete Works, Newly Edited by Roger Ingpen and Walter Peck. 10 vols. London, 1926-30.

——The Poems of Percy Bysshe Shelley, Edited with Notes by C. D. Locock. 2 vols. London, 1911.

Smith, Joseph. The Book of Mormon; an Account Written by the Hand of Mormon upon Plates Taken from the Plates of Nephi . . . Translated by Joseph Smith, Jun. Salt Lake City, Utah, The Church of Jesus Christ of Latter-Day Saints, 1921.

Smith, William. Dictionary of Greek and Roman Geography, by Various Writers, Edited by William Smith. 2 vols. London, 1873.

——Dictionary of Greek and Roman Biography and Mythology, Edited by William Smith. 3 vols. Boston, 1849.

Solinus. C. Iulii Solini memorabilia mundi . . . ed. Georginus Dravidius. Frankfort, 1603.

Sophocles. Oedipus Coloneus, with Critical Notes, Commentary, and Translation in English Prose by R. C. Jebb. Cambridge, 1889.

Southey, Robert. The Poetical Works. 10 vols. London, 1837-40.

Spaulding, Solomon. The "Manuscript Found," or, "Manuscript Story" of the Late Rev. Solomon Spaulding; from a Verbatim Copy of the Original. Lamoni, Iowa, 1885.

Strabo. The Geography of Strabo, with an English Translation by Horace Leonard Jones. 8 vols. London, 1917-32.

Stukeley, William. Abury, a Temple of the British Druids, with Some Others, Described. London, 1743.

——Stonehenge, a Temple Restor'd to the British Druids. London, 1740.

Suidas. Suidae lexicon edidit Ada Adler. 5 vols. Leipzig, 1928-38.

Tzetzes. Joannis Tzetzae Antehomerica, Homerica, et Posthomerica . . . edidit Fredericus Jacobs. Leipzig, 1803.

Ulloa, Antonio de.   Noticias americanas. Madrid, 1772.

Valerius Flaccus.   Valerius Flaccus with an English Translation by J. H. Mozley. London, 1934.

Vallancey, Charles.   Collectanea de rebus Hibernicis . . . Published from the Manuscripts by Major Charles Vallancey. 6 vols. Dublin, 1770-1804. 2d ed., 4 vols. Dublin, 1786.

——An Essay on the Antiquity of the Irish Language; with a Preface, Proving Ireland to Be the Thule of the Ancients. London, 1822. (Reprinted verbatim from the second edition of Collectanea.)

——A Vindication of the Ancient History of Ireland; Wherein Is Shewn, I, The Descent of the Old Inhabitants from the Phaeno-Scythians of the East, II, The Early Skill of the Phaeno-Scythians, in Navigation, Arts, and Letters, III, Several Accounts of the Ancient Irish Bards. Dublin, 1786.

Voss, Johann Heinrich, the Elder.   Antisymbolik. 2 vols. Stuttgart, 1824-26.

Warren, Herbert.   "Keats as a Classical Scholar," *The Nineteenth Century*, XCIII (Jan., 1923), 62-68.

Wilford, Francis.   *For the various essays of Wilford see:*

Asiatic Researches; or, Transactions of the Society, Instituted in Bengal, for Inquiry into the History and Antiquities, the Arts, Sciences, and Literature of Asia, Vols. I-XX. Calcutta, 1788-1839.

Index to the First Eighteen Volumes of the Asiatic Researches, etc. Calcutta, 1835.

Note: the original quarto edition of the Asiatic Researches was issued at Calcutta. A pirated edition was brought out in England in 1798 and within the next few years various editions were issued, together with the following reprint:

Asiatic Researches.   Vol. I-XI, printed verbatim from the Calcutta edition. London, 1801-12.

Wordsworth, William.   The Ecclesiastical Sonnets of William Wordsworth; a Critical Edition by Abbie Findlay Potts. New Haven, 1922.

——The Letters of William and Dorothy Wordsworth; the Middle Years. Arranged and Edited by Ernest de Selincourt. Oxford, 1937.

——The Poetical Works of William Wordsworth, Edited by William Knight. 8 vols. London, 1896.

Index

303

EDWARD BUELL HUNGERFORD was born in New Britain, Connecticut, in 1900. He took his A.B. at Trinity College, Hartford, in 1921, and his Ph.D. at Harvard in 1928. He has been a professor of English at Northwestern University since 1928, except for the war years when he was a Lieutenant Commander in the United States Naval Reserve. Professor Hungerford has contributed to *American Literature*, *New England Quarterly*, and *Chicago Schools Journal*. He is the author of five historical novels for children *(Fighting Frigate,* 1947; *Emergency Run,* 1948; *Escape to Danger,* 1949; *Forbidden Island,* 1950; and *Four for Heroes,* 1952)*, and the editor of *Poets in Progress*, published in 1962. He is also editor of the periodical *Tri-Quarterly*, published at Northwestern. Professor Hungerford and his wife make their home in Kenilworth, Illinois.